FOUR ENGLISH TRAGEDIES OF THE
16TH AND 17TH CENTURIES

FOUR
ENGLISH TRAGEDIES

*of the 16th and 17th
Centuries*

———

EDWARD THE SECOND
A WOMAN KILLED WITH KINDNESS
THE DUCHESS OF MALFY
ALL FOR LOVE

———

Edited by J. M. Morrell

PENGUIN BOOKS
MELBOURNE · LONDON · BALTIMORE

Penguin Books Ltd, Harmondsworth, Middlesex
U.S.A.: Penguin Books Inc., 3300 Clipper Mill Road, Baltimore 11, Md
[*Educational Representative:*
D. C. Heath & Co., 285 Columbus Avenue, Boston 16, Mass]
AUSTRALIA: Penguin Books Pty Ltd, 200 Normanby Road,
Melbourne, S.C.5, Victoria
AGENT IN CANADA: Riverside Books Ltd, 47 Green Street,
Saint Lambert, Montreal, P.Q.

—

Made and printed in Great Britain by
Hazell, Watson and Viney, Ltd
Aylesbury and London

—

This collection first published in
Penguin Books 1953

CONTENTS

PREFACE   7

EDWARD THE SECOND   9

A WOMAN KILLED WITH KINDNESS   103

THE DUCHESS OF MALFY   173

ALL FOR LOVE   285

PREFACE

*These four English tragedies are intended as a companion volume
to* Four English Comedies. *They have been selected from plays
which in their time were acceptable on the stage, and one at least
of them –* The Duchess of Malfy *– has in our own time shown
that it has lost nothing during the intervening centuries.*

*It is at once obvious that the tragedies are drawn from a much
more restricted field than the comedies. It would be easy to confine
a selection of this kind to the period from, roughly,* 1590 *to* 1620.
*The first three, indeed, lie within these years. When the eclipse of
drama during the interregnum ceased the stream of comedy flowed
strongly and that flow has never really ceased. Yet, apart from
Dryden's work, tragedy of worth comparable to the comedy did not
appear. True, 'literary' tragedy has been written, Shelley's* Cenci,
for instance, and Tennyson's Becket, *but for tragedy which is also
good theatre we have had to wait until our own time.*

*It has therefore been impossible to cover as wide a range
chronologically: the XVIth and XVIIth centuries offered a goodly
company, Marlowe and Webster inevitably leading the way.*
Edward II *has been chosen to represent Marlowe rather than*
Dr Faustus *because, though it never reaches the translunary
heights of that play, neither does it contain anything as tiresome
as the clowning.* Edward II *contains, also, the element of human
suffering which gives it a poignancy lacking in Marlowe's other
tragedies.*

A Woman Killed with Kindness *is here to represent a kind
of tragedy little developed in its time. The setting is domestic, the
people private persons. Heywood has built up a picture of a happy
domestic life, based on the trust of a husband in his wife; so con-
vincing is it that its destruction by Mistress Frankford's almost
accidental lapse from virtue is tragic. Bloody revenge would be
unthinkable, and it is this which makes the play remarkable for
its time. This play, almost contemporary with* The Duchess of
Malfy *yet completely unlike it, and so many other tragedies of the
time, should, for that very reason, be especially interesting.*

The Duchess of Malfy *has been included because of the finer shades of variety than can be found in the oppressive and thunderous climate of* The White Devil. *Evil appears in so many forms, all subtly studied and all credible. Ferdinand is perfect material for the psycho-analyst's case-history. In shining contrast is the Duchess and her mild majesty. The verse has a haunting quality rising to moments of* 'dazzling darkness':

> I know death hath ten thousand several doors
> For men to take their exits; and 'tis found
> They go on such strange geometrical hinges,
> You may open them both ways; any way, for Heaven sake,
> So I were out of your whispering.

To find a tragedy later in date and of general interest was difficult. Dryden's All for Love *has been chosen as it is, probably, the best-known of his plays, and because it inevitably leads back to Shakespeare.* 'Comparisons are odorous'; *if the reader chooses to make them he may be surprised to find that they smell less than he might expect.*

Edward the Second *was written about 1592;* A Woman Killed with Kindness, *first published in 1603, appeared in quarto in 1607;* The Duchess of Malfy, *written probably in 1613–14, and acted in 1614, was published in 1623;* All for Love *is dated 1677.*

Christopher Marlowe

EDWARD THE SECOND

DRAMATIS PERSONAE

KING EDWARD THE SECOND

PRINCE EDWARD, *his Son, afterwards* KING EDWARD
THE THIRD

EARL OF KENT, *Brother of King Edward the Second*

GAVESTON

WARWICK

LANCASTER

PEMBROKE

ARUNDEL

LEICESTER

BERKELEY

MORTIMER *senior*

MORTIMER *junior, his Nephew*

SPENCER *senior*

SPENCER *junior, his Son*

ARCHBISHOP OF CANTERBURY

BISHOP OF COVENTRY

BISHOP OF WINCHESTER

BALDOCK

BEAUMONT

TRUSSEL

GURNEY

MATREVIS

LIGHTBORN

SIR JOHN OF HAINAULT

LEVUNE

RICE AP HOWEL

ABBOT, MONKS, HERALD, LORDS, POOR MEN,
JAMES, MOWER, CHAMPION, MESSENGERS,
SOLDIERS AND ATTENDANTS

QUEEN ISABELLA, *Wife of King Edward the Second*

NIECE TO KING EDWARD THE SECOND, *daughter of
the Duke of Gloucester*

LADIES

EDWARD THE SECOND

ACT I, SCENE 1

A Street in London

Enter GAVESTON, *reading on a letter that was brought him from the King.*

Gaveston. 'My father is deceased. Come, Gaveston,
And share the kingdom with thy dearest friend.'
Ah, words that make me surfeit with delight!
What greater bliss can hap to Gaveston
Than live and be the favourite of a king?
Sweet prince, I come; these, these thy amorous lines
Might have enforced me to have swum from France,
And, like Leander, gasped upon the sand,
So thou wouldst smile, and take me in thy arms.
The sight of London to my exiled eyes
Is as Elysium to a new-come soul;
Not that I love the city, or the men,
But that it harbours him I hold so dear,
The king, upon whose bosom let me die,
And with the world be still at enmity.
What need the arctic people love starlight,
To whom the sun shines both by day and night?
Farewell base stooping to the lordly peers.
My knee shall bow to none but to the king.
As for the multitude that are but sparks,
Raked up in embers of their poverty –
Tanti; I'll fawn first on the wind
That glanceth at my lips, and flieth away.
But how now, what are these?

Enter three POOR MEN

Poor Men. Such as desire your worship's service.

Gaveston. What canst thou do?

1*st Poor Man.* I can ride.

Gaveston. But I have no horses. What art thou?

2*nd Poor Man.* A traveller.

Gaveston. Let me see – thou wouldst do well
To wait at my trencher and tell me lies at dinner-
time;
And as I like your discoursing, I'll have you.
And what art thou?

3*rd Poor Man.* A soldier, that hath served against the
Scot,

Gaveston. Why, there are hospitals for such as you;
I have no war, and therefore, sir, be gone.

3*rd Poor Man.* Farewell, and perish by a soldier's hand,
That wouldst reward them with an hospital.

Gaveston. Ay, ay, these words of his move me as much
As if a goose should play the porpintine,
And dart her plumes, thinking to pierce my breast.
But yet it is no pain to speak men fair;
I'll flatter these and make them live in hope. [*Aside.*
You know that I came lately out of France,
And yet I have not viewed my lord the king.
If I speed well, I'll entertain you all.

Omnes. We thank your worship.

Gaveston. I have some business, leave me to myself.

Omnes. We will wait here about the court.   [*Exeunt.*

Gaveston. Do; these are not men for me:
I must have wanton poets, pleasant wits,
Musicians, that with touching of a string
May draw the pliant king which way I please.
Music and poetry is his delight;
Therefore I'll have Italian masques by night,
Sweet speeches, comedies, and pleasing shows;
And in the day, when he shall walk abroad,
Like sylvan nymphs my pages shall be clad;

My men, like satyrs grazing on the lawns,
Shall with their goat-feet dance an antic hay.
Sometime a lovely boy in Dian's shape
With hair that gilds the water as it glides,
Crownets of pearl about his naked arms,
And in his sportful hands an olive-tree,
To hide those parts which men delight to see,
Shall bathe him in a spring; and there, hard by,
One like Actaeon peeping through the grove,
Shall by the angry goddess be transformed,
And running in the likeness of an hart
By yelping hounds pulled down shall seem to die;
Such things as these best please his majesty.
My lord! Here comes the king, and the nobles
From the parliament. I'll stand aside.   [*Retires.*

Enter the KING, LANCASTER, MORTIMER *senior,* MOR-
TIMER *junior,* EDMUND, *Earl of Kent,* GUY, *Earl of
Warwick, etc.*

Edward. Lancaster!
Lancaster. My lord.
Gaveston. That Earl of Lancaster do I abhor.   [*Aside.*
Edward. Will you not grant me this? In spite of them
  I'll have my will; and these two Mortimers,
  That cross me thus, shall know I am displeased. [*Aside.*
Mortimer sen. If you love us, my lord, hate Gaveston.
Gaveston. That villain Mortimer! I'll be his death [*Aside.*
Mortimer jun. Mine uncle here, this earl, and I myself,
  Were sworn to your father at his death,
  That he should ne'er return into the realm:
  And know, my lord, ere I will break my oath,
  This sword of mine, that should offend your foes,
  Shall sleep within the scabbard at thy need,
  And underneath thy banners march who will,
  For Mortimer will hang his armour up.
Gaveston. Mort Dieu!   [*Aside.*

Edward. Well, Mortimer, I'll make thee rue these words.
Beseems it thee to contradict thy king?
Frownst thou thereat, aspiring Lancaster?
The sword shall plane the furrows of thy brows,
And hew these knees that now are grown so stiff.
I will have Gaveston; and you shall know
What danger 'tis to stand against your king.

Gaveston. Well done, Ned!   [*Aside.*

Lancaster. My lord, why do you thus incense your peers,
That naturally would love and honour you
But for that base and obscure Gaveston?
Four earldoms have I besides Lancaster,
Derby, Salisbury, Lincoln, Leicester;
These will I sell to give my soldiers pay,
Ere Gaveston shall stay within the realm;
Therefore, if he be come, expel him straight.

Kent. Barons and earls, your pride hath made me
mute;
But now I'll speak, and to the proof, I hope.
I do remember, in my father's days,
Lord Percy of the north, being highly moved,
Braved Mowbery in presence of the king;
For which, had not his highness loved him well,
He should have lost his head; but with his look
The undaunted spirit of Percy was appeased,
And Mowbery and he were reconciled:
Yet dare you brave the king unto his face.
Brother, revenge it, and let these their heads
Preach upon poles, for trespass of their tongues.

Warwick. O, our heads!

Edward. Ay, yours; and therefore I would wish you
grant —

Warwick. Bridle thy anger, gentle Mortimer.

Mortimer jun. I cannot, nor I will not: I must speak.
Cousin, our hands I hope shall fence our heads,
And strike off his that makes you threaten us.

Come, uncle, let us leave the brain-sick king,
And henceforth parley with our naked swords.

Mortimer sen. Wiltshire hath men enough to save our
heads.

Warwick. All Warwickshire will love him for my sake.

Lancaster. And northward Gaveston hath many friends.
Adieu, my lord; and either change your mind,
Or look to see the throne, where you should sit,
To float in blood; and at thy wanton head,
The glozing head of thy base minion thrown.

   [Exeunt all except King Edward, Kent, Gaveston, and
                Attendants

Edward. I cannot brook these haughty menaces;
Am I a king, and must be overruled?
Brother, display my ensigns in the field;
I'll bandy with the barons and the earls,
And either die, or live with Gaveston.

Gaveston. I can no longer keep me from my lord.
             [Comes forward.

Edward. What, Gaveston! welcome! – Kiss not my hand,
Embrace me, Gaveston, as I do thee.
Why shouldst thou kneel? knowest thou not who I am?
Thy friend, thyself, another Gaveston!
Not Hylas was more mourned of Hercules,
Than thou hast been of me since thy exile.

Gaveston. And since I went from hence, no soul in hell
Hath felt more torment than poor Gaveston.

Edward. I know it. Brother, welcome home my friend.
Now let the treacherous Mortimers conspire,
And that high-minded Earl of Lancaster.
I have my wish, in that I joy thy sight;
And sooner shall the sea o'erwhelm my land,
Than bear the ship that shall transport thee hence.
I here create thee Lord High Chamberlain,
Chief Secretary to the state and me,
Earl of Cornwall, King and Lord of Man.

Gaveston. My lord, these titles far exceed my worth.
Kent. Brother, the least of these may well suffice
  For one of greater birth than Gaveston.
Edward. Cease, brother: for I cannot brook these words.
  Thy worth, sweet friend, is far above my gifts,
  Therefore, to equal it, receive my heart.
  If for these dignities thou be envied,
  I'll give thee more; for but to honour thee
  Is Edward pleased with kingly regiment.
  Fearst thou thy person? thou shalt have a guard:
  Wantest thou gold? go to my treasury:
  Wouldst thou be loved and feared? receive my seal;
  Save or condemn, and in our name command
  Whatso thy mind affects, or fancy likes.
Gaveston. It shall suffice me to enjoy your love,
  Which whiles I have, I think myself as great
  As Caesar riding in the Roman street,
  With captive kings at his triumphant car.

Enter the BISHOP OF COVENTRY

Edward. Whither goes my lord of Coventry so fast?
Bishop. To celebrate your father's exequies.
  But is that wicked Gaveston returned?
Edward. Ay, priest, and lives to be revenged on thee,
  That wert the only cause of his exile.
Gaveston. 'Tis true; and but for reverence of these robes,
  Thou shouldst not plod one foot beyond this place.
Bishop. I did no more than I was bound to do;
  And, Gaveston, unless thou be reclaimed,
  As then I did incense the parliament,
  So will I now and thou shalt back to France.
Gaveston. Saving your reverence, you must pardon me.
Edward. Throw off his golden mitre, rend his stole,
  And in the channel christen him anew.
Kent. Ah, brother, lay not violent hands on him!
  For he'll complain unto the see of Rome.

Gaveston. Let him complain unto the see of Hell;
  I'll be revenged on him for my exile.
Edward. No, spare his life, but seize upon his goods;
  Be thou lord bishop and receive his rents,
  And make him serve thee as thy chaplain:
  I give him thee; here, use him as thou wilt.
Gaveston. He shall to prison, and there die in bolts.
Edward. Ay, to the Tower, the Fleet, or where thou wilt.
Bishop. For this offence, be thou accurst of God!
Edward. Who's there? Convey this priest to the Tower.
Bishop. True, true.
Edward. But in the meantime, Gaveston, away.
  And take possession of his house and goods.
  Come, follow me, and thou shalt have my guard
  To see it done, and bring thee safe again.
Gaveston. What should a priest do with so fair a house?
  A prison may beseem his holiness.   [*Exeunt.*

ACT I, SCENE 2

Near the King's Palace

Enter on one side the elder MORTIMER, *and the younger*
MORTIMER; *on the other,* WARWICK *and* LANCASTER

Warwick. 'Tis true, the Bishop is in the Tower,
  And goods and body given to Gaveston.
Lancaster. What! will they tyrannize upon the church?
  Ah, wicked king! accursed Gaveston!
  This ground, which is corrupted with their steps,
  Shall be their timeless sepulchre, or mine.
Mortimer jun. Well, let that peevish Frenchman guard him
    sure;
  Unless his breast be sword-proof he shall die.
Mortimer sen. How now! why droops the Earl of Lancas-
    ter?

Mortimer jun. Wherefore is Guy of Warwick discontent?

Lancaster. That villain Gaveston is made an earl.

Mortimer sen. An earl!

Warwick. Ay, and besides Lord Chamberlain of the realm,
And Secretary too, and Lord of Man.

Mortimer sen. We may not, nor we will not suffer this.

Mortimer jun. Why post we not from hence to levy men?

Lancaster. 'My Lord of Cornwall' now at every word!
And happy is the man whom he vouchsafes,
For vailing of his bonnet, one good look.
Thus arm in arm the king and he doth march:
Nay more, the guard upon his lordship waits,
And all the court begins to flatter him.

Warwick. Thus leaning on the shoulder of the king,
He nods, and scorns, and smiles at those that pass.

Mortimer sen. Doth no man take exceptions at the slave?

Lancaster. All stomach him, but none dare speak a word!

Mortimer jun. Ah, that bewrays their baseness, Lancaster.
Were all the earls and barons of my mind,
We'll hale him from the bosom of the king
And at the court-gate hang the peasant up,
Who, swoln with venom of ambitious pride,
Will be the ruin of the realm and us.

Warwick. Here comes my lord of Canterbury's grace.

Lancaster. His countenance bewrays he is displeased.

Enter the ARCHBISHOP OF CANTERBURY *and an*
ATTENDANT

Canterbury. First were his sacred garments rent and torn,
Then laid they violent hands upon him; next
Himself imprisoned, and his goods asseized. –
This certify the Pope; away, take horse.

　　　　　　　　　　　　　　　　[Exit Attendant.

Lancaster. My lord, will you take arms against the king?

Canterbury. What need I? God himself is up in arms,
When violence is offered to the church.

Mortimer jun. Then will you join with us that be his peers,
   To banish or behead that Gaveston?
Canterbury. What else, my lords? for it concerns me near;
   The bishopric of Coventry is his.

Enter the QUEEN

Mortimer jun. Madam, whither walks your majesty so
   fast?
Queen. Unto the forest, gentle Mortimer,
   To live in grief and baleful discontent;
   For now my lord the king regards me not,
   But doats upon the love of Gaveston.
   He claps his cheeks, and hangs about his neck,
   Smiles in his face, and whispers in his ears;
   And when I come, he frowns, as who would say,
   Go whither thou wilt, seeing I have Gaveston.
Mortimer sen. Is it not strange, that he is thus bewitched?
Mortimer jun. Madam, return unto the court again:
   That sly inveigling Frenchman we'll exile,
   Or lose our lives; and yet, ere that day come,
   The king shall lose his crown, for we have power,
   And courage too, to be revenged at full.
Canterbury. But yet lift not your swords against the king.
Lancaster. No; but we'll lift Gaveston from hence.
Warwick. And war must be the means, or he'll stay still.
Queen. Then let him stay, for rather than my lord
   Shall be oppressed by civil mutinies,
   I will endure a melancholy life,
   And let him frolic with his minion.
Canterbury. My lords, to ease all this, but hear me speak:
   We and the rest that are his counsellors,
   Will meet, and with a general consent,
   Confirm his banishment with our hands and seals.
Lancaster. What we confirm the king will frustrate.
Mortimer jun. Then may we lawfully revolt from him.
Warwick. But say, my lord, where shall this meeting be?

Canterbury. At the New Temple.

Mortimer jun. Content.

Canterbury. And, in the meantime, I'll entreat you all
  To cross to Lambeth, and there stay with me.

Lancaster. Come then, let's away.

Mortimer jun. Madam, farewell.

Queen, Farewell, sweet Mortimer; and for my sake,
  Forbear to levy arms against the king.

Mortimer jun. Ay, if words will serve; if not, I must.

                                [Exeunt.

ACT I, SCENE 3

A Street in London

Enter GAVESTON *and the* EARL OF KENT

Gaveston. Edmund, the mighty prince of Lancaster,
  That hath more earldoms than an ass can bear,
  And both the Mortimers, two goodly men,
  With Guy of Warwick, that redoubted knight,
  Are gone towards Lambeth. There let them remain.

                                [Exeunt.

ACT I, SCENE 4

The New Temple

Enter LANCASTER, WARWICK, PEMBROKE, MOR-
TIMER *senior*, MORTIMER *junior*, ARCHBISHOP OF
CANTERBURY *and* ATTENDANTS

Lancaster. Here is the form of Gaveston's exile:
  May it please your lordship to subscribe your name.

Canterbury. Give me the paper.

          [He subscribes, as do the others after him.

Lancaster. Quick, quick, my lord; I long to write my
   name.

Warwick. But I long more to see him banished hence.

Mortimer jun. The name of Mortimer shall fright the king,
   Unless he be declined from that base peasant.

Enter the KING, GAVESTON, *and* KENT

Edward. What? are you moved that Gaveston sits here?
   It is our pleasure: we will have it so.

Lancaster. Your grace doth well to place him by your side,
   For nowhere else the new earl is so safe.

Mortimer sen. What man of noble birth can brook this
     sight?
   Quam male conveniunt!
   See what a scornful look the peasant casts.

Pembroke. Can kingly lions fawn on creeping ants?

Warwick. Ignoble vassal, that like Phaeton
   Aspirest unto the guidance of the sun.

Mortimer jun. Their downfall is at hand, their forces down:
   We will not thus be faced and over-peered.

Edward. Lay hands on that traitor Mortimer!

Mortimer sen. Lay hands on that traitor Gaveston!

Kent. Is this the duty that you owe your king?

Warwick. We know our duties; let him know his peers.

Edward. Whither will you bear him? Stay, or ye shall die.

Mortimer sen. We are no traitors; therefore threaten not.

Gaveston. No, threaten not, my lord, but pay them home!
   Were I a king —

Mortimer jun. Thou villain, wherefore talks thou of a king,
   That hardly art a gentleman by birth?

Edward. Were he a peasant, being my minion,
   I'll make the proudest of you stoop to him.

Lancaster. My lord, you may not thus disparage us.
   Away, I say, with hateful Gaveston!

Mortimer sen. And with the Earl of Kent that favours him.
                    [*Attendants remove Kent and Gaveston.*

Edward. Nay, then lay violent hands upon your king:
  Here, Mortimer, sit thou in Edward's throne:
  Warwick and Lancaster, wear you my crown:
  Was ever king thus over-ruled as I?

Lancaster. Learn then to rule us better, and the realm.

Mortimer jun. What we have done, our heart-blood shall
    maintain.

Warwick. Think you that we can brook this upstart pride?

Edward. Anger and wrathful fury stops my speech.

Canterbury. Why are you moved? be patient, my lord,
  And see what we your counsellors have done.

Mortimer jun. My lords, now let us all be resolute,
  And either have our wills, or lose our lives.

Edward. Meet you for this, proud overdaring peers?
  Ere my sweet Gaveston shall part from me,
  This isle shall fleet upon the ocean,
  And wander to the unfrequented Inde.

Canterbury. You know that I am legate to the Pope?
  On your allegiance to the see of Rome,
  Subscribe as we have done to his exile.

Mortimer jun. Curse him, if he refuse, and then may we
  Depose him and elect another king.

Edward. Ay, there it goes: but yet I will not yield:
  Curse me, depose me, do the worst you can.

Lancaster. Then linger not, my lord, but do it straight.

Canterbury. Remember how the bishop was abused:
  Either banish him that was the cause thereof,
  Or I will presently discharge these lords
  Of duty and allegiance due to thee.

Edward. It boots me not to threat; I must speak fair:
  The legate of the Pope will be obeyed.   *[Aside.*
  My lord, you shall be Chancellor of the realm;
  Thou, Lancaster, High Admiral of our fleet;
  Young Mortimer and his uncle shall be earls;
  And you, Lord Warwick, President of the North;
  And thou of Wales. If this content you not,

Make several kingdoms of this monarchy,
And share it equally amongst you all,
So I may have some nook or corner left,
To frolic with my dearest Gaveston.

Canterbury. Nothing shall alter us: we are resolved.

Lancaster. Come, come, subscribe.

Mortimer jun. Why should you love him whom the world
  hates so?

Edward. Because he loves me more than all the world.
Ah, none but rude and savage-minded men
Would seek the ruin of my Gaveston;
You that be noble-born should pity him.

Warwick. You that are princely-born should shake him
  off:
For shame subscribe, and let the lown depart.

Mortimer sen. Urge him, my lord.

Canterbury. Are you content to banish him the realm?

Edward. I see I must, and therefore am content:
Instead of ink I'll write it with my tears.   [*Subscribes.*

Mortimer jun. The king is love-sick for his minion.

Edward. 'Tis done, and now, accursed hand, fall off!

Lancaster. Give it me; I'll have it published in the streets.

Mortimer jun. I'll see him presently dispatched away.

Canterbury. Now is my heart at ease.

Warwick.   And so is mine.

Pembroke. This will be good news to the common sort.

Mortimer sen. Be it or no, he shall not linger here.

                        [*Exeunt all except King Edward.*

Edward. How fast they run to banish him I love.
They would not stir, were it to do me good.
Why should a king be subject to a priest?
Proud Rome, that hatchest such imperial grooms,
For these thy superstitious taper-lights,
Wherewith thy antichristian churches blaze,
I'll fire thy crazed buildings, and enforce
The papal towers to kiss the lowly ground.

With slaughtered priests may Tiber's channel swell,
And banks raised higher with their sepulchres.
As for the peers that back the clergy thus,
If I be king, not one of them shall live.

Re-enter GAVESTON

Gaveston. My lord, I hear it whispered everywhere,
  That I am banished, and must fly the land.
Edward. 'Tis true, sweet Gaveston – O! were it false!
  The legate of the Pope will have it so,
  And thou must hence, or I shall be deposed.
  But I will reign to be revenged of them,
  And therefore, sweet friend, take it patiently.
  Live where thou wilt, I'll send thee gold enough;
  And long thou shalt not stay, or if thou dost,
  I'll come to thee; my love shall ne'er decline.
Gaveston. Is all my hope turned to this hell of grief?
Edward. Rend not my heart with thy too-piercing words:
  Thou from this land, I from myself am banished.
Gaveston. To go from hence grieves not poor Gaveston;
  But to forsake you, in whose gracious looks
  The blessedness of Gaveston remains:
  For nowhere else seeks he felicity.
Edward. And only this torments my wretched soul,
  That whether I will or no, thou must depart.
  Be governor of Ireland in my stead,
  And there abide till fortune call thee home.
  Here take my picture, and let me wear thine.

  [They exchange pictures.
  O, might I keep thee here as I do this,
  Happy were I: but now most miserable.
Gaveston. 'Tis something to be pitied of a king.
Edward. Thou shalt not hence; I'll hide thee, Gaveston.
Gaveston. I shall be found, and then 'twill grieve me more.
Edward. Kind words and mutual talk makes our grief
    greater:

Therefore, with dumb embracement, let us part –
Stay, Gaveston, I cannot leave thee thus.
Gaveston. For every look, my lord, drops down a tear:
Seeing I must go, do not renew my sorrow.
Edward. The time is little that thou hast to stay,
And therefore give me leave to look my fill:
But come, sweet friend, I'll bear thee on thy way.
Gaveston. The peers will frown.
Edward. I pass not for their anger. Come, let's go.
O that we might as well return as go.

Enter the QUEEN

Queen. Whither goes my lord?
Edward. Fawn not on me, French strumpet; get thee
gone.
Queen. On whom but on my husband should I fawn?
Gaveston. On Mortimer, with whom, ungentle queen –
I say no more, judge you the rest, my lord.
Queen. In saying this, thou wrongest me, Gaveston;
Is't not enough that thou corrupt'st my lord,
And art a bawd to his affections,
But thou must call mine honour thus in question?
Gaveston. I mean not so; your grace must pardon me.
Edward. Thou art too familiar with that Mortimer,
And by thy means is Gaveston exiled;
But I would wish thee reconcile the lords,
Or thou shalt ne'er be reconciled to me.
Queen. Your highness knows it lies not in my power.
Edward. Away then; touch me not. Come, Gaveston.
Queen. Villain! 'tis thou that robb'st me of my lord.
Gaveston. Madam, 'tis you that rob me of my lord.
Edward. Speak not unto her; let her droop and pine.
Queen. Wherein, my lord, have I deserved these words?
Witness the tears that Isabella sheds,
Witness this heart, that sighing for thee breaks,
How dear my lord is to poor Isabel.

Edward. And witness heaven how dear thou art to
  me.
   There weep: for till my Gaveston be repealed,
   Assure thyself thou com'st not in my sight.

                    [*Exeunt Edward and Gaveston.*

Queen. O miserable and distressed queen!
   Would, when I left sweet France and was embarked,
   That charming Circe, walking on the waves,
   Had changed my shape, or at the marriage-day
   The cup of Hymen had been full of poison,
   Or with those arms that twined about my neck
   I had been stifled, and not lived to see
   The king my lord thus to abandon me.
   Like frantic Juno will I fill the earth
   With ghastly murmur of my sighs and cries;
   For never doted Jove on Ganymede
   So much as he on cursed Gaveston. –
   But that will more exasperate his wrath;
   I must entreat him, I must speak him fair,
   And be a means to call home Gaveston:
   And yet he'll ever dote on Gaveston;
   And so am I for ever miserable.

Re-enter LANCASTER, WARWICK, PEMBROKE,
   MORTIMER *senior, and* MORTIMER *junior*

Lancaster. Look where the sister of the king of France
   Sits wringing of her hands, and beats her breast!
Warwick. The king, I fear, hath ill intreated her.
Pembroke. Hard is the heart that injures such a saint.
Mortimer jun. I know 'tis 'long of Gaveston she weeps.
Mortimer sen. Why? He is gone.
Mortimer jun.   Madam, how fares your grace?
Queen. Ah, Mortimer! now breaks the king's hate forth,
   And he confesseth that he loves me not.
Mortimer jun. Cry quittance, madam, then, and love not
   him.

Queen. No, rather will I die a thousand deaths:
  And yet I love in vain; he'll ne'er love me.
Lancaster. Fear ye not, madam; now his minion's gone,
  His wanton humour will be quickly left.
Queen. O never, Lancaster! I am enjoined
  To sue unto you all for his repeal;
  This wills my lord, and this must I perform,
  Or else be banished from his highness' presence.
Lancaster. For his repeal, madam! He comes not back,
  Unless the sea cast up his shipwracked body.
Warwick. And to behold so sweet a sight as that,
  There's none here but would run his horse to death.
Mortimer jun. But, madam, would you have us call him
    home?
Queen. Ay, Mortimer, for till he be restored,
  The angry king hath banished me the court;
  And therefore, as thou lovest and tendrest me,
  Be thou my advocate unto these peers.
Mortimer jun. What, would ye have me plead for Gaves-
    ton?
Mortimer sen. Plead for him he that will, I am re-
    solved.
Lancaster. And so am I, my lord: dissuade the queen.
Queen. O Lancaster, let him dissuade the king,
  For 'tis against my will he should return.
Warwick. Then speak not for him, let the peasant go.
Queen. 'Tis for myself I speak, and not for him.
Pembroke. No speaking will prevail, and therefore cease.
Mortimer jun. Fair queen, forbear to angle for the fish
  Which, being caught, strikes him that takes it dead;
  I mean that vile torpedo, Gaveston,
  That now, I hope, floats on the Irish seas.
Queen. Sweet Mortimer, sit down by me awhile,
  And I will tell thee reasons of such weight
  As thou wilt soon subscribe to his repeal.
Mortimer jun. It is impossible; but speak your mind.

Queen. Then thus, but none shall hear it but ourselves.
                              [*Talks to Mortimer junior apart.*
Lancaster. My lords, albeit the queen win Mortimer,
  Will you be resolute and hold with me?
Mortimer sen. Not I, against my nephew.
Pembroke. Fear not, the queen's words cannot alter him.
Warwick. No? Do but mark how earnestly she pleads.
Lancaster. And see how coldly his looks make denial.
Warwick. She smiles; now for my life his mind is changed.
Lancaster. I'll rather lose his friendship, I, than grant.
Mortimer jun. Well, of necessity it must be so.
  My lords, that I abhor base Gaveston,
  I hope your honours make no question,
  And therefore, though I plead for his repeal,
  'Tis not for his sake, but for our avail;
  Nay for the realm's behoof, and for the king's.
Lancaster. Fie, Mortimer, dishonour not thyself!
  Can this be true, 'twas good to banish him?
  And is this true, to call him home again?
  Such reasons make white black, and dark night day.
Mortimer jun. My lord of Lancaster, mark the respect.
Lancaster. In no respect can contraries be true.
Queen. Yet, my good lord, hear what he can allege.
Warwick. All that he speaks is nothing; we are resolved.
Mortimer jun. Do you not wish that Gaveston were dead?
Pembroke. I would he were.
Mortimer jun. Why then, my lord, give me but leave to speak.
Mortimer sen. But, nephew, do not play the sophister.
Mortimer jun. This which I urge is of a burning zeal
  To mend the king, and do our country good.
  Know you not Gaveston hath store of gold,
  Which may in Ireland purchase him such friends
  As he will front the mightiest of us all?
  And whereas he shall live and be beloved,
  'Tis hard for us to work his overthrow.
Warwick. Mark you but that, my lord of Lancaster.

Mortimer jun. But were he here, detested as he is,
   How easily might some base slave be suborned
   To greet his lordship with a poniard,
   And none so much as blame the murtherer,
   But rather praise him for that brave attempt,
   And in the chronicle enrol his name
   For purging of the realm of such a plague.

Pembroke. He saith true.

Lancaster. Ay, but how chance was not this done before?

Mortimer jun. Because, my lords, it was not thought upon.
   Nay, more, when he shall know it lies in us
   To banish him and then to call him home,
   'Twill make him vail the top-flag of his pride,
   And fear to offend the meanest nobleman.

Mortimer sen. But how if he do not, nephew?

Mortimer jun. Then may we with some colour rise in arms;
   For howsoever we have borne it out,
   'Tis treason to be up against the king;
   So shall we have the people of our side,
   Which for his father's sake lean to the king,
   But cannot brook a night-grown mushroom,
   Such a one as my lord of Cornwall is,
   Should bear us down of the nobility.
   And when the commons and the nobles join,
   'Tis not the king can buckler Gaveston;
   We'll pull him from the strongest hold he hath.
   My lords, if to perform this I be slack,
   Think me as base a groom as Gaveston.

Lancaster. On that condition, Lancaster will grant.

Warwick. And so will Pembroke and I.

Mortimer sen.   And I.

Mortimer jun. In this I count me highly gratified,
   And Mortimer will rest at your command.

Queen. And when this favour Isabel forgets,
   Then let her live abandoned and forlorn.
   But see, in happy time, my lord the king,

Having brought the Earl of Cornwall on his way,
Is new returned; this news will glad him much,
Yet not so much as me; I love him more
Than he can Gaveston; would he loved me
But half so much, then were I treble-blessed!

Re-enter KING EDWARD, *mourning*

Edward. He's gone, and for his absence thus I mourn.
Did never sorrow go so near my heart
As doth the want of my sweet Gaveston;
And could my crown's revenue bring him back,
I would freely give it to his enemies,
And think I gained, having bought so dear a friend.
Queen. Hark, how he harps upon his minion.
Edward. My heart is as an anvil unto sorrow,
Which beats upon it like the Cyclops' hammers,
And with the noise turns up my giddy brain,
And makes me frantic for my Gaveston.
Ah, had some bloodless Fury rose from hell,
And with my kingly sceptre struck me dead,
When I was forced to leave my Gaveston.
Lancaster. Diablo! What passions call you these?
Queen. My gracious lord, I come to bring you news.
Edward. That you have parled with your Mortimer.
Queen. That Gaveston, my lord, shall be repealed.
Edward. Repealed! The news is too sweet to be true.
Queen. But will you love me, if you find it so?
Edward. If it be so, what will not Edward do?
Queen. For Gaveston, but not for Isabel.
Edward. For thee, fair queen, if thou lovest Gaveston;
I'll hang a golden tongue about thy neck,
Seeing thou hast pleaded with so good success.
Queen. No other jewels hang about my neck
Than these, my lord; nor let me have more wealth
Than I may fetch from this rich treasury:
O how a kiss revives poor Isabel!

Edward. Once more receive my hand, and let this be
  A second marriage 'twixt thyself and me.
Queen. And may it prove more happy than the first.
  My gentle lord, bespeak these nobles fair,
  That wait attendance for a gracious look,
  And on their knees salute your majesty.
Edward. Courageous Lancaster, embrace thy king,
  And, as gross vapours perish by the sun,
  Even so let hatred with thy sovereign's smile.
  Live thou with me as my companion.
Lancaster. This salutation overjoys my heart.
Edward. Warwick shall be my chiefest counsellor:
  These silver hairs will more adorn my court
  Than gaudy silks, or rich embroidery,
  Chide me, sweet Warwick, if I go astray.
Warwick. Slay me, my lord, when I offend your grace.
Edward. In solemn triumphs, and in public shows,
  Pembroke shall bear the sword before the king.
Pembroke. And with this sword Pembroke will fight for
  you.
Edward. But wherefore walks young Mortimer aside?
  Be thou commander of our royal fleet;
  Or, if that lofty office like thee not,
  I make thee here Lord Marshal of the realm.
Mortimer jun. My lord, I'll marshal so your enemies,
  As England shall be quiet, and you safe.
Edward. And as for you, Lord Mortimer of Chirke,
  Whose great achievements in our foreign war
  Deserve no common place, nor mean reward;
  Be you the general of the levied troops,
  That now are ready to assail the Scots.
Mortimer sen. In this your grace hath highly honoured
  me,
  For with my nature war doth best agree.
Queen. Now is the king of England rich and strong,
  Having the love of his renowned peers.

Edward. Ay, Isabel, ne'er was my heart so light.
   Clerk of the crown, – direct our warrant forth
   For Gaveston to Ireland:

Enter BEAUMONT *with warrant.*

                   Beaumont, fly
   As fast as Iris or Jove's Mercury.
Beaumont. It shall be done, my gracious lord.   [*Exit.*
Edward. Lord Mortimer, we leave you to your charge.
   Now let us in, and feast it royally.
   Against our friend the earl of Cornwall comes,
   We'll have a general tilt and tournament;
   And then his marriage shall be solemnized.
   For wot you not that I have made him sure
   Unto our cousin, the earl of Gloucester's heir?
Lancaster. Such news we hear, my lord.
Edward. That day, if not for him, yet for my sake
   Who in the triumph will be challenger,
   Spare for no cost; we will requite your love.
Warwick. In this or aught your highness shall command
   us.
Edward. Thanks, gentle Warwick. Come, let's in and
   revel.   [*Exeunt. Manent Mortimers.*
Mortimer sen. Nephew, I must to Scotland; thou stayest
   here.
   Leave now to oppose thyself against the king.
   Thou seest by nature he is mild and calm,
   And, seeing his mind so dotes on Gaveston,
   Let him without controlment have his will.
   The mightiest kings have had their minions:
   Great Alexander loved Hephaestion;
   The conquering Hercules for Hylas wept;
   And for Patroclus stern Achilles drooped.
   And not kings only, but the wisest men:
   The Roman Tully loved Octavius;
   Grave Socrates, wild Alcibiades.

A hall in Gloucester's house

Enter SPENCER *junior and* BALDOCK

Baldock. Spencer,
    Seeing that our lord th' earl of Gloucester's dead,
    Which of the nobles dost thou mean to serve?
Spencer jun. Not Mortimer, nor any of his side;
    Because the king and he are enemies.
    Baldock, learn this of me, a factious lord
    Shall hardly do himself good, much less us;
    But he that hath the favour of a king,
    May with one word advance us while we live:
    The liberal earl of Cornwall is the man
    On whose good fortune Spencer's hope depends.
Baldock. What, mean you then to be his follower?
Spencer jun. No, his companion, for he loves me well,
    And would have once preferred me to the king.
Baldock. But he is banished; there's small hope of him.
Spencer jun. Ay, for a while; but, Baldock, mark the end.
    A friend of mine told me in secrecy
    That he's repealed, and sent for back again;
    And even now a post came from the court
    With letters to our lady from the king;
    And as she read she smiled, which makes me think
    It is about her lover Gaveston.
Baldock. 'Tis like enough, for since he was exiled
    She neither walks abroad, nor comes in sight.
    But I had thought the match had been broke off,
    And that his banishment had changed her mind.
Spencer jun. Our lady's first love is not wavering;
    My life for thine she will have Gaveston.
Baldock. Then hope I by her means to be preferred,
    Having read unto her since she was a child.

Then let his grace, whose youth is flexible,
And promiseth as much as we can wish,
Freely enjoy that vain, light-headed earl;
For riper years will wean him from such toys.

Mortimer jun. Uncle, his wanton humour grieves not me;
But this I scorn, that one so basely born
Should by his sovereign's favour grow so pert,
And riot it with the treasure of the realm.
While soldiers mutiny for want of pay,
He wears a lord's revenue on his back,
And, Midas-like, he jets it in the court,
With base outlandish cullions at his heels,
Whose proud fantastic liveries make such show,
As if that Proteus, god of shapes, appeared,
I have not seen a dapper Jack so brisk;
He wears a short Italian hooded cloak,
Larded with pearl, and in his Tuscan cap
A jewel of more value than the crown.
Whiles other walk below, the king and he
From out a window laugh at such as we,
And flout our train, and jest at our attire.
Uncle, 'tis this that makes me impatient.

Mortimer sen. But, nephew, now you see the king is
changed.

Mortimer jun. Then so am I, and live to do him service:
But whiles I have a sword, a hand, a heart,
I will not yield to any such upstart.
You know my mind; come, uncle, let's away.

                                        [*Exeunt.*

Spencer jun. Then, Baldock, you must cast the scholar off,
    And learn to court it like a gentleman.
    'Tis not a black cloak and a little band,
    A velvet-caped cloak, faced before with serge,
    And smelling to a nosegay all the day,
    Or holding of a napkin in your hand,
    Or saying a long grace at a table's end,
    Or making low legs to a nobleman,
    Or looking downward with your eyelids close,
    And saying, 'Truly, an't may please your honour,'
    Can get you any favour with great men;
    You must be proud, bold, pleasant, resolute,
    And now and then stab, as occasion serves.
Baldock. Spencer, thou knowest I hate such formal toys,
    And use them but of mere hypocrisy.
    Mine old lord while he lived was so precise,
    That he would take exceptions at my buttons,
    And being like pin's heads, blame me for the bigness;
    Which made me curate-like in mine attire,
    Though inwardly licentious enough,
    And apt for any kind of villainy.
    I am none of these common pedants, I,
    That cannot speak without *propterea quod*.
Spencer jun. But one of those that saith, *quando-quidem*,
    And hath a special gift to form a verb.
Baldock. Leave off this jesting, here my lady comes.

Enter the KING'S NIECE

Niece. The grief for his exile was not so much,
    As is the joy of his returning home.
    This letter came from my sweet Gaveston:
    What needst thou, love, thus to excuse thyself?
    I know thou couldst not come and visit me:
    [*Reads.*] 'I will not long be from thee, though I die.'
    This argues the entire love of my lord;
    [*Reads.*] 'When I forsake thee, death seize on my heart.':

But rest thee here where Gaveston shall sleep.

[Placing the letter in her bosom.

Now to the letter of my lord the king.
He wills me to repair unto the court,
And meet my Gaveston. Why do I stay,
Seeing that he talks thus of my marriage-day?
Who's there? Baldock!
See that my coach be ready, I must hence.

Baldock. It shall be done, madam.

Niece. And meet me at the park-pale presently.

[Exit Baldock.

Spencer, stay you and bear me company,
For I have joyful news to tell thee of;
My lord of Cornwall is a-coming over,
And will be at the court as soon as we.

Spencer jun. I knew the king would have him home again

Niece. If all things sort out as I hope they will,
Thy service, Spencer, shall be thought upon.

Spencer jun. I humbly thank your ladyship.

Niece. Come, lead the way; I long till I am there.

[Exeunt.

ACT II, SCENE 2

Before Tynemouth Castle

Enter KING EDWARD, *the* QUEEN, LANCASTER,
MORTIMER *junior*, WARWICK, PEMBROKE, KENT,
ATTENDANTS

Edward [aside]. The wind is good, I wonder why he stays;
I fear me he is wracked upon the sea.

Queen. Look, Lancaster, how passionate he is,
And still his mind runs on his minion.

Lancaster. My lord, —

Edward. How now! what news? is Gaveston arrived?

Mortimer jun. Nothing but Gaveston! what means your
    grace?
  You have matters of more weight to think upon;
  The King of France sets foot in Normandy.
Edward. A trifle! we'll expel him when we please.
  But tell me, Mortimer, what's thy device
  Against the stately triumph we decreed?
Mortimer jun. A homely one, my lord, not worth the tell-
    ing.
Edward. Prithee let me know it.
Mortimer jun. But seeing you are so desirous, thus it is:
  A lofty cedar-tree, fair flourishing,
  On whose top-branches kingly eagles perch,
  And by the bark a canker creeps me up,
  And gets unto the highest bough of all:
  The motto, *Aeque tandem.*
Edward. And what is yours, my lord of Lancaster?
Lancaster. My lord, mine's more obscure than Mortimer's.
  Pliny reports there is a flying fish
  Which all the other fishes deadly hate,
  And therefore, being pursued, it takes the air:
  No sooner is it up, but there's a fowl
  That seizeth it; this fish, my lord, I bear,
  The motto this: *Undique mors est.*
Edward. Proud Mortimer! ungentle Lancaster!
  Is this the love you bear your sovereign?
  Is this the fruit your reconcilement bears?
  Can you in words make show of amity,
  And in your shields display your rancorous minds?
  What call you this but private libelling
  Against the earl of Cornwall and my brother?
Queen. Sweet husband, be content, they all love you.
Edward. They love me not that hate my Gaveston.
  I am that cedar – shake me not too much –
  And you the eagles: soar ye ne'er so high,
  I have the jesses that will pull you down;

    And *Aeque tandem* shall that canker cry
    Unto the proudest peer of Britainy.
    Though thou compar'st him to a flying fish,
    And threatenest death whether he rise or fall,
    'Tis not the hugest monster of the sea,
    Nor foulest harpy that shall swallow him.
Mortimer jun. If in his absence thus he favours him,
    What will he do whenas he shall be present?
Lancaster. That shall we see; look where his lordship comes.

Enter GAVESTON

Edward. My Gaveston!
    Welcome to Tynemouth, welcome to thy friend!
    Thy absence made me droop and pine away;
    For, as the lovers of fair Danaë,
    When she was locked up in a brazen tower,
    Desired her more, and waxed outrageous,
    So did it sure with me: and now thy sight
    Is sweeter far than was thy parting hence
    Bitter and irksome to my sobbing heart.
Gaveston. Sweet lord and king, your speech preventeth
      mine,
    Yet have I words left to express my joy:
    The shepherd nipt with biting winter's rage
    Frolics not more to see the painted spring,
    Than I do to behold your majesty.
Edward. Will none of you salute my Gaveston?
Lancaster. Salute him? yes; welcome Lord Chamberlain.
Mortimer jun. Welcome is the good earl of Cornwall.
Warwick. Welcome, Lord Governor of the Isle of Man.
Pembroke. Welcome, Master Secretary.
Kent. Brother, do you hear them?
Edward. Still will these earls and barons use me thus?
Gaveston. My lord, I cannot brook these injuries.
Queen. Ay me, poor soul, when these begin to jar.
                                [Aside.

Edward. Return it to their throats, I'll be thy warrant.

Gaveston. Base, leaden earls, that glory in your birth,
  Go sit at home and eat your tenants' beef;
  And come not here to scoff at Gaveston,
  Whose mounting thoughts did never creep so low
  As to bestow a look on such as you.

Lancaster. Yet I disdain not to do this for you.

                                    [*Draws his sword.*

Edward. Treason, treason! where's the traitor?

Pembroke. Here! here!

Edward. Convey hence Gaveston; they'll murder him.

Gaveston. The life of thee shall salve this foul disgrace.

Mortimer jun. Villain, thy life, unless I miss mine aim.

                                    [*Wounds Gaveston.*

Queen. Ah! furious Mortimer, what hast thou done?

Mortimer jun. No more than I would answer, were he
  slain.   [*Exit Gaveston with Attendants.*

Edward. Yes, more than thou canst answer, though he
  live;
  Dear shall you both aby this riotous deed.
  Out of my presence, come not near the court.

Mortimer jun. I'll not be barred the court for Gaveston.

Lancaster. We'll hale him by the ears unto the block.

Edward. Look to your own heads; his is sure enough.

Warwick. Look to your own crown, if you back him
  thus.

Kent. Warwick, these words do ill beseem thy years.

Edward. Nay, all of them conspire to cross me thus;
  But if I live, I'll tread upon their heads
  That think with high looks thus to tread me down.
  Come, Edmund, let's away and levy men,
  'Tis war that must abate these barons' pride.

          [*Exeunt King Edward, Queen Isabella, and Kent.*

Warwick. Let's to our castles, for the king is moved.

Mortimer jun. Moved may he be, and perish in his
  wrath!

Lancaster. Cousin, it is no dealing with him now,
  He means to make us stoop by force of arms:
  And therefore let us jointly here protest,
  To prosecute that Gaveston to the death.
Mortimer jun. By heaven, the abject villain shall not live.
Warwick. I'll have his blood, or die in seeking it.
Pembroke. The like oath Pembroke takes.
Lancaster.   And so doth Lancaster.
  Now send our heralds to defy the king;
  And make the people swear to put him down.

Enter a POST

Mortimer jun. Letters: from whence?
Messenger.   From Scotland, my lord.
Lancaster. Why, how now, cousin, how fares all our
    friends?
Mortimer jun. My uncle's taken prisoner by the Scots.
Lancaster. We'll have him ransomed, man; be of good
    cheer.
Mortimer jun. They rate his ransom at five thousand
    pound.
  Who should defray the money but the king,
  Seeing he is taken prisoner in his wars?
  I'll to the king.
Lancaster. Do, cousin, and I'll bear thee company.
Warwick. Meantime, my lord of Pembroke and myself
  Will to Newcastle here, and gather head.
Mortimer jun. About it then, and we will follow you.
Lancaster. Be resolute and full of secrecy.
Warwick. I warrant you.
                    [*Exeunt all but Mortimer and Lancaster.*
Mortimer jun. Cousin, and if he will not ransom him,
  I'll thunder such a peal into his ears,
  As never subject did unto his king.
Lancaster. Content, I'll bear my part. Holla! who's there?

Enter GUARD

Mortimer jun. Ay, marry, such a guard as this doth well.

Lancaster. Lead on the way.

Guard. Whither will your lordships?

Mortimer jun. Whither else but to the king?

Guard. His highness is disposed to be alone.

Lancaster. Why, so he may, but we will speak to him.

Guard. You may not in, my Lord.

Mortimer jun. May we not?

Enter the KING and KENT

Edward. How now! – What noise is this?
  Who have we there, is't you?   [*Going.*

Mortimer jun. Nay, stay, my lord, I come to bring you news;
  Mine uncle's taken prisoner by the Scots.

Edward. Then ransom him.

Lancaster. 'Twas in your wars; you should ransom him.

Mortimer jun. And you shall ransom him, or else —

Kent. What, Mortimer! you will not threaten him?

Edward. Quiet yourself, you shall have the broad seal,
  To gather for him throughout the realm.

Lancaster. Your minion Gaveston hath taught you this.

Mortimer jun. My lord, the family of the Mortimers
  Are not so poor, but, would they sell their land,
  Would levy men enough to anger you.
  We never beg, but use such prayers as these.
                    [*Putting his hand on his sword.*

Edward. Shall I still be haunted thus?

Mortimer jun. Nay, now you are here alone, I'll speak my
  mind.

Lancaster. And so will I, and then, my lord, farewell.

Mortimer jun. The idle triumphs, masks, lascivious shows,
  And prodigal gifts bestowed on Gaveston,
  Have drawn thy treasure dry, and made thee weak,
  The murmuring commons overstretched have.

Lancaster. Look for rebellion, look to be deposed;
  Thy garrisons are beaten out of France,

And, lame and poor, lie groaning at the gates.
The wild O'Neil, with swarms of Irish kerns,
Lives uncontrolled within the English pale.
Unto the walls of York the Scots made road,
And unresisted drave away rich spoils.

Mortimer jun. The haughty Dane commands the narrow
    seas,
While in the harbour ride thy ships unrigged.

Lancaster. What foreign prince sends thee ambassadors?

Mortimer jun. Who loves thee, but a sort of flatterers?

Lancaster. Thy gentle queen, sole sister to Valois,
Complains that thou hast left her all forlorn.

Mortimer jun. Thy court is naked, being bereft of those
That makes a king seem glorious to the world;
I mean the peers, whom thou shouldst dearly love:
Libels are cast again thee in the street,
Ballads and rhymes, made of thy overthrow.

Lancaster. The Northern borderers seeing their houses
    burnt,
Their wives and children slain, run up and down,
Cursing the name of thee and Gaveston.

Mortimer jun. When wert thou in the field with banner
    spread?
But once, and then thy soldiers marched like players,
With garish robes, not armour, and thyself,
Bedaubed with gold, rode laughing at the rest,
Nodding and shaking of thy spangled crest.
Where women's favours hung like labels down.

Lancaster. And thereof came it that the fleering Scots
To England's high disgrace, have made this jig;
'Maids of England, sore may you mourn,
For your lemans you have lost at Bannocksbourn,
    With a heave and a ho!
What weeneth the King of England,
So soon to have won Scotland? –
    With a rombelow.'

Mortimer jun. Wigmore shall fly to set my uncle free.

Lancaster. And when 'tis gone, our swords shall purchase
    more.

  If ye be moved, revenge it as you can;

  Look next to see us with our ensigns spread.

                           [Exit with Mortimer junior.

Edward. My swelling heart for very anger breaks.

  How oft have I been baited by these peers?

  And dare not be revenged, for their power is great.

  Yet, shall the crowing of these cockerels

  Affright a lion? Edward, unfold thy paws,

  And let their lives' blood slake thy fury's hunger.

  If I be cruel and grow tyrannous,

  Now let them thank themselves, and rue too late.

Kent. My lord, I see your love to Gaveston

  Will be the ruin of the realm and you,

  For now the wrathful nobles threaten wars,

  And therefore, brother, banish him for ever.

Edward. Art thou an enemy to my Gaveston?

Kent. Ay, and it grieves me that I favoured him.

Edward. Traitor, begone! whine thou with Mortimer.

Kent. So will I, rather than with Gaveston.

Edward. Out of my sight, and trouble me no more.

Kent. No marvel though thou scorn thy noble peers,

  When I thy brother am rejected thus.

Edward. Away!   *[Exit Kent.*

  Poor Gaveston, that hast no friend but me,

  Do what they can, we'll live in Tynemouth here,

  And, so I walk with him about the walls,

  What care I though the earls begirt us round?

  Here comes she that's cause of all these jars.

Enter the QUEEN *with the* KING'S NIECE, *two* LADIES,
    GAVESTON, BALDOCK, *and* SPENCER *junior*

Queen. My lord, 'tis thought the earls are up in arms.

Edward. Ay, and 'tis likewise thought you favour him.

Queen. Thus do you still suspect me without cause?

Niece. Sweet uncle, speak more kindly to the queen.

Gaveston. My lord, dissemble with her, speak her fair.

Edward. Pardon me, sweet, I forgot myself.

Queen. Your pardon is quickly got of Isabel.

Edward. The younger Mortimer is grown so brave,
That to my face he threatens civil wars.

Gaveston. Why do you not commit him to the Tower?

Edward. I dare not, for the people love him well.

Gaveston. Why, then we'll have him privily made
away.

Edward. Would Lancaster and he had both caroused
A bowl of poison to each other's health.
But let them go, and tell me what are these.

Niece. Two of my father's servants whilst he lived;
May't please your grace to entertain them now?

Edward. Tell me, where wast thou born? what is thine
arms?

Baldock. My name is Baldock, and my gentry
I fetch from Oxford, not from heraldry.

Edward. The fitter art thou, Baldock, for my turn.
Wait on me, and I'll see thou shalt not want.

Baldock. I humbly thank your majesty.

Edward. Knowest thou him, Gaveston?

Gaveston.   Ay, my lord;
His name is Spencer, he is well allied;
For my sake, let him wait upon your grace;
Scarce shall you find a man of more desert.

Edward. Then, Spencer, wait upon me; for his sake
I'll grace thee with a higher style ere long.

Spencer jun. No greater titles happen unto me,
Than to be favoured of your majesty.

Edward. Cousin, this day shall be your marriage-feast.
And, Gaveston, think that I love thee well,
To wed thee to our niece, the only heir
Unto the Earl of Gloucester late deceased

Gaveston. I know, my lord, many will stomach me,
  But I respect neither their love nor hate.
Edward. The headstrong barons shall not limit me;
  He that I list to favour shall be great.
  Come, let's away; and when the marriage ends,
  Have at the rebels, and their complices.

                                    [*Exeunt omnes.*

───

ACT II, SCENE 3

Near Tynemouth Castle

Enter LANCASTER, MORTIMER *junior*, WARWICK,
      PEMBROKE, KENT, *and others*

Kent. My lords, of love to this our native land
  I come to join with you and leave the king;
  And in your quarrel and the realm's behoof
  Will be the first that shall adventure life.
Lancaster. I fear me you are sent of policy,
  To undermine us with a show of love.
Warwick. He is your brother, therefore have we cause
  To cast the worst, and doubt of your revolt.
Kent. Mine honour shall be hostage of my truth:
  If that will not suffice, farewell, my lords.
Mortimer jun. Stay, Edmund; never was Plantagenet
  False of his word, and therefore trust we thee.
Pembroke. But what's the reason you should leave him
    now?
Kent. I have informed the Earl of Lancaster.
Lancaster. And it sufficeth. Now, my lords, know this,
  That Gaveston is secretly arrived,
  And here in Tynemouth frolics with the king.
  Let us with these our followers scale the walls,
  And suddenly surprise them unawares.
Mortimer jun. I'll give the onset.

Warwick.   And I'll follow thee.

Mortimer jun. This tattered ensign of my ancestors,
  Which swept the desert shore of that dead sea
  Whereof we got the name of Mortimer,
  Will I advance upon this castle's walls.
  Drums, strike alarum, raise them from their sport,
  And ring aloud the knell of Gaveston.

Lancaster. None be so hardy as to touch the king;
  But neither spare you Gaveston nor his friends.

                              [*Exeunt.*

━━━

ACT II, SCENE 4

In Tynemouth Castle

Enter severally the KING *and* SPENCER *junior*

Edward. O tell me, Spencer, where is Gaveston?

Spencer jun. I fear me he is slain, my gracious lord.

Edward. No, here he comes; now let them spoil and kill.

Enter the QUEEN, *the* KING'S NIECE, GAVESTON, *and* NOBLES

  Fly, fly, my lords, the earls have got the hold;
  Take shipping and away to Scarborough;
  Spencer and I will post away by land.

Gaveston. O stay, my lord, they will not injure you.

Edward. I will not trust them, Gaveston; away.

Gaveston. Farewell, my lord.

Edward. Lady, farewell.

Niece. Farewell, sweet uncle, till we meet again.

Edward. Farewell, sweet Gaveston, and farewell, niece.

Queen. No farewell to poor Isabel thy queen?

Edward. Yes, yes, for Mortimer, your lover's sake.

Queen. Heavens can witness I love none but you;

                    [*Exeunt omnes, manet Isabella.*
  From my embracements thus he breaks away.

O that mine arms could close this isle about,
That I might pull him to me where I would;
Or that these tears, that drizzle from mine eyes,
Had power to mollify his stony heart,
That when I had him we might never part.

Enter LANCASTER, WARWICK, MORTIMER *junior,*
and others. Alarums within

Lancaster. I wonder how he scaped?
Mortimer jun.   Who's this? the queen!
Queen. Ay, Mortimer, the miserable queen,
  Whose pining heart her inward sighs have blasted,
  And body with continual mourning wasted;
  These hands are tired with haling of my lord
  From Gaveston, from wicked Gaveston,
  And all in vain; for, when I speak him fair,
  He turns away, and smiles upon his minion.
Mortimer jun. Cease to lament, and tell us where's the
  king?
Queen. What would you with the King? is't him you seek?
Lancaster. No, madam, but that cursed Gaveston.
  Far be it from the thought of Lancaster
  To offer violence to his sovereign.
  We would but rid the realm of Gaveston:
  Tell us where he remains, and he shall die.
Queen. He's gone by water unto Scarborough;
  Pursue him quickly, and he cannot scape;
  The king hath left him, and his train is small.
Warwick. Forslow no time; sweet Lancaster, let's march.
Mortimer jun. How comes it that the king and he is parted?
Queen. That this your army, going several ways
  Might be of lesser force: and with the power
  That he intendeth presently to raise,
  Be easily suppressed; and therefore be gone.
Mortimer jun. Here in the river rides a Flemish hoy;
  Let's all aboard, and follow him amain.

Lancaster. The wind that bears him hence will fill our
    sails.
  Come, come aboard, 'tis but an hour's sailing.
Mortimer jun. Madam, stay you within this castle here.
Queen. No, Mortimer, I'll to my lord the king.
Mortimer jun. Nay, rather sail with us to Scarborough.
Queen. You know the king is so suspicious,
  As if he hear I have talked with you,
  Mine honour will be called in question;
  And therefore, gentle Mortimer, be gone.
Mortimer jun. Madam, I cannot stay to answer you,
  But think of Mortimer as he deserves.

                    [Exeunt all but the Queen.

Queen. So well hast thou deserved, sweet Mortimer,
  As Isabel could live with thee for ever.
  In vain I look for love at Edward's hand,
  Whose eyes are fixed on none but Gaveston,
  Yet once more I'll importune him with prayers:
  If he be strange and not regard my words,
  My son and I will over into France,
  And to the king my brother there complain,
  How Gaveston hath robbed me of his love:
  But yet I hope my sorrows will have end,
  And Gaveston this blessed day be slain.   *[Exit.*

───

ACT II, SCENE 5

The Open Country

Enter GAVESTON, *pursued*

Gaveston. Yet, lusty lords, I have escaped your hands,
  Your threats, your larums, and your hot pursuits;
  And though divorced from king Edward's eyes,
  Yet liveth Pierce of Gaveston unsurprised,
  Breathing, in hope [*malgrado* all your beards,

That muster rebels thus against your king],
To see his royal sovereign once again.

Enter WARWICK, LANCASTER, PEMBROKE, MOR-
TIMER *junior*, SOLDIERS, JAMES, *and other* ATTEND-
ANTS *of* PEMBROKE

Warwick. Upon him, soldiers, take away his weapons.
Mortimer jun. Thou proud disturber of thy country's peace,
  Corrupter of thy king, cause of these broils,
  Base flatterer, yield! and were it not for shame,
  Shame and dishonour to a soldier's name,
  Upon my weapon's point here shouldst thou fall,
  And welter in thy gore.
Lancaster.   Monster of men!
  That, like the Greekish strumpet, trained to arms
  And bloody wars so many valiant knights;
  Look for no other fortune, wretch, than death.
  Kind Edward is not here to buckler thee.
Warwick. Lancaster, why talkst thou to the slave?
  Go, soldiers, take him hence, for, by my sword,
  His head shall off: Gaveston, short warning
  Shall serve thy turn: it is our country's cause,
  That here severely we will execute
  Upon thy person. Hang him at a bough.
Gaveston. My lord! —
Warwick. Soldiers, have him away;
  But for thou wert the favourite of a king,
  Thou shalt have so much honour at our hands.
Gaveston. I thank you all, my lords: then I perceive,
  That heading is one, and hanging is the other,
  And death is all.

Enter EARL OF ARUNDEL

Lancaster. How now, my lord of Arundel?
Arundel. My lords, King Edward greets you all by me.
Warwick. Arundel, say your message.

Arundel.   His majesty,
  Hearing that you had taken Gaveston,
  Entreateth you by me, yet but he may
  See him before he dies; for why, he says,
  And send you word, he knows that die he shall;
  And if you gratify his grace so far,
  He will be mindful of the courtesy.
Warwick. How now?
Gaveston.   Renowmed Edward, how thy name
  Revives poor Gaveston.
Warwick.   ·   No, it needeth not;
  Arundel, we will gratify the king
  In other matters; he must pardon us in this.
  Soldiers, away with him.
Gaveston. Why, my lord of Warwick,
  Will not these delays beget my hopes?
  I know it, lords, it is this life you aim at;
  Yet grant King Edward this.
Mortimer jun.   Shalt thou appoint
  What we shall grant? Soldiers, away with him:
  Thus we'll gratify the king,
  We'll send his head by thee; let him bestow
  His tears on that, for that is all he gets
  Of Gaveston, or else his senseless trunk.
Lancaster. Not so, my lord, lest he bestow more cost
  In burying him than he hath ever earned.
Arundel. My lords, it is his majesty's request,
  And in the honour of a king he swears,
  He will but talk with him, and send him back.
Warwick. When, can you tell? Arundel, no; we wot,
  He that the care of realm remits,
  And drives his nobles to these exigents
  For Gaveston, will, if he sees him once,
  Violate any promise to possess him.
Arundel. Then if you will not trust his grace in keep,
  My lords, I will be pledge for his return.

Mortimer jun. It is honourable in thee to offer this;
  But for we know thou art a noble gentleman,
  We will not wrong thee so, to make away
  A true man for a thief.
Gaveston. How mean'st thou, Mortimer? that is over-
    base.
Mortimer jun. Away, base groom, robber of king's renowm.
  Question with thy companions and thy mates.
Pembroke. My lord Mortimer, and you, my lords, each
    one,
  To gratify the king's request therein,
  Touching the sending of this Gaveston,
  Because his majesty so earnestly
  Desires to see the man before his death,
  I will upon mine honour undertake
  To carry him, and bring him back again;
  Provided this, that you my lord of Arundel
  Will join with me.
Warwick.   Pembroke, what wilt thou do?
  Cause yet more bloodshed: it is not enough
  That we have taken him, but must we now
  Leave him on 'had I wist,' and let him go?
Pembroke. My lords, I will not over-woo your honours,
  But if you dare trust Pembroke with the prisoner,
  Upon mine oath, I will return him back.
Arundel. My lord of Lancaster, what say you in this?
Lancaster. Why, I say, let him go on Pembroke's word.
Pembroke. And you, lord Mortimer?
Mortimer jun. How say you, my lord of Warwick?
Warwick. Nay, do your pleasures, I know how 'twill
  prove.
Pembroke. Then give him me.
Gaveston.   Sweet sovereign, yet I come
  To see thee ere I die.
Warwick [*aside*].   Yet not perhaps,
  If Warwick's wit and policy prevail.

Mortimer jun. My lord of Pembroke, we deliver him you;
   Return him on your honour. Sound, away!

        [Exeunt. Manent Pembroke, Arundel, Gaveston, James,
                      and other Attendants of Pembroke

Pembroke. My lord, you shall go with me.
   My house is not far hence, out of the way
   A little, but our men shall go along.
   We that have pretty wenches to our wives,
   Sir, must not come so near and baulk their lips.

Arundel. 'Tis very kindly spoke, my lord of Pembroke;
   Your honour hath an adamant of power
   To draw a prince.

Pembroke.   So, my lord. Come hither, James:
   I do commit this Gaveston to thee,
   Be thou this night his keeper; in the morning
   We will discharge thee of thy charge: be gone.

Gaveston. Unhappy Gaveston, whither goest thou now?

               [Exit cum servis Pembroke.

Horse-boy. My lord, we'll quickly be at Cobham.

                     [Exeunt.

ACT III, SCENE 1

The Open Country

Enter GAVESTON *mourning,* JAMES, *and other*
ATTENDANTS *of* PEMBROKE

Gaveston. O treacherous Warwick, thus to wrong thy
friend.
James. I see it is your life these arms pursue.
Gaveston. Weaponless must I fall, and die in bands?
O, must this day be period of my life?
Centre of all my bliss! An ye be men,
Speed to the king.

Enter WARWICK *and* SOLDIERS

Warwick. My lord of Pembroke's men,
Strive you no longer; I will have that Gaveston.
James. Your lordship doth dishonour to yourself,
And wrong our lord, your honourable friend.
Warwick. No, James, it is my country's cause I follow.
Go, take the villain; soldiers, come away.
We'll make quick work. Commend me to your master,
My friend, and tell him that I watched it well.
Come, let thy shadow parley with King Edward.
Gaveston. Treacherous earl, shall I not see the King?
Warwick. The king of heaven perhaps, no other king.
Away! [*Exeunt Warwick and Soldiers with Gaveston.*
James. Come, fellows, it booted not for us to strive,
We will in haste go certify our lord. [*Exeunt.*

ACT III, SCENE 2

Near Boroughbridge, in Yorkshire

Enter KING EDWARD *and* SPENCER *junior,* BALDOCK,
and NOBLES *of the King's side, and* SOLDIERS *with
drums and fifes.*

Edward. I long to hear an answer from the barons
Touching my friend, my dearest Gaveston.
Ah! Spencer, not the riches of my realm
Can ransom him; ah, he is marked to die.
I know the malice of the younger Mortimer,
Warwick I know is rough, and Lancaster
Inexorable, and I shall never see
My lovely Pierce, my Gaveston again!
The barons overbear me with their pride.
Spencer jun. Were I King Edward, England's sovereign,
Son to the lovely Eleanor of Spain,
Great Edward Longshanks' issue, would I bear
These braves, this rage, and suffer uncontrolled
These barons thus to beard me in my land,
In mine own realm? My lord, pardon my speech:
Did you retain your father's magnanimity,
Did you regard the honour of your name,
You would not suffer thus your majesty
Be counterbuft of your nobility.
Strike off their heads, and let them preach on poles.
No doubt, such lessons they will teach the rest,
As by their preachments they will profit much,
And learn obedience to their lawful king.
Edward. Yea, gentle Spencer, we have been too mild,
Too kind to them; but now have drawn our sword,
And if they send me not my Gaveston,
We'll steel it on their crest, and poll their tops.

Baldock. This haught resolve becomes your majesty,
   Not to be tied to their affection,
   As though your highness were a schoolboy still,
   And must be awed and governed like a child.

Enter SPENCER *senior with his truncheon and*
SOLDIERS

Spencer sen. Long live my sovereign, the noble Edward,
   In peace triumphant, fortunate in wars!
Edward. Welcome, old man, com'st thou in Edward's
   aid?
   Then tell thy prince of whence, and what thou art.
Spencer sen. Lo, with a band of bowmen and of pikes,
   Brown bills and targeteers, four hundred strong,
   Sworn to defend King Edward's royal right,
   I come in person to your majesty,
   Spencer, the father of Hugh Spencer there,
   Bound to your highness everlastingly,
   For favours done, in him, unto us all.
Edward. Thy father, Spencer?
Spencer jun.   True, an it like your grace,
   That pours, in lieu of all your goodness shown,
   His life, my lord, before your princely feet.
Edward. Welcome ten thousand times, old man, again.
   Spencer, this love, this kindness to thy king,
   Argues thy noble mind and disposition.
   Spencer, I here create thee earl of Wiltshire,
   And daily will enrich thee with our favour,
   That, as the sunshine, shall reflect o'er thee.
   Beside, the more to manifest our love,
   Because we hear Lord Bruce doth sell his land,
   And that the Mortimers are in hand withal,
   Thou shalt have crowns of us t' outbid the barons:
   And, Spencer, spare them not, but lay it on.
   Soldiers, a largess, and thrice welcome all.
Spencer jun. My lord, here comes the queen.

Enter the QUEEN, PRINCE EDWARD, *and* LEVUNE,
a Frenchman

Edward.   Madam, what news?
Queen. News of dishonour, lord, and discontent.
　　Our friend Levune, faithful and full of trust,
　　Informeth us, by letters and by words,
　　That lord Valois our brother, King of France,
　　Because your highness hath been slack in homage,
　　Hath seized Normandy into his hands,
　　These be the letters, this the messenger.
Edward. Welcome, Levune. [*To the* QUEEN.] Tush, Sib,
　　if this be all,
　　Valois and I will soon be friends again.
　　But to my Gaveston; shall I never see,
　　Never behold thee now? Madam, in this matter,
　　We will employ you and your little son;
　　You shall go parley with the king of France.
　　Boy, see you bear you bravely to the king,
　　And do your message with a majesty.
Prince. Commit not to my youth things of more weight
　　Than fits a prince so young as I to bear,
　　And fear not, lord and father, heaven's great beams
　　On Atlas' shoulder shall not lie more safe,
　　Than shall your charge committed to my trust.
Queen. Ah, boy! this towardness makes thy mother fear
　　Thou art not marked to many days on earth.
Edward. Madam, we will that you with speed be shipped,
　　And this our son; Levune shall follow you
　　With all the haste we can despatch him hence.
　　Choose of our lords to bear you company;
　　And go in peace, leave us in wars at home.
Queen. Unnatural wars, where subjects brave their king;
　　God end them once! My lord, I take my leave,
　　To make my preparation for France.
　　　　　　　　　　　　　[*Exit with Prince Edward.*

Enter ARUNDEL

Edward. What, lord Arundel, dost thou come alone?
Arundel. Yea, my good lord, for Gaveston is dead.
Edward. Ah, traitors! have they put my friend to death?
  Tell me, Arundel, died he ere thou cam'st,
  Or didst thou see my friend to take his death?
Arundel. Neither, my lord; for as he was surprised,
  Begirt with weapons, and with enemies round,
  I did your highness' message to them all;
  Demanding him of them, entreating rather,
  And said, upon the honour of my name,
  That I would undertake to carry him
  Unto your highness, and to bring him back.
Edward. And tell me, would the rebels deny me that?
Spencer jun. Proud recreants.
Edward.   Yea, Spencer, traitors all.
Arundel. I found them at the first inexorable;
  The earl of Warwick would not bide the hearing,
  Mortimer hardly; Pembroke and Lancaster
  Spake least: and when they flatly had denied,
  Refusing to receive me pledge for him,
  The earl of Pembroke mildly thus bespake;
  'My lords, because our sovereign sends for him,
  And promiseth he shall be safe returned,
  I will this undertake, to have him hence,
  And see him re-delivered to your hands.'
Edward. Well, and how fortunes that he came not?
Spencer jun. Some treason, or some villainy, was cause.
Arundel. The Earl of Warwick seized him on his way;
  For being delivered unto Pembroke's men,
  Their lord rode home thinking his prisoner safe;
  But ere he came, Warwick in ambush lay,
  And bare him to his death; and in a trench
  Strake off his head, and marched unto the camp.
Spencer iun. A bloody part, flatly against law of arms.

Edward. O shall I speak, or shall I sigh and die!
Spencer jun. My lord, refer your vengeance to the sword
  Upon these barons; hearten up your men;
  Let them not unrevenged murther your friends!
  Advance your standard, Edward, in the field,
  And march to fire them from their starting holes.

Edward kneels and saith

Edward. By earth, the common mother of us all,
  By heaven, and all the moving orbs thereof,
  By this right hand, and by my father's sword,
  And all the honours longing to my crown,
  I will have heads, and lives for him, as many
  As I have manors, castles, towns, and towers.

                                              [*Rises.*

  Treacherous Warwick! traitorous Mortimer!
  If I be England's king, in lakes of gore
  Your headless trunks, your bodies will I trail,
  That you may drink your fill, and quaff in blood,
  And stain my royal standard with the same,
  That so my bloody colours may suggest
  Remembrance of revenge immortally
  On your accursed traitorous progeny,
  You villains, that have slain my Gaveston.
  And in this place of honour and of trust,
  Spencer, sweet Spencer, I adopt thee here:
  And merely of our love we do create thee
  Earl of Gloucester, and Lord Chamberlain,
  Despite of times, despite of enemies.
Spencer jun. My lord, here's a messenger from the barons
  Desires access unto your majesty.
Edward. Admit him near.

Enter the HERALD, *with his coat of arms*

Messenger. Long live King Edward, England's lawful lord.
Edward. So wish not they, I wis, that sent thee hither.
  Thou comst from Mortimer and his complices,

A ranker rout of rebels never was.
Well, say thy message.
Messenger. The barons up in arms by me salute
  Your highness with long life and happiness;
  And bid me say, as plainer to your grace,
  That if without effusion of blood
  You will this grief have ease and remedy,
  That from your princely person you remove
  This Spencer, as a putrifying branch,
  That deads the royal vine, whose golden leaves
  Empale your princely head, your diadem,
  Whose brightness such pernicious upstarts dim,
  Say they; and lovingly advise your grace,
  To cherish virtue and nobility,
  And have old servitors in high esteem,
  And shake off smooth dissembling flatterers:
  This granted, they, their honours, and their lives,
  Are to your highness vowed and consecrate.
Spencer jun. Ah, traitors! will they still display their pride?
Edward. Away, tarry no answer, but be gone.
  Rebels, will they appoint their sovereign
  His sports, his pleasures, and his company?
  Yet, ere thou go, see how I do divorce
                              [*Embraces Spencer.*
  Spencer from me. Now get thee to thy lords,
  And tell them I will come to chastise them
  For murthering Gaveston; hie thee, get thee gone.
  Edward with fire and sword follows at thy heels.
                              [*Exit Herald.*
  My lord, perceive you how these rebels swell?
  Soldiers, good hearts, defend your sovereign's right,
  For now, even now, we march to make them stoop.
  Away!
            [*Exeunt. Alarums, excursions, a great fight, and a
                    retreat sounded, within.*

ACT III, SCENE 3

The battlefield, Boroughbridge

Enter the KING, SPENCER *senior*, SPENCER *junior*,
and the NOBLEMEN *of the King's side*

Edward. Why do we sound retreat? upon them, lords!
This day I shall pour vengeance with my sword
On those proud rebels that are up in arms,
And do confront and countermand their king.
Spencer jun. I doubt it not, my lord, right will prevail.
Spencer sen. 'Tis not amiss, my liege, for either part
To breathe awhile; our men, with sweat and dust
All choked well near, begin to faint for heat;
And this retire refresheth horse and man.
Spencer jun. Here come the rebels.

Enter MORTIMER *junior*, LANCASTER, WARWICK,
PEMBROKE, *and others*

Mortimer jun. Look, Lancaster, yonder is Edward
Among his flatterers.
Lancaster.   And there let him be
Till he pay dearly for their company.
Warwick. And shall, or Warwick's sword shall smite in
vain.
Edward. What, rebels, do you shrink and sound retreat?
Mortimer jun. No, Edward, no, thy flatterers faint and fly.
Lancaster. They'd best betimes forsake thee, and their
trains.
For they'll betray thee, traitors as they are.
Spencer jun. Traitor on thy face, rebellious Lancaster!
Pembroke. Away, base upstart, brav'st thou nobles thus?
Spencer sen. A noble attempt, and honourable deed,
Is it not, trow ye, to assemble aid,
And levy arms against your lawful king?

Edward. For which ere long their heads shall satisfy,
  T' appease the wrath of their offended king.

Mortimer jun. Then, Edward, thou wilt fight it to the
    last,
  And rather bathe thy sword in subjects' blood,
  Than banish that pernicious company?

Edward. Ay, traitors all, rather than thus be braved,
  Make England's civil towns huge heaps of stones,
  And ploughs to go about our palace-gates.

Warwick. A desperate and unnatural resolution.
  Alarum! to the fight! St George for England,
  And the barons' right.

Edward. Saint George for England, and King Edward's
    right.   [*Alarums. Exeunt the two parties severally.*

  Enter KING EDWARD *and his followers, with the*
        BARONS, *captives*

Edward. Now, lusty lords, now, not by chance of war,
  But justice of the quarrel and the cause,
  Vailed is your pride; methinks you hang the heads,
  But we'll advance them, traitors; now 'tis time
  To be avenged on you for all your braves,
  And for the murther of my dearest friend,
  To whom right well you knew our soul was knit,
  Good Pierce of Gaveston, my sweet favourite.
  Ah, rebels, recreants, you made him away!

Kent. Brother, in regard of thee, and of thy land,
  Did they remove that flatterer from thy throne.

Edward. So, sir, you have spoke; away, avoid our pre-
    sence.   [*Exit Kent.*
  Accursed wretches, was't in regard of us,
  When we had sent our messenger to request
  He might be spared to come to speak with us,
  And Pembroke undertook for his return,
  That thou, proud Warwick, watched the prisoner,
  Poor Pierce, and headed him against law of arms?

For which thy head shall overlook the rest,
  As much as thou in rage outwentst the rest.
Warwick. Tyrant, I scorn thy threats and menaces;
  'Tis but temporal that thou canst inflict.
Lancaster. The worst is death, and better die to live
  Than live in infamy under such a king.
Edward. Away with them, my lord of Winchester.
  These lusty leaders, Warwick and Lancaster,
  I charge you roundly – off with both their heads.
  Away!
Warwick. Farewell, vain world.
Lancaster.   Sweet Mortimer, farewell.
Mortimer jun. England, unkind to thy nobility,
  Groan for this grief, behold how thou art maimed.
Edward. Go, take that haughty Mortimer to the
    Tower,
  There see him safe bestowed; and for the rest,
  Do speedy execution on them all.
  Begone!
Mortimer jun. What, Mortimer! can ragged stony walls
  Immure thy virtue that aspires to heaven?
  No, Edward, England's scourge, it may not be;
  Mortimer's hope surmounts his fortune far.
                    [*The captive Barons are led off.*
Edward. Sound drums and trumpets! March with me,
    my friends,
  Edward this day hath crowned him king anew.
        [*Exeunt all except Spencer junior, Levune, and Baldock.*
Spencer jun. Levune, the trust that we repose in thee,
  Begets the quiet of King Edward's land.
  Therefore begone in haste, and with advice
  Bestow that treasure on the lords of France,
  That therewith all enchanted, like the guard
  That suffered Jove to pass in showers of gold
  To Danaë, all aid may be denied
  To Isabel, the queen, that now in France

Makes friends, to cross the seas with her young son,
And step into his father's regiment.

Levune. That's it these barons and the subtle queen
Long levell'd at.

Baldock.   Yea, but, Levune, thou seest
These barons lay their heads on blocks together;
What they intend, the hangman frustrates clean.

Levune. Have you no doubts, my lords, I'll clap so close
Among the lords of France with England's gold,
That Isabel shall make her plaints in vain,
And France shall be obdurate with her tears.

Spencer jun. Then make for France amain; Levune, away.
Proclaim King Edward's wars and victories.

                                        [*Exeunt.*

ACT IV, SCENE 1

Near the Tower of London

Enter KENT

Kent. Fair blows the wind for France; blow, gentle gale,
    Till Edmund be arrived for England's good.
    Nature, yield to my country's cause in this.
    A brother, no, a butcher of thy friends,
    Proud Edward, dost thou banish me thy presence?
    But I'll to France, and cheer the wronged queen,
    And certify what Edward's looseness is.
    Unnatural king, to slaughter noble men
    And cherish flatterers. Mortimer, I stay
    Thy sweet escape: stand gracious, gloomy night,
    To his device.

Enter MORTIMER *junior, disguised*

Mortimer jun. Holla! who walketh there?
    Is't you, my lord?
Kent.   Mortimer, 'tis I;
    But hath thy potion wrought so happily?
Mortimer jun. It hath, my lord; the warders all asleep,
    I thank them, gave me leave to pass in peace.
    But hath your grace got shipping unto France?
Kent. Fear it not.   [*Exeunt.*

ACT IV, SCENE 2

Paris

Enter the QUEEN *and* PRINCE EDWARD

Queen Ah, boy, our friends do fail us all in France:
    The lords are cruel, and the king unkind;
    What shall we do?

Prince.　　　　　　　　Madam, return to England,
　And please my father well, and then a fig
　For all my uncle's friendship here in France.
　I warrant you, I'll win his highness quickly;
　'A loves me better than a thousand Spencers.
Queen. Ah, boy, thou art deceived, at least in this,
　To think that we can yet be tuned together;
　No, no, we jar too far. Unkind Valois,
　Unhappy Isabel, when France rejects,
　Whither, oh, whither dost thou bend thy steps?

　　　　　Enter SIR JOHN OF HAINAULT

Sir John. Madam, what cheer?
Queen.　　　　　　Ah, good Sir John of Hainault,
　Never so cheerless, nor so far distrest.
Sir John. I hear, sweet lady, of the king's unkindness;
　But droop not, madam; noble minds contemn
　Despair: will your grace with me to Hainault,
　And there stay time's advantage with your son?
　How say you, my lord, will you go with your friends,
　And shake off all our fortunes equally?
Prince. So pleaseth the queen, my mother, me it likes;
　The King of England, nor the court of France,
　Shall have me from my gracious mother's side,
　Till I be strong enough to break a staff;
　And then have at the proudest Spencer's head.
Sir John. Well said, my lord.
Queen. O, my sweet heart, how do I moan thy wrongs,
　Yet triumph in the hope of thee, my joy.
　Ah, sweet Sir John, even to the utmost verge
　Of Europe, or the shore of Tanais,
　Will we with thee to Hainault, so we will;
　The marquis is a noble gentleman;
　His grace, I dare presume, will welcome me.
　But who are these?

　　　　　Enter KENT *and* MORTIMER *junior*

F.T.—3

Kent.   Madam, long may you live,
    Much happier than your friends in England do.
Queen. Lord Edmund and lord Mortimer alive!
    Welcome to France; the news was here, my lord,
    That you were dead, or very near your death.
Mortimer jun. Lady, the last was truest of the twain:
    But Mortimer, reserved for better hap,
    Hath shaken off the thraldom of the Tower,
    And lives t' advance your standard, good my lord.
Prince. How mean you? and the king, my father, lives!
    No, my Lord Mortimer, not I, I trow.
Queen. Not, son! why not? I would it were no worse.
    But, gentle lords, friendless we are in France.
Mortimer jun. Monsieur le Grand, a noble friend of yours,
    Told us, at our arrival, all the news –
    How hard the nobles, how unkind the king
    Hath showed himself; but, madam, right makes room
    Where weapons want; and, though a many friends
    Are made away, as Warwick, Lancaster,
    And others of our party and faction;
    Yet have we friends, assure your grace, in England
    Would cast up caps, and clap their hands for joy,
    To see us there appointed for our foes.
Kent. Would all were well, and Edward well reclaimed,
    For England's honour, peace, and quietness.
Mortimer jun. But by the sword, my lord, it must be
        deserved;
    The king will ne'er forsake his flatterers.
Sir John. My lords of England, sith the ungentle king
    Of France refuseth to give aid of arms
    To this distressed queen his sister here,
    Go you with her to Hainault; doubt ye not,
    We will find comfort, money, men and friends
    Ere long, to bid the English king a base.
    How say, young prince, what think you of the match?
Prince. I think King Edward will outrun us all.

Queen. Nay, son, not so; and you must not discourage
  Your friends, that are so forward in your aid.
Kent. Sir John of Hainault, pardon us, I pray;
  These comforts that you give our woful queen
  Bind us in kindness all at your command.
Queen. Yea, gentle brother; and the God of heaven
  Prosper your happy motion, good Sir John.
Mortimer jun. This noble gentleman, forward in arms,
  Was born, I see, to be our anchor-hold.
  Sir John of Hainault, be it thy renown,
  That England's Queen, and nobles in distress,
  Have been by thee restored and comforted.
Sir John. Madam, along, and you, my lord, with me,
  That England's peers may Hainault's welcome see.
                                        [*Exeunt.*

———

ACT IV, SCENE 3

The Royal Palace, London

Enter the KING, ARUNDEL, *the* SPENCERS,
and others

Edward. Thus after many threats of wrathful war,
  Triumpheth England's Edward with his friends;
  And triumph, Edward, with his friends uncontrolled.
  My lord of Gloucester, do you hear the news?
Spencer jun. What news, my lord?
Edward. Why, man, they say there is great execution
  Done through the realm; my lord of Arundel,
  You have the note, have you not?
Arundel. From the lieutenant of the Tower, my lord.
Edward. I pray let us see it. [*Takes the note.*] What have
  we there?
  Read it, Spencer.
            [*Hands it to Spencer junior, who reads the names.*

Why, so; they barked apace a month ago:
Now, on my life, they'll neither bark nor bite.
Now, sirs, the news from France? Gloucester, I trow
These lords of France love England's gold so well
As Isabella gets no aid from thence.
What now remains? Have you proclaimed, my lord,
Reward for them can bring in Mortimer?

Spencer jun. My lord, we have; and if he be in England,
'A will be had ere long, I doubt it not.

Edward. If, dost thou say? Spencer, as true as death,
He is in England's ground; our portmasters
Are not so careless of their king's command.

Enter a POST

How now, what news with thee? from whence come
    these?

Post. Letters, my lord, and tidings forth of France;
To you, my lord of Gloucester, from Levune.
                    [*Gives letters to Spencer junior.*

Edward. Read.

Spencer junior reads the letter:

   'My duty to your honour premised, &c. I have, according to instructions in that behalf, dealt with the king
of France his lords, and effected, that the Queen, all
discontented and discomforted, is gone: whither, if you
ask, with Sir John of Hainault, brother to the marquis,
into Flanders. With them are gone lord Edmund, and
the lord Mortimer, having in their company divers of
your nation, and others; and, as constant report goeth,
they intend to give King Edward battle in England,
sooner than he can look for them. This is all the news of
import.

                    Your honour's in all service, LEVUNE.'

dward. Ah, villains, hath that Mortimer escaped?
With him is Edmund gone associate?

And will Sir John of Hainault lead the round?
Welcome, a God's name, madam, and your son;
England shall welcome you and all your rout.
Gallop apace, bright Phoebus, through the sky,
And dusky night, in rusty iron car,
Between you both shorten the time, I pray,
That I may see that most desired day
When we may meet these traitors in the field.
Ah, nothing grieves me, but my little boy
Is thus misled to countenance their ills.
Come, friends, to Bristow, there to make us strong;
And, winds, as equal be to bring them in,
As you injurious were to bear them forth.

                                                          [Exeunt.

ACT IV, SCENE 4

Near Harwich

Enter the QUEEN, PRINCE EDWARD, KENT,
MORTIMER *junior, and* SIR JOHN OF HAINAULT

Queen. Now, lords, our loving friends and countrymen,
Welcome to England all, with prosperous winds.
Our kindest friends in Belgia have we left,
To cope with friends at home; a heavy case
When force to force is knit, and sword and glaive
In civil broils makes kin and countrymen
Slaughter themselves in others, and their sides
With their own weapons gored. But what's the help?
Misgoverned kings are cause of all this wrack;
And, Edward, thou art one among them all,
Whose looseness hath betrayed thy land to spoil,
And made the channels overflow with blood
Of thine own people; patron shouldst thou be,
But thou —

Mortimer jun. Nay, madam, if you be a warrior,
  You must not grow so passionate in speeches.
  Lords, sith that we are by sufferance of heaven
  Arrived, and armed in this prince's right,
  Here for our country's cause swear we to him
  All homage, fealty, and forwardness;
  And for the open wrongs and injuries
  Edward hath done to us, his queen and land,
  We come in arms to wreck it with the swords,
  That England's queen in peace may repossess
  Her dignities and honours: and withal
  We may remove these flatterers from the king,
  That havocks England's wealth and treasury.
Sir John. Sound trumpets, my lord, and forward let us march.
  Edward will think we come to flatter him.
Kent. I would he never had been flattered more.

                                              [*Exeunt.*

———

ACT IV, SCENE 5

Near Bristol

Enter the KING, BALDOCK, *and* SPENCER *junior,
  flying about the stage*

Spencer jun. Fly, fly, my lord, the queen is overstrong;
  Her friends do multiply, and yours do fail.
  Shape we our course to Ireland, there to breathe.
Edward. What, was I born to fly and run away,
  And leave the Mortimers conquerors behind?
  Give me my horse, and let's r'enforce our troops:
  And in this bed of honour die with fame.
Baldock. O no, my lord, this princely resolution
  Fits not the time; away, we are pursued.

                                              [*Exeunt.*

  Enter KENT *alone, with a sword and target*

Kent. This way he fled, but I am come too late.
 Edward, alas, my heart relents for thee.
 Proud traitor, Mortimer, why dost thou chase
 Thy lawful king, thy sovereign, with thy sword?
 Vile wretch, and why hast thou, of all unkind,
 Borne arms against thy brother and thy king?
 Rain showers of vengeance on my cursed head,
 Thou God, to whom in justice it belongs
 To punish this unnatural revolt.
 Edward, this Mortimer aims at thy life.
 O fly him, then! But, Edmund, calm this rage,
 Dissemble, or thou diest; for Mortimer
 And Isabel do kiss, while they conspire:
 And yet she bears a face of love forsooth.
 Fie on that love that hatcheth death and hate.
 Edmund, away. Bristow to Longshanks' blood
 Is false; be not found single for suspect:
 Proud Mortimer pries near into thy walks.

Enter the QUEEN, PRINCE EDWARD, MORTIMER
iunior, and SIR JOHN OF HAINAULT

Queen. Successful battles gives the God of kings
 To them that fight in right and fear his wrath.
 Since then successfully we have prevailed,
 Thanks be heaven's great architect, and you.
 Ere farther we proceed, my noble lords,
 We here create our well-beloved son,
 Of love and care unto his royal person,
 Lord Warden of the realm, and sith the fates
 Have made his father so infortunate,
 Deal you, my lords, in this, my loving lords,
 As to your wisdoms fittest seems in all.
Kent. Madam, without offence, if I may ask,
 How will you deal with Edward in his fall?
Prince. Tell me, good uncle, what Edward do you mean?
Kent. Nephew, your father: I dare not call him king.

Mortimer jun. My lord of Kent, what needs these ques-
    tions?
  'Tis not in her controlment, nor in ours,
  But as the realm and parliament shall please,
  So shall your brother be disposed of.
  I like not this relenting mood in Edmund.
  Madam, 'tis good to look to him betimes.
                          [Aside to the Queen.
Queen. My lord, the Mayor of Bristow knows our mind.
Mortimer jun. Yea, madam, and they scape not easily
  That fled the field.
Queen.   Baldock is with the King.
  A goodly chancellor, is he not my lord?
Sir John. So are the Spencers, the father and the son.
Kent. This, Edward, is the ruin of the realm.

Enter RICE AP HOWELL, *and the* MAYOR OF BRISTOW,
  with SPENCER *senior*, PRISONER, *and* ATTENDANTS

Rice. God save Queen Isabel, and her princely son.
  Madam, the mayor and citizens of Bristow,
  In sign of love and duty to this presence,
  Present by me this traitor to the state,
  Spencer, the father to that wanton Spencer,
  That, like the lawless Catiline of Rome,
  Revelled in England's wealth and treasury.
Queen. We thank you all.
Mortimer jun.   Your loving care in this
  Deserveth princely favours and rewards.
  But where's the king and the other Spencer fled?
Rice. Spencer the son, created Earl of Gloucester,
  Is with that smooth-tongued scholar Baldock gone,
  And shipped but late for Ireland with the King.
Mortimer jun. Some whirlwind fetch them back or sink
    them all: *[Aside.*
  They shall be started thence, I doubt it not.
Prince. Shall I not see the king my father yet?

Kent. Unhappy is Edward, chased from England's
　　bounds.　　　　　　　　　　　　　　　[*Aside.*

Sir John. Madam, what resteth, why stand you in a
　　muse?

Queen. I rue my lord's ill-fortune; but alas,
　Care of my country called me to this war.

Mortimer jun. Madam, have done with care and sad com-
　　plaint;
　Your king hath wronged your country and himself,
　And we must seek to right it as we may.
　Meanwhile, have hence this rebel to the block.
　Your lordship cannot privilege your head.

Spencer sen. Rebel is he that fights against his prince;
　So fought not they that fought in Edward's right.

Mortimer jun. Take him away, he prates;
　　　　　　　　　[*Exeunt Attendants with Spencer senior.*
　　　　　　　　　　　　You, Rice ap Howell,
　Shall do good service to her majesty,
　Being of countenance in your country here,
　To follow these rebellious runagates.
　We in meanwhile, madam, must take advice,
　How Baldock, Spencer, and their complices,
　May in their fall be followed to their end.
　　　　　　　　　　　　　　　　[*Exeunt omnes.*

━━━

ACT IV, SCENE 6

The Abbey of Neath, Glamorganshire

Enter the ABBOT, MONKS, KING EDWARD, SPENCER
junior, and BALDOCK [*the three latter disguised*]

Abbot. Have you no doubt, my lord; have you no fear;
　As silent and as careful will we be,
　To keep your royal person safe with us,
　Free from suspect, and fell invasion

Of such as have your majesty in chase,
Yourself, and those your chosen company,
As danger of this stormy time requires.

Edward. Father, thy face should harbour no deceit.
O, hadst thou ever been a king, thy heart,
Pierced deeply with sense of my distress,
Could not but take compassion of my state.
Stately and proud, in riches and in train,
Whilom I was, powerful and full of pomp:
But what is he whom rule and empery
Have not in life or death made miserable?
Come, Spencer; come, Baldock, come, sit down by
    me;
Make trial now of that philosophy,
That in our famous nurseries of arts
Thou suckedst from Plato and from Aristotle.
Father, this life contemplative is heaven.
O that I might this life in quiet lead.
But we, alas, are chased; and you, my friends,
Your lives and my dishonour they pursue.
Yet, gentle monks, for treasure, gold nor fee,
Do you betray us and our company.

Monks. Your grace may sit secure, if none but we
Do wot of your abode.

Spencer jun. Not one alive; but shrewdly I suspect
A gloomy fellow in a mead below.
'A gave a long look after us, my lord;
And all the land I know is up in arms,
Arms that pursue our lives with deadly hate.

Baldock. We were embarked for Ireland, wretched we,
With awkward winds and sore tempests driven
To fall on shore, and here to pine in fear
Of Mortimer and his confederates.

Edward. Mortimer, who talks of Mortimer?
Who wounds me with the name of Mortimer,
That bloody man? Good father, on thy lap

Lay I this head, laden with mickle care.
O might I never open these eyes again,
Never again lift up this drooping head,
O never more lift up this dying heart!
Spencer jun. Look up, my lord. Baldock, this drowsiness
  Betides no good; here even we are betrayed.

Enter, with Welsh hooks, RICE AP HOWELL, *a* MOWER,
    and the EARL OF LEICESTER

Mower. Upon my life, those be the men ye seek.
Rice. Fellow, enough. My lord, I pray be short,
  A fair commission warrants what we do.
Leicester. The Queen's commission, urged by Mortimer.
  What cannot gallant Mortimer with the queen?
  Alas, see where he sits, and hopes unseen
  T' escape their hands that seek to reave his life.
  Too true it is, *Quem dies vidit veniens superbum,*
  Hunc dies vidit fugiens jacentem.
  But, Leicester, leave to grow so passionate.
  Spencer and Baldock, by no other names,
  I arrest you of high treason here.
  Stand not on titles, but obey th' arrest;
  'Tis in the name of Isabel the Queen.
  My lord, why droop you thus?
Edward. O day! the last of all my bliss on earth,
  Centre of all misfortune! O my stars!
  Why do you lour unkindly on a king?
  Comes Leicester, then, in Isabella's name
  To take my life, my company from me?
  Here, man, rip up this panting breast of mine,
  And take my heart in rescue of my friends!
Rice. Away with them.
Spencer jun.   It may become thee yet
  To let us take our farewell of his grace.
Abbot. My heart with pity earns to see this sight,
  A king to bear these words and proud commands.

Edward. Spencer, ah, sweet Spencer, thus then must we part.

Spencer jun. We must, my lord; so will the angry heavens.

Edward. Nay, so will hell and cruel Mortimer;
The gentle heavens have not to do in this.

Baldock. My lord, it is in vain to grieve or storm.
Here humbly of your grace we take our leaves;
Our lots are cast; I fear me, so is thine.

Edward. In heaven we may, in earth never shall we meet:
And, Leicester, say, what shall become of us?

Leicester. Your majesty must go to Killingworth.

Edward. Must! 'tis somewhat hard, when kings must go.

Leicester. Here is a litter ready for your grace,
That waits your pleasure, and the day grows old.

Rice. As good be gone, as stay and be benighted.

Edward. A litter hast thou? lay me in a hearse,
And to the gates of hell convey me hence;
Let Pluto's bells ring out my fatal knell,
And hags howl for my death at Charon's shore,
For friends hath Edward none but these and these,
And these must die under a tyrant's sword.

Rice. My lord, be going; care not for these,
For we shall see them shorter by the heads.

Edward. Well, that shall be, shall be: part we must.
Sweet Spencer, gentle Baldock, part we must.
Hence feigned weeds! unfeigned are my woes;
                              [*Throws off his disguise.*
Father, farewell. Leicester, thou stay'st for me,
And go I must. Life, farewell, with my friends.
                     [*Exeunt King Edward and Leicester.*

Spencer jun. O, is he gone? is noble Edward gone?
Parted from hence? never to see us more?
Rend, sphere of heaven, and, fire, forsake thy orb,
Earth, melt to air! gone is my sovereign,
Gone, gone, alas, never to make return.

Baldock. Spencer, I see our souls are fleeted hence;
  We are deprived the sunshine of our life:
  Make for a new life, man; throw up thy eyes
  And heart and hand to heaven's immortal throne,
  Pay nature's debts with cheerful countenance;
  Reduce we all our lessons unto this,
  To die, sweet Spencer, therefore live we all;
  Spencer, all live to die, and rise to fall.

Rice. Come, come, keep these preachments till you come
  to the place appointed. You, and such as you are, have
  made wise work in England. Will your lordships away?

Mower. Your worship, I trust, will remember me?

Rice. Remember thee, fellow! what else? Follow me to
  the town.   *[Exeunt.*

ACT V, SCENE 1

Kenilworth Castle

Enter the KING, LEICESTER, *the* BISHOP OF
WINCHESTER, *and* TRUSSEL

Leicester. Be patient, good my lord, cease to lament,
Imagine Killingworth Castle were your court,
And that you lay for pleasure here a space,
Not of compulsion or necessity.
Edward. Leicester, if gentle words might comfort me,
Thy speeches long ago had eased my sorrows;
For kind and loving hast thou always been.
The griefs of private men are soon allayed,
But not of kings. The forest deer, being struck,
Runs to an herb that closeth up the wounds;
But when the imperial lion's flesh is gored,
He rends and tears it with his wrathful paw,
And highly scorning that the lowly earth
Should drink his blood, mounts up into the air.
And so it fares with me, whose dauntless mind
The ambitious Mortimer would seek to curb,
And that unnatural queen, false Isabel,
That thus hath pent and mewed me in a prison;
For such outrageous passions cloy my soul,
As with the wings of rancour and disdain
Full often am I soaring up to heaven,
To plain me to the gods against them both.
But when I call to mind I am a king,
Methinks I should revenge me of the wrongs
That Mortimer and Isabel have done.
But what are kings, when regiment is gone,
But perfect shadows in a sunshine day?
My nobles rule, I bear the name of king;
I wear the crown, but am controlled by them,

By Mortimer, and my unconstant queen,
Who spots my nuptial bed with infamy;
Whilst I am lodged within this cave of care,
Where sorrow at my elbow still attends,
To company my heart with sad laments,
That bleeds within me for this strange exchange.
But tell me, must I now resign my crown,
To make usurping Mortimer a king?

Bishop. Your grace mistakes; it is for England's good,
And princely Edward's right we crave the crown.

Edward. No, 'tis for Mortimer, not Edward's head;
For he's a lamb, encompassed by wolves,
Which in a moment will abridge his life.
But if proud Mortimer do wear this crown,
Heavens turn it to a blaze of quenchless fire;
Or, like the snaky wreath of Tisiphon,
Engird the temples of his hateful head;
So shall not England's vine be perished,
But Edward's name survives, though Edward dies.

Leicester. My lord, why waste you thus the time away?
They stay your answer; will you yield your crown?

Edward. Ah, Leicester, weigh how hardly I can brook
To lose my crown and kingdom without cause;
To give ambitious Mortimer my right,
That like a mountain overwhelms my bliss,
In which extreme my mind here murthered is.
But what the heavens appoint, I must obey!
Here, take my crown; the life of Edward too;
                              [*Taking off the crown.*
Two kings in England cannot reign at once.
But stay awhile, let me be king till night,
That I may gaze upon this glittering crown;
So shall my eyes receive their last content,
My head, the latest honour due to it,
And jointly both yield up their wished right.
Continue ever thou celestial sun;

Let never silent night possess this clime:
Stand still you watches of the element;
All times and seasons, rest you at a stay,
That Edward may be still fair England's king.
But day's bright beams doth vanish fast away,
And needs I must resign my wished crown.
Inhuman creatures, nursed with tiger's milk,
Why gape you for your sovereign's overthrow?
My diadem I mean, and guiltless life.
See, monsters, see, I'll wear my crown again!

                        [He puts on the crown.

What, fear you not the fury of your king?
But, hapless Edward, thou art fondly led;
They pass not for thy frowns as late they did,
But seek to make a new-elected king;
Which fills my mind with strange despairing thoughts,
Which thoughts are martyred with endless torments,
And in this torment comfort find I none,
But that I feel the crown upon my head,
And therefore let me wear it yet awhile.

Trussel. My lord, the parliament must have present news,
And therefore say, will you resign or no?

                        [The King rageth.

Edward. I'll not resign; but whilst I live be king.
Traitors, be gone! and join you with Mortimer!
Elect, conspire, instal, do what you will,
Their blood and yours shall seal these treacheries!

Bishop. This answer we'll return, and so farewell.

Leicester. Call them again, my lord, and speak them fair;
For if they go, the prince shall lose his right.

Edward. Call thou them back, I have no power to speak.

Leicester. My lord, the king is willing to resign.

Bishop. If he be not, let him choose.

Edward. O would I might! but heavens and earth conspire
To make me miserable. Here receive my crown;

Receive it? no, these innocent hands of mine
Shall not be guilty of so foul a crime.
He of you all that most desires my blood,
And will be called the murtherer of a king,
Take it. What, are you moved? pity you me?
Then send for unrelenting Mortimer,
And Isabel, whose eyes, being turned to steel,
Will sooner sparkle fire than shed a tear.
Yet stay, for rather than I will look on them,
Here, here!   [*Gives the crown.*
    Now, sweet God of heaven,
Make me despise this transitory pomp,
And sit for aye enthronized in heaven.
Come, death, and with thy fingers close my eyes,
Of if I live, let me forget myself.
Bishop. My lord —
Edward. Call me not lord; away – out of my sight:
 Ah, pardon me: grief makes me lunatic.
 Let not that Mortimer protect my son;
 More safety is there in a tiger's jaws,
 Than his embracements. Bear this to the queen,
 Wet with my tears, and dried again with sighs;
      [*Gives a handkerchief.*
 If with the sight thereof she be not moved,
 Return it back and dip it in my blood.
 Commend me to my son, and bid him rule
 Better than I. Yet how have I transgressed,
 Unless it be with too much clemency?
Trussel. And thus most humbly do we take our leave.
    [*Exeunt the Bishop of Winchester and Trussel.*
Edward. Farewell; I know the next news that they
  bring
 Will be my death; and welcome shall it be;
 To wretched men death is felicity.

Enter BERKELEY, *who gives a paper to* LEICESTER

Leicester. Another post. What news brings he?

Edward. Such news as I expect: come, Berkeley, come,
  And tell thy message to my naked breast.

Berkeley. My lord, think not a thought so villainous
  Can harbour in a man of noble birth.
  To do your highness service and devoir,
  And save you from your foes, Berkeley would die.

Leicester. My lord, the council of the queen commands
  That I resign my charge.

Edward. And who must keep me now? Must you, my
  lord?

Berkeley. Ay, my most gracious lord, so 'tis decreed.

Edward [*taking the paper*]. By Mortimer, whose name is
  written here.
  Well may I rend his name that rends my heart!
                                        [*Tears it.*
  This poor revenge hath something eased my mind.
  So may his limbs be torn, as is this paper.
  Hear me, immortal Jove, and grant it too.

Berkeley. Your grace must hence with me to Berkeley
  straight.

Edward. Whither you will; all places are alike,
  And every earth is fit for burial.

Leicester. Favour him, my lord, as much as lieth in you.

Berkeley. Even so betide my soul as I use him.

Edward. Mine enemy hath pitied my estate,
  And that's the cause that I am now removed.

Berkeley. And thinks your grace that Berkeley will be
  cruel?

Edward. I know not; but of this am I assured,
  That death ends all, and I can die but once.
  Leicester, farewell.

Leicester. Not yet, my lord; I'll bear you on your way.
                                        [*Exeunt.*

ACT V, SCENE 2

The Royal Palace, London

Enter MORTIMER *junior and* QUEEN ISABEL

Mortimer jun. Fair Isabel, now have we our desire;
  The proud corrupters of the light-brained king
  Have done their homage to the lofty gallows,
  And he himself lies in captivity.
  Be ruled by me, and we will rule the realm.
  In any case take heed of childish fear,
  For now we hold an old wolf by the ears,
  That, if he slip, will seize upon us both,
  And gripe the sorer, being griped himself.
  Think therefore, madam, that imports us much
  To erect your son with all the speed we may,
  And that I be protector over him;
  For our behoof will bear the greater sway
  Whenas a king's name shall be under writ.
Queen. Sweet Mortimer, the life of Isabel,
  Be thou persuaded that I love thee well,
  And therefore, so the prince my son be safe,
  Whom I esteem as dear as these mine eyes,
  Conclude against his father what thou wilt,
  And I myself will willingly subscribe.
Mortimer jun. First would I hear news that he were
    deposed,
  And then let me alone to handle him.

Enter MESSENGER

  Letters! from whence?
Messenger.   From Killingworth, my lord.
Queen. How fares my lord the king?
Messenger. In health, madam, but full of pensiveness.
Queen. Alas, poor soul, would I could ease his grief.

Enter the BISHOP OF WINCHESTER *with the crown*

Thanks, gentle Winchester.
[*To the Messenger.*] Sirrah, be gone.   [*Exit Messenger.*
Bishop. The king hath willingly resigned his crown.
Queen. O happy news! send for the prince, my son.
Bishop. Further, ere this letter was sealed, Lord Berkeley
    came,
  So that he now is gone from Killingworth;
  And we have heard that Edmund laid a plot
  To set his brother free; no more but so.
  The lord of Berkeley is so pitiful
  As Leicester that had charge of him before.
Queen. Then let some other be his guardian.
Mortimer jun. Let me alone, here is the Privy Seal.
                         [*Exit the Bishop of Winchester.*
  Who's there? – Call hither Gurney and Matrevis.
                         [*To Attendants, within.*
  To dash the heavy-headed Edmund's drift,
  Berkeley shall be discharged, the king removed,
  And none but we shall know where he lieth.
Queen. But, Mortimer, as long as he survives,
  What safety rests for us, or for my son?
Mortimer jun. Speak, shall he presently be dispatched and
    die?
Queen. I would he were, so it were not by my means.

Enter MATREVIS *and* GURNEY

Mortimer jun. Enough.
  Matrevis, write a letter presently
  Unto the lord of Berkeley from ourself
  That he resign the king to thee and Gurney;
  And when 'tis done, we will subscribe our name.
Matrevis. It shall be done, my lord.   [*Writes.*
Mortimer jun.   Gurney!
Gurney.   My lord.

Mortimer jun. As thou intendest to rise by Mortimer,
   Who now makes Fortune's wheel turn as he please,
   Seek all the means thou canst to make him droop,
   And neither give him kind word nor good look.
Gurney. I warrant you, my lord.
Mortimer jun. And this above the rest: because we hear
   That Edmund casts to work his liberty,
   Remove him still from place to place by night,
   Till at the last he come to Killingworth,
   And then from thence to Berkeley back again;
   And by the way, to make him fret the more,
   Speak curstly to him; and in any case
   Let no man comfort him if he chance to weep,
   But amplify his grief with bitter words.
Matrevis. Fear not, my lord, we'll do as you command.
Mortimer jun. So now away; post thitherwards amain.
Queen. Whither goes this letter? to my lord the king?
   Commend me humbly to his majesty,
   And tell him that I labour all in vain
   To ease his grief, and work his liberty;
   And bear him this as witness of my love.   [*Gives a ring.*
Matrevis. I will, madam.

        [*Exeunt Matrevis and Gurney. Manent Isabella and
                             Mortimer.*

Mortimer jun. Finely dissembled. Do so still, sweet queen.
   Here comes the young prince with the Earl of Kent.
Queen. Something he whispers in his childish ears.
Mortimer jun. If he have such access unto the prince,
   Our plots and stratagems will soon be dashed.
Queen. Use Edmund friendly as if all were well.

 Enter PRINCE EDWARD, *and* KENT, *talking with him*

Mortimer jun. How fares my honourable lord of Kent?
Kent. In health, sweet Mortimer: how fares your grace?
Queen. Well, if my lord your brother were enlarged.
Kent. I hear of late he hath deposed himself.

Queen. The more my grief.

Mortimer jun. And mine.

Kent. Ah, they do dissemble.   [*Aside.*

Queen. Sweet son, come hither, I must talk with thee.

Mortimer jun. Thou being his uncle, and the next of
     blood,
  Do look to be protector over the prince.

Kent. Not I, my lord; who should protect the son,
  But she that gave him life? I mean the queen.

Prince. Mother, persuade me not to wear the crown:
  Let him be king. I am too young to reign.

Queen. But be content, seeing it his highness' pleasure.

Prince. Let me but see him first, and then I will.

Kent. Ay, do, sweet nephew.

Queen. Brother, you know it is impossible.

Prince. Why, is he dead?

Queen. No, God forbid.

Kent. I would those words proceeded from your heart.

Mortimer jun. Inconstant Edmund, dost thou favour him,
  That wast a cause of his imprisonment?

Kent. The more cause have I now to make amends.

Mortimer jun. I tell thee, 'tis not meet that one so false
  Should come about the person of a prince.
  My lord, he hath betrayed the king his brother,
  And therefore trust him not.

Prince. But he repents, and sorrows for it now.

Queen. Come, son, and go with this gentle lord and me.

Prince. With you I will, but not with Mortimer.

Mortimer jun. Why, youngling, 'sdain'st thou so of
     Mortimer?
  Then I will carry thee by force away.

Prince. Help, Uncle Kent, Mortimer will wrong me.

Queen. Brother Edmund, strive not; we are his friends;
  Isabel is nearer than the Earl of Kent.

Kent. Sister, Edward is my charge, redeem him.

Queen. Edward is my son, and I will keep him.

Kent. Mortimer shall know that he hath wronged me.
   Hence will I haste to Killingworth Castle,
   And rescue aged Edward from his foes,
   To be revenged on Mortimer and thee.

> [*Exeunt one side the Queen, Prince Edward, and
> Mortimer junior; on the other, Kent.*

ACT V, SCENE 3

Near Kenilworth Castle

Enter MATREVIS *and* GURNEY *and* SOLDIERS,
with the KING

Matrevis. My lord, be not pensive, we are your friends;
   Men are ordained to live in misery,
   Therefore come: dalliance dangereth our lives.
Edward. Friends, whither must unhappy Edward go?
   Will hateful Mortimer appoint no rest?
   Must I be vexed like the nightly bird,
   Whose sight is loathsome to all winged fowls?
   When will the fury of his mind assuage?
   When will his heart be satisfied with blood?
   If mine will serve, unbowel straight this breast,
   And give my heart to Isabel and him;
   It is the chiefest mark they level at.
Gurney. Not so, my liege, the queen hath given this charge
   To keep your grace in safety;
   Your passions make your dolours to increase.
Edward. This usage makes my misery increase.
   But can my air of life continue long
   When all my senses are annoyed with stench?
   Within a dungeon England's king is kept,
   Where I am starved for want of sustenance.

My daily diet is heart-breaking sobs,
That almost rents the closet of my heart;
Thus lives old Edward not relieved by any,
And so must die, though pitied by many.
O, water, gentle friends, to cool my thirst,
And clear my body from foul excrements.

Matrevis. Here's channel water, as our charge is given;
Sit down, for we'll be barbers to your grace.

Edward. Traitors, away! what, will you murther me,
Or choke your sovereign with puddle water?

Gurney. No; but wash your face, and shave away your
beard,
Lest you be known and so be rescued.

Matrevis. Why strive you thus? your labour is in vain.

Edward. The wren may strive against the lion's strength,
But all in vain: so vainly do I strive
To seek for mercy at a tyrant's hand.

[*They wash him with puddle water, and shave his beard*
away.

Immortal powers! that know the painful cares
That waits upon my poor distressed soul,
O level all your looks upon these daring men,
That wrongs their liege and sovereign, England's king.
O Gaveston, it is for thee that I am wronged,
For me, both thou and both the Spencers died!
And for your sakes a thousand wrongs I'll take.
The Spencers' ghosts, wherever they remain,
Wish well to mine; then tush, for them I'll die.

Matrevis. 'Twixt theirs and yours shall be no enmity.
Come, come away; now put the torches out,
We'll enter in by darkness to Killingworth.

Enter KENT

Gurney. How now, who comes there?

Matrevis. Guard the king sure: it is the Earl of Kent.

Edward. O gentle brother, help to rescue me.

Matrevis. Keep them asunder; thrust in the king.

Kent. Soldiers, let me but talk to him one word.

Gurney. Lay hands upon the earl for this assault.

Kent. Lay down your weapons, traitors; yield the king.

Matrevis. Edmund, yield thou thyself, or thou shalt die.

Kent. Base villains, wherefore do you gripe me thus?

Gurney. Bind him and so convey him to the court.

Kent. Where is the court but here? he is the king;
   And I will visit him; why stay you me?

Matrevis. The court is where lord Mortimer remains;
   Thither shall your honour go; and so farewell.

> [*Exeunt Matrevis and Gurney, with the King.*

Kent. O miserable is that commonweal,
   Where lords keep courts, and kings are locked in
      prison!

Soldier. Wherefore stay we? On, sirs, to the court.

Kent. Ay, lead me whither you will, even to my death,
   Seeing that my brother cannot be released.

> [*Exeunt.*

ACT V, SCENE 4

The Royal Palace, London

Enter MORTIMER *junior*

Mortimer jun. The king must die, or Mortimer goes down;
   The commons now begin to pity him:
   Yet he that is the cause of Edward's death,
   Is sure to pay for it when his son is of age;
   And therefore will I do it cunningly.
   This letter, written by a friend of ours,
   Contains his death, yet bids them save his life.

> [*Reads.*

'*Edwardum occidere nolite timere bonum est:*
Fear not to kill the king, 'tis good he die.'

But read it thus, and that's another sense:
'*Edwardum occidere nolite timere bonum est:*
Kill not the king, 'tis good to fear the worst.'
Unpointed as it is, thus shall it go,
That, being dead, if it chance to be found,
Matrevis and the rest may bear the blame,
And we be quit that caused it to be done.
Within this room is locked the messenger
That shall convey it, and perform the rest:
And by a secret token that he bears,
Shall he be murthered when the deed is done.
Lightborn, come forth!

Enter LIGHTBORN

Art thou as resolute as thou wast?
Lightborn. What else, my lord? and far more resolute.
Mortimer jun. And hast thou cast how to accomplish it?
Lightborn. Ay, ay, and none shall know which way he
    died.
Mortimer jun. But at his looks, Lightborn, thou wilt relent.
Lightborn. Relent! ha, ha! I use much to relent.
Mortimer jun. Well, do it bravely, and be secret.
Lightborn. You shall not need to give instructions;
    'Tis not the first time I have killed a man.
    I learned in Naples how to poison flowers;
    To strangle with a lawn thrust through the throat;
    To pierce the windpipe with a needle's point;
    Or whilst one is asleep, to take a quill
    And blow a little powder in his ears:
    Or open his mouth and pour quicksilver down.
    But yet I have a braver way than these.
Mortimer jun. What's that?
Lightborn. Nay, you shall pardon me; none shall know
    my tricks.
Mortimer jun. I care not how it is, so it be not spied.
    Deliver this to Gurney and Matrevis.   [*Gives a letter.*

At every ten miles' end thou hast a horse.

Take this; [*Gives money*] away, and never see me more.

Lightborn. No.

Mortimer jun. No.

Unless thou bring me news of Edward's death.

Lightborn. That will I quickly do. Farewell, my lord.

[*Exit.*

Mortimer jun. The prince I rule, the queen do I command,
And with a lowly conge to the ground,
The proudest lords salute me as I pass;
I seal, I cancel, I do what I will.
Feared am I more than loved; – let me be feared,
And when I frown, make all the court look pale.
I view the prince with Aristarchus' eyes,
Whose looks were as a breeching to a boy.
They thrust upon me the protectorship,
And sue to me for that that I desire.
While at the council-table, grave enough,
And not unlike a bashful puritan,
First I complain of imbecility,
Saying it is *onus quam gravissimum*;
Till, being interrupted by my friends,
Suscepi that *provinciam* as they term it;
And to conclude, I am Protector now.
Now is all sure: the queen and Mortimer
Shall rule the realm, the king; and none rule us.
Mine enemies will I plague, my friends advance;
And what I list command who dare control?
Major sum quam cui possit fortuna nocere.
And that this be the coronation-day,
It pleaseth me, and Isabel the queen.

[*Trumpets within.*

The trumpets sound, I must go take my place.

Enter the young KING, *the* BISHOP OF CANTERBURY,
CHAMPION, NOBLES, QUEEN

Bishop of Canterbury. Long live King Edward, by the grace
    of God,
  King of England and lord of Ireland.

Champion. If any Christian, Heathen, Turk, or Jew,
  Dares but affirm that Edward's not true king,
  And will avouch his saying with the sword,
  I am the champion that will combat him.

Mortimer jun. None comes, sound trumpets.

                                  [Trumpets sound.

King Edward III.   Champion, here's to thee.

                                     [Gives a purse.

Queen. Lord Mortimer, now take him to your charge.

        Enter SOLDIERS, *with* KENT *prisoner*

Mortimer jun. What traitor have we there with blades and
  bills?

Soldier. Edmund, the Earl of Kent.

King Edward III.   What hath he done?

Soldier. 'A would have taken the king away perforce,
  As we were bringing him to Killingworth.

Mortimer jun. Did you attempt his rescue, Edmund?
  Speak.

Kent. Mortimer, I did; he is our king,
  And thou compellst this prince to wear the crown.

Mortimer jun. Strike off his head! he shall have martial
  law.

Kent. Strike off my head! base traitor, I defy thee.

King Edward III. My lord, he is my uncle, and shall live.

Mortimer jun. My lord, he is your enemy, and shall die.

Kent. Stay, villains!

King Edward III. Sweet mother, if I cannot pardon him,
  Entreat my lord Protector for his life.

Queen. Son, be content; I dare not speak a word.

King Edward III. Nor I, and yet methinks I should
  command;
  But, seeing I cannot, I'll entreat for him.

My lord, if you will let my uncle live,
I will requite it when I come to age.

Mortimer jun. 'Tis for your highness' good, and for the
realm's.
How often shall I bid you bear him hence?

Kent. Art thou king? must I die at thy command?

Mortimer jun. At our command. Once more away with
him.

Kent. Let me but stay and speak; I will not go.
Either my brother or his son is king,
And none of both them thirst for Edmund's blood:
And therefore, soldiers, whither will you hale me?

> [*They hale Kent away and carry him to be beheaded.*

King Edward III. What safety may I look for at his hands,
If that my uncle shall be murthered thus?

Queen. Fear not, sweet boy, I'll guard thee from thy foes;
Had Edmund lived, he would have sought thy death.
Come, son, we'll ride a-hunting in the park.

King Edward III. And shall my uncle Edmund ride with
us?

Queen. He is a traitor; think not on him; come.

> [*Exeunt omnes.*

━━━

ACT V, SCENE 5

Berkeley Castle

Enter MATREVIS *and* GURNEY

Matrevis. Gurney, I wonder the king dies not,
Being in a vault up to the knees in water,
To which the channels of the castle run,
From whence a damp continually ariseth,
That were enough to poison any man,
Much more a king brought up so tenderly.

Gurney. And so do I, Matrevis: yesternight
  I opened but the door to throw him meat,
  And I was almost stifled with the savour.
Matrevis. He hath a body able to endure
  More than we can inflict: and therefore now
  Let us assail his mind another while.
Gurney. Send for him out thence, and I will anger
    him.
Matrevis. But stay, who's this?

Enter LIGHTBORN

Lightborn. My lord Protector greets you.   [*Gives letter.*
Gurney. What's here? I know not how to conster it.
Matrevis. Gurney, it was left unpointed for the nonce;
  'Edwardum occidere nolite timere,'
  That's his meaning.
Lightborn. Know you this token? I must have the king.
                                          [*Gives token.*
Matrevis. Ay, stay awhile, thou shalt have answer straight.
  This villain's sent to make away the king.   [*Aside.*
Gurney. I thought as much.   [*Aside.*
Matrevis.   And when the murther's done,
  See how he must be handled for his labour.
  Pereat iste! Let him have the king.   [*Aside.*
  What else? here is the keys, this is the lake,
  Do as you are commanded by my lord.
Lightborn. I know what I must do. Get you away.
  Yet be not far off, I shall need your help;
  See that in the next room I have a fire,
  And get me a spit, and let it be red-hot.
Matrevis. Very well.
Gurney.   Need you anything besides?
Lightborn. What else? A table and a feather-bed.
Gurney. That's all?
Lightborn. Ay, ay; so, when I call you, bring it in.
Matrevis. Fear not you that.

Gurney [*Gives a light, and then exit with Matrevis*]. Here's a
   light, to go into the dungeon.

Lightborn. So now
   Must I about this gear; ne'er was there any
   So finely handled as this king shall be.
   Foh, here's a place indeed, with all my heart.

Edward. Who's there? What light is that? Wherefore
    comest thou?

Lightborn. To comfort you, and bring you joyful news.

Edward. Small comfort finds poor Edward in thy looks.
   Villain, I know thou comst to murther me.

Lightborn. To murther you, my most gracious lord,
   Far is it from my heart to do you harm.
   The queen sent me to see how you were used,
   For she relents at this your misery:
   And what eyes can refrain from shedding tears,
   To see a king in this most piteous state?

Edward. Weepst thou already? List awhile to me
   And then thy heart, were it as Gurney's is,
   Or as Matrevis', hewn from the Caucasus,
   Yet will it melt, ere I have done my tale.
   This dungeon where they keep me is the sink
   Wherein the filth of all the castle falls.

Lightborn. O villains!

Edward. And there in mire and puddle have I stood
   This ten days' space; and, lest that I should sleep,
   One plays continually upon a drum.
   They give me bread and water, being a king;
   So that, for want of sleep and sustenance,
   My mind's distempered, and my body's numbed,
   And whether I have limbs or no I know not.
   O, would my blood dropped out from every vein,
   As doth this water from my tattered robes.
   Tell Isabel, the queen, I looked not thus,
   When for her sake I ran at tilt in France,
   And there unhorsed the Duke of Cleremont.

Lightborn. O speak no more, my lord; this breaks my
heart.
Lie on this bed, and rest yourself awhile.
Edward. These looks of thine can harbour nought but
death:
I see my tragedy written in thy brows.
Yet stay awhile; forbear thy bloody hand,
And let me see the stroke before it comes,
That even then when I shall lose my life,
My mind may be more steadfast on my God.
Lightborn. What means your highness to mistrust me thus?
Edward. What meanst thou to dissemble with me thus?
Lightborn. These hands were never stained with innocent
blood,
Nor shall they now be tainted with a king's.
Edward. Forgive my thought for having such a thought.
One jewel have I left; receive thou this. [*Giving jewel.*
Still fear I, and I know not what's the cause,
But every joint shakes as I give it thee.
O, if thou harbourst murther in thy heart,
Let this gift change thy mind, and save thy soul.
Know that I am a king: O, at that name
I feel a hell of grief! Where is my crown?
Gone, gone, and do I remain alive?
Lightborn. You're overwatched, my lord; lie down and
rest.
Edward. But that grief keeps me waking, I should sleep;
For not these ten days have these eyes' lids closed.
Now as I speak they fall, and yet with fear
Open again. O wherefore sits thou here?
Lightborn. If you mistrust me, I'll begone, my lord.
Edward. No, no, for if thou meanst to murther me,
Thou wilt return again, and therefore stay.   [*Sleeps.*
Lightborn. He sleeps.
Edward [*waking*]. O let me not die yet: stay, O stay a
while!

Lightborn. How now, my lord?

Edward. Something still buzzeth in mine ears,
  And tells me if I sleep I never wake;
  This fear is that which makes me tremble thus;
  And therefore tell me, wherefore art thou come?

Lightborn. To rid thee of thy life. Matrevis, come!

Enter MATREVIS *and* GURNEY

Edward. I am too weak and feeble to resist:
  Assist me, sweet God, and receive my soul!

Lightborn. Run for the table.

Edward. O spare me, or despatch me in a trice.
                              [*Matrevis brings in a table.*

Lightborn. So, lay the table down, and stamp on it,
  But not too hard, lest that you bruise his body.
                              [*King Edward is murdered.*

Matrevis. I fear me that this cry will raise the town,
  And therefore let us take horse and away.

Lightborn. Tell me, sirs, was it not bravely done?

Gurney. Excellent well: take this for thy reward.
                        [*Then Gurney stabs Lightborn.*
  Come, let us cast the body in the moat,
  And bear the king's to Mortimer our lord:
  Away!   [*Exeunt with the bodies.*

———

ACT V, SCENE 6

The Royal Palace, London

Enter MORTIMER *junior and* MATREVIS

Mortimer jun. Is't done, Matrevis, and the murtherer
  dead?

Matrevis. Ay, my good lord; I would it were undone.

Mortimer jun. Matrevis, if thou now growest penitent
  I'll be thy ghostly father; therefore choose,

F.T.—4

Whether thou wilt be secret in this,
Or else die by the hand of Mortimer.
Matrevis. Gurney, my lord, is fled, and will, I fear,
Betray us both, therefore let me fly.
Mortimer jun. Fly to the savages.
Matrevis. I humbly thank your honour.   [*Exit.*
Mortimer jun. As for myself, I stand as Jove's huge tree,
And others are but shrubs compared to me.
All tremble at my name, and I fear none;
Let's see who dare impeach me for his death.

Enter the QUEEN

Queen. Ah, Mortimer, the king my son hath news
His father's dead, and we have murthered him!
Mortimer jun. What if we have? the king is yet a child.
Queen. Ay, ay, but he tears his hair, and wrings his hands,
And vows to be revenged upon us both.
Into the council-chamber he is gone,
To crave the aid and succour of his peers.
Ay me, see where he comes, and they with him;
Now, Mortimer, begins our tragedy.

Enter KING EDWARD THE THIRD, LORDS,
and ATTENDANTS

1st Lord. Fear not, my lord, know that you are a king.
King Edward III. Villain! –
Mortimer jun. How now, my lord?
King Edward III. Think not that I am frighted with thy
words.
My father's murthered through thy treachery;
And thou shalt die, and on his mournful hearse
Thy hateful and accursed head shall lie,
To witness to the world that by thy means
His kingly body was too soon interred.
Queen. Weep not, sweet son.

King Edward III. Forbid not me to weep; he was my
    father;
   And had you loved him half so well as I,
   You could not bear his death thus patiently.
   But you, I fear, conspired with Mortimer.
1st Lord. Why speak you not unto my lord the king?
Mortimer jun. Because I think scorn to be accused.
   Who is the man dare say I murthered him?
King Edward III. Traitor, in me my loving father speaks,
   And plainly saith, 'twas thou that murthredst him.
Mortimer jun. But hath your grace no other proof than
    this?
King Edward III [*showing letter*]. Yes, if this be the hand o.
   Mortimer.
Mortimer jun. [*aside*]. False Gurney hath betrayed me and
   himself.
Queen [*aside*]. I feared as much; murther cannot be hid.
Mortimer jun. 'Tis my hand; what gather you by this?
King Edward III. That thither thou didst send a mur-
   therer.
Mortimer jun. What murtherer? Bring forth the man I sent.
King Edward III. Ah, Mortimer, thou knowest that he is
   slain;
   And so shalt thou be too. Why stays he here,
   Bring him unto a hurdle, drag him forth;
   Hang him, I say, and set his quarters up;
   But bring his head back presently to me.
Queen. For my sake, sweet son, pity Mortimer.
Mortimer jun. Madam, entreat not, I will rather die,
   Than sue for life unto a paltry boy.
King Edward III. Hence with the traitor, with the
   murtherer!
Mortimer jun. Base Fortune, now I see, that in thy wheel
   There is a point, to which when men aspire,
   They tumble headlong down: that point I touched,
   And, seeing there was no place to mount up higher,

Why should I grieve at my declining fall?
Farewell, fair queen. Weep not for Mortimer,
That scorns the world, and, as a traveller,
Goes to discover countries yet unknown.

King Edward III. What! suffer you the traitor to delay?

            [*Mortimer junior is taken away by 1st Lord and
                                                Attendants.*

Queen. As thou receivedst thy life from me,
Spill not the blood of gentle Mortimer!

King Edward III. This argues that you spilt my father's
blood,
Else would you not entreat for Mortimer.

Queen. I spill his blood? no.

King Edward III. Ay, madam, you; for so the rumour
runs.

Queen. That rumour is untrue; for loving thee,
Is this report raised on poor Isabel.

King Edward III. I do not think her so unnatural.

2nd Lord. My lord, I fear me it will prove too true.

King Edward III. Mother, you are suspected for his death,
And therefore we commit you to the Tower
Till further trial may be made thereof;
If you be guilty, though I be your son,
Think not to find me slack or pitiful.

Queen. Nay, to my death, for too long have I lived,
Whenas my son thinks to abridge my days.

King Edward III. Away with her, her words enforce these
tears,
And I shall pity her if she speak again.

Queen. Shall I not mourn for my beloved lord,
And with the rest accompany him to his grave?

2nd Lord. Thus, madam, 'tis the king's will you shall hence.

Queen. He hath forgotten me; stay, I am his mother.

2nd Lord. That boots not; therefore, gentle madam, go.

Queen. Then come, sweet death, and rid me of this grief.

                                                [*Exit.*

Re-enter 1st LORD, *with the head of* MORTIMER *junior*

1st Lord. My lord, here is the head of Mortimer.
King Edward III. Go fetch my father's hearse, where it
    shall lie;
  And bring my funeral robes.   *[Exeunt Attendants.*
                        Accursed head,
  Could I have ruled thee then, as I do now,
  Thou hadst not hatched this monstrous treachery!
  Here comes the hearse; help me to mourn, my lords.

Re-enter ATTENDANTS *with the hearse and funeral robes*

  Sweet father, here unto thy murthered ghost
  I offer up this wicked traitor's head;
  And let these tears, distilling from mine eyes,
  Be witness of my grief and innocency.

Thomas Heywood

——

A WOMAN
KILLED WITH KINDNESS

DRAMATIS PERSONAE

SIR FRANCIS ACTON, *Brother of Mistress Frankford*
SIR CHARLES MOUNTFORD
MASTER FRANKFORD
MASTER WENDOLL, *Friend to Frankford*
MASTER MALBY, *Friend to Sir Francis*
MASTER CRANWELL
SHAFTON, *a False Friend to Sir Charles*
OLD MOUNTFORD, *Uncle to Sir Charles*
TIDY, *Cousin to Sir Charles*
SANDY
RODER
NICHOLAS
JENKIN
ROGER BRICKBAT } SERVANTS *to Frankford*
JACK SLIME
SPIGOT, A BUTLER
SHERIFF
A SERGEANT, A KEEPER, OFFICERS, FALCONERS,
    HUNTSMEN, A COACHMAN, CARTERS, SERVANTS,
    MUSICIANS

MISTRESS FRANKFORD
SUSAN, *Sister of Sir Charles*
CICELY, *Maid to Mistress Frankford*
WOMEN SERVANTS

A WOMAN
KILLED WITH KINDNESS

THE PROLOGUE

I come but like a harbinger, being sent
To tell you what these preparations mean:
Look for no glorious state; our Muse is bent
Upon a barren subject, a bare scene.
We could afford this twig a timber tree,
Whose strength might boldly on your favours build;
Our russet, tissue; drone, a honey-bee;
Our barren plot, a large and spacious field;
Our coarse fare, banquets; our thin water, wine;
Our brook, a sea; our bat's eyes, eagle's sight;
Our poet's dull and earthy Muse, divine;
Our ravens, doves; our crow's black feathers, white.
  But gentle thoughts, when they may give the foil,
  Save them that yield, and spare where they may spoil.

ACT I, SCENE 1

Enter MASTER JOHN FRANKFORD, MISTRESS FRANK-
FORD, SIR FRANCIS ACTON, SIR CHARLES
MOUNTFORD, MASTER MALBY, MASTER WEN-
DOLL, *and* MASTER CRANWELL

Sir Fran. Some music there: none lead the bride a dance?
Sir Char. Yes, would she dance *The Shaking of the Sheets;*
  But that's the dance her husband means to lead her.
Wen. That's not the dance that every man must dance,
  According to the ballad.

Sir Fran.   Music, ho!
 By your leave, sister — by your husband's leave,
 I should have said — the hand that but this day
 Was given you in the church I'll borrow: sound!
 This marriage music hoists me from the ground.
Frank. Ay, you may caper, you are light and free:
 Marriage hath yoked my heels; pray then pardon me.
Sir Fran. I'll have you dance too, brother.
Sir Char.   Master Frankford,
 You are a happy man, sir; and much joy
 Succeed your marriage mirth! You have a wife
 So qualified, and with such ornaments
 Both of the mind and body. First, her birth
 Is noble, and her education such
 As might become the daughter of a prince:
 Her own tongue speaks all tongues, and her own hand
 Can teach all strings to speak in their best grace,
 From the shrill treble to the hoarsest bass.
 To end her many praises in one word,
 She's beauty and perfection's eldest daughter,
 Only found by yours, though many a heart hath sought
  her.
Frank. But that I know your virtues and chaste thoughts,
 I should be jealous of your praise, Sir Charles.
Cran. He speaks no more than you approve.
Mal. Nor flatters he that gives to her her due.
Mis. Frank. I would your praise could find a fitter theme
 Than my imperfect beauties to speak on;
 Such as they be, if they my husband please,
 They suffice me now I am married:
 His sweet content is like a flattering glass,
 To make my face seem fairer to mine eye;
 But the least wrinkle from his stormy brow
 Will blast the roses in my cheeks that grow.
Sir Fran. A perfect wife already, meek and patient;
 How strangely the word 'husband' fits your mouth,

Not married three hours since! Sister, 'tis good;
You, that begin betimes thus, must needs prove
Pliant and duteous in your husband's love. –
Godamercies, brother, wrought her to 't already;
'Sweet husband,' and a curtsey, the first day!
Mark this, mark this, you that are bachelors,
And never took the grace of honest man;
Mark this, against you marry, this one phrase:
'In a good time that man both wins and woos,
That takes his wife down in her wedding shoes.'

Frank. Your sister takes not after you, Sir Francis,
All his wild blood your father spent on you:
He got her in his age, when he grew civil;
All his mad tricks were to his land entailed,
And you are heir to all; your sister, she
Hath to her dower her mother's modesty.

Sir Char. Lord, sir, in what a happy state live you!
This morning, which to many seems a burthen
Too heavy to bear, is unto you a pleasure.
This lady is no clog, as many are:
She doth become you like a well-made suit,
In which the tailor hath used all his art:
Not like a thick coat of unseasoned frieze,
Forced on your back in summer; she's no chain
To tie your neck, and curb you to the yoke;
But she's a chain of gold to adorn your neck.
You both adorn each other, and your hands,
Methinks, are matches: there's equality
In this fair combination; you are both
Scholars, both young, both being descended nobly.
There's music in this sympathy; it carries
Consort, and expectation of much joy,
Which God bestow on you, from this first day
Until your dissolution; that's for aye.

Sir Fran. We keep you here too long, good brother Frankford.

Into the hall; away! go cheer your guests.
What, bride and bridegroom both withdrawn at
    once?
If you be missed, the guests will doubt their welcome,
And charge you with unkindness.

Frank.   To prevent it,
I'll leave you here, to see the dance within.

Mis. Frank. And so will I.

           [Exeunt Frankford and Mistress Frankford.

Sir Fran.   To part you, it were sin.
Now, gallants, while the town-musicians
Finger their frets within; and the mad lads
And country-lasses, every mother's child,
With nosegays and bridelaces in their hats,
Dance all their country measures, rounds, and jigs,
What shall we do? Hark, they are all on the hoigh;
They toil like mill-horses, and turn as round, –
Marry, not on the toe. Ay, and they caper,
Not without cutting; you shall see, to-morrow,
The hall-floor pecked and dinted like a mill-stone,
Made with their high shoes: though their skill be
    small,
Yet they tread heavy where their hob-nails fall.

Sir Char. Well, leave them to their sports. Sir Francis
    Acton,
I'll make a match with you; meet me to-morrow
At Chevy-chase, I'll fly my hawk with yours.

Sir Fran. For what? For what?

Sir Char.   Why, for a hundred pound.

Sir Fran. Pawn me some gold of that.

Sir Char.   Here are ten angels;
I'll make them good a hundred pound to-morrow
Upon my hawk's wing.

Sir Fran.   'Tis a match, 'tis done.
Another hundred pound upon your dogs,
Dare ye, Sir Charles?

Sir Char.   I dare: were I sure to lose,
I durst do more than that: here's my hand,
The first course for a hundred pound.

Sir Fran.   A match.

Wen. Ten angels on Sir Francis Acton's hawk;
As much upon his dogs.

Cran. I am for Sir Charles Mountford; I have seen
His hawk and dog both tried. What, clap you hands?
Or is't no bargain?

Wen.   .   Yes, and stake them down:
Were they five hundred, they were all my own.

Sir Fran. Be stirring early with the lark to-morrow;
I'll rise into my saddle ere the sun
Rise from his bed.

Sir Char.   If there you miss me, say
I am no gentleman: I'll hold my day.

Sir Fran. It holds on all sides. Come, to-night let's dance,
Early to-morrow let's prepare to ride;
We had need be three hours up before the bride.

                                        [*Exeunt.*

—————

ACT I, SCENE 2

Enter NICHOLAS *and* JENKIN, JACK SLIME, *and*
ROGER BRICKBAT, *with* COUNTRY WENCHES,
and two or three MUSICIANS

Jenk. Come, Nick, take you Joan Miniver to trace withal;
Jack Slime, traverse you with Cicely Milk-pail; I will
take Jane Trubkin, and Roger Brickbat shall have
Isbel Motley; and now that they are busy in the
parlour, come, strike up, we'll have a crash here in
the yard.

Nic. My humour is not compendious; dancing I possess
not, though I can foot it; yet, since I am fallen into
the hands of Cicely Milk-pail, I consent.

Slime. Truly Nick, though we were never brought up like serving courtiers, yet we have been brought up with serving creatures, ay, and God's creatures too; for we have been brought up to serve sheep, oxen, horses, and hogs, and such like; and, though we be but country fellows, it may be in the way of dancing we can do the horse-trick as well as serving-men.

Brick. Ay, and the cross-point too.

Jenk. O Slime, O Brickbat, do not you know that comparisons are odious? now we are odious ourselves, too, therefore there are no comparisons to be made betwixt us.

Nic. I am sudden, and not superfluous.

I am quarrelsome, and not seditious;

I am peaceable, and not contentious;

I am brief, and not compendious.

Slime. Foot it quickly: if the music overcome not my melancholy, I shall quarrel; and if they do not suddenly strike up, I shall presently strike thee down.

Jenk. No quarrelling, for God's sake: truly, if you do, I shall set a knave between ye.

Slime. I come to dance, not to quarrel. Come, what shall it be? *Rogero?*

Jenk. Rogero! no, we will dance *The Beginning of the World.*

Cicely. I love no dance so well as *John come kiss me now.*

Nic. I, that have ere now deserved a cushion, call for the *Cushion-dance.*

Brick. For my part, I like nothing so well as *Tom Tyler.*

Jenk. No, we'll have *The Hunting of the Fox.*

Slime. The Hay, The Hay; there's nothing like *The Hay.*

Nic. I have said, I do say, and I will say again —

Jenk. Every man agree to have it as Nick says.

All. Content.

Nic. It hath been, it now is, and it shall be —

Cicely. What, Master Nicholas, what?

Nic. Put on your smock a' Monday.

Jenk. So the dance will come cleanly off. Come, for God's
    sake agree of something; if you like not that, put it to
    the musicians; or let me speak for all, and we'll have
    Sellenger's round.

All. That, that, that.

Nic. No, I am resolved, thus it shall be:
    First take hands, then take you to your heels.

Jenk. Why, would you have us run away?

Nic. No but I would have you shake your heels.
    Music, strike up!

        [*They dance. Nick dancing speaks stately and scurvily,*
                  the rest after the country fashion.

Jenk. Hey! lively, my lasses! here's a turn for thee!

                              [*Exeunt.*

———

ACT I, SCENE 3

Wind horns. Enter Sir Charles Mountford, Sir
    Francis Acton, Malby, Cranwell, Wen-
    doll, Falconers, *and* Huntsmen

Sir Char. So; well cast off: aloft, aloft! well flown!
    Oh, now she takes her at the sowse, and strikes her
    Down to the earth, like a swift thunder-clap.

Wen. She hath struck ten angels out of my way.

Sir Fran. A hundred pound from me.

Sir Char.   What, falconer!

Fal. At hand, sir.

Sir Char. Now she hath seized the fowl, and 'gins to plume
    her,
    Rebeck her not; rather stand still and check her.
    So, seize her gets, her jesses, and her bells:
    Away!

Sir Fran. My hawk killed too.

Sir Char.   Ay, but 'twas at the querre,

Not at the mount, like mine.

Sir Fran.   Judgement, my masters.

Cran. Yours missed her at the ferre.

Wen. Ay, but our merlin first had plumed the fowl,
And twice renewed her from the river too;
Her bells, Sir Francis, had not both one weight,
Nor was one semi-tune above the other:
Methinks these Milan bells do sound too full,
And spoil the mounting of your hawk.

Sir Char.   'Tis lost.

Sir Fran. I grant it not. Mine likewise seized a fowl
Within her talons; and you saw her paws
Full of the feathers: both her petty singles,
And her long singles gripped her more than other;
The terrials of her legs were stained with blood:
Not of the fowl only she did discomfit
Some of her feathers; but she brake away.
Come, come, your hawk is but a rifler.

Sir Char.   How!

Sir Fran. Ay, and your dogs are trindle-tails and curs.

Sir Char. You stir my blood.
You keep not a good hound in all your kennel,
Nor one good hawk upon your perch.

Sir Fran.   How, knight!

Sir Char. So, knight: you will not swagger, sir?

Sir Fran. Why, say I did?

Sir Char. Why, sir,
I say you would gain as much by swaggering
As you have got by wagers on your dogs;
You will come short in all things.

Sir Fran.   Not in this:
Now I'll strike home.

Sir Char.   Thou shalt to thy long home,
Or I will want my will.

Sir Fran. All they that love Sir Francis, follow me.

Sir Char. All that affect Sir Charles, draw on my part.

Cran. On this side heaves my hand.
Wen.   Here goes my heart.

> [*They divide themselves. Sir Charles Mountford, Cran-*
> *well, Falconer, and Huntsman, fight against Sir*
> *Francis Acton, Wendoll, his Falconer, and Huntsman;*
> *and Sir Charles's side gets the better, beating the*
> *others away, and killing both of Sir Francis's men.*
> *Exeunt all except Sir Charles.*

Sir Char. My God! what have I done? what have I done?
My rage hath plunged into a sea of blood,
In which my soul lies drowned. Poor innocents,
For whom we are to answer! Well, 'tis done,
And I remain the victor. A great conquest,
When I would give this right hand, nay, this head,
To breathe in them new life whom I have slain!
Forgive me, God! 'twas in the heat of blood,
And anger quite removes me from myself:
It was not I, but rage, did this vile murther;
Yet I, and not my rage, must answer it.
Sir Francis Acton he is fled the field;
With him all those that did partake his quarrel,
And I am left alone, with sorrow dumb,
And in my height of conquest overcome.

Enter SUSAN

Susan. O God! my brother wounded 'mong the dead!
Unhappy jest, that in such earnest ends;
The rumour of this fear stretched to my ears,
And I am come to know if you be wounded.
Sir Char. Oh, sister, sister, wounded at the heart!
Susan. My God forbid!
Sir Char. In doing that thing which He forbad,
I am wounded, sister.
Susan.   I hope not at the heart.
Sir Char. Yes, at the heart.
Susan.   O God! a surgeon there!

Sir Char. Call me a surgeon, sister, for my soul;
   The sin of murther it hath pierced my heart,
   And made a wide wound there: but for these scratches,
   They are nothing, nothing.
Susan.   Charles, what have you done?
   Sir Francis hath great friends, and will pursue you
   Unto the utmost danger of the law.
Sir Char. My conscience is become mine enemy,
   And will pursue me more than Acton can.
Susan. Oh, fly, sweet brother.
Sir Char.   Shall I fly from thee?
   Why, Sue, art weary of my company?
Susan. Fly from your foe.
Sir Char.   You, sister, are my friend,
   And, flying you, I shall pursue my end.
Susan. Your company is as my eye-ball dear;
   Being far from you, no comfort can be near;
   Yet fly to save your life: what would I care
   To spend my future age in black despair,
   So you were safe? and yet to live one week
   Without my brother Charles, through every cheek
   My streaming tears would downwards run so rank,
   Till they could set on either side a bank,
   And in the midst a channel; so my face
   For two salt-water brooks shall still find place.
Sir Char. Thou shalt not weep so much, for I will stay
   In spite of danger's teeth; I'll live with thee,
   Or I'll not live at all. I will not sell
   My country and my father's patrimony,
   Nor thy sweet sight, for a vain hope of life.

Enter SHERIFF, *with* OFFICERS

Sher. Sir Charles, I am made the unwilling instrument
   Of your attach and apprehension:
   I am sorry that the blood of innocent men
   Should be of you exacted. It was told me

That you were guarded with a troop of friends,
And therefore I come thus armed.

Sir Char.   O, Master Sheriff,
I came into the field with many friends,
But see, they all have left me: only one
Clings to my sad misfortune, my dear sister.
I know you for an honest gentleman;
I yield my weapons, and submit to you;
Convey me where you please.

Sher.   To prison then,
To answer for the lives of these dead men.

Susan. O God! O God!

Sir Char.   Sweet sister, every strain
Of sorrow from your heart augments my pain;
Your grief abounds, and hits against my breast.

Sher. Sir, will you go?

Sir Char.   Even where it likes you best.

                                        [*Exeunt.*

ACT II, SCENE 1

Enter MASTER FRANKFORD *in a study*

Frank. How happy am I amongst other men,
That in my mean estate embrace content!
I am a gentleman, and by my birth,
Companion with a king; a king's no more.
I am possessed of many fair revenues,
Sufficient to maintain a gentleman.
Touching my mind, I am studied in all arts;
The riches of my thoughts, and of my time,
Have been a good proficient; but the chief
Of all the sweet felicities on earth,
I have a fair, a chaste, and loving wife;
Perfection all, all truth, all ornament;
If man on earth may truly happy be,
Of these at once possessed, sure I am he.

Enter NICHOLAS

Nic. Sir, there's a gentleman attends without
To speak with you.
Frank.   On horseback?
Nic.   Ay, on horseback.
Frank. Entreat him to alight, I will attend him.
Know'st thou him, Nick?
Nic.   Know him, yes: his name's Wendoll:
It seems he comes in haste: his horse is booted
Up to the flank in mire, himself all spotted
And stained with splashing. Sure he rid in fear,
Or for a wager: horse and man both sweat;
I ne'er saw two in such a smoking heat.
Frank. Entreat him in: about it instantly.
                                        [*Exit Nicholas.*
This Wendoll I have noted, and his carriage
Hath pleased me much; by observation

I have noted many good deserts in him:
He's affable, and seen in many things,
Discourses well, a good companion;
And though of small means, yet a gentleman
Of a good house, though somewhat pressed by want:
I have preferred him to a second place
In my opinion, and my best regard.

Enter WENDOLL, MISTRESS FRANKFORD, *and*
NICHOLAS

Mis. Frank. O Master Frankford, Master Wendoll here
　Brings you the strangest news that e'er you heard.
Frank. What news, sweet wife? What news, good Master
　　Wendoll?
Wen. You knew the match made 'twixt Sir Francis Acton
　And Sir Charles Mountford.
Frank.　　　　　True, with their hounds and hawks.
Wen. The matches were both played.
Frank.　　　　　　　　Ha, and which won?
Wen. Sir Francis, your wife's brother, had the worst,
　And lost the wager.
Frank.　　　　　Why, the worse his chance;
　Perhaps the fortune of some other day
　Will change his luck.
Mis. Frank.　　　　　Oh, but you hear not all.
　Sir Francis lost, and yet was loth to yield:
　In brief the two knights grew to difference,
　From words to blows, and so to banding sides;
　Where valorous Sir Charles slew in his spleen
　Two of your brother's men; his falconer,
　And his good huntsman, whom he loved so well;
　More men were wounded, no more slain outright.
Frank. Now, trust me, I am sorry for the knight;
　But is my brother safe?
Wen.　　　　　All whole and sound,
　His body not being blemished with one wound:

But poor Sir Charles is to the prison led,
To answer at th' assize for them that's dead.

Frank. I thank your pains, sir; had the news been
better
Your will was to have brought it, Master Wendoll.
Sir Charles will find hard friends; his case is heinous,
And will be most severely censured on;
I am sorry for him. Sir, a word with you:
I know you, sir, to be a gentleman
In all things; your possibilities but mean:
Please you to use my table and my purse,
They are yours.

Wen.   O Lord, sir, I shall never deserve it.

Frank. O sir, disparage not your worth too much,
You are full of quality and fair desert;
Choose of my men which shall attend on you
And he is yours. I will allow you, sir,
Your man, your gelding, and your table, all
At my own charge: be my companion.

Wen. Master Frankford, I have oft been bound to you
By many favours; this exceeds them all,
That I shall never merit your least favour:
But, when your last remembrance I forget,
Heaven at my soul exact that weighty debt!

Frank. There needs no protestation; for I know you
Virtuous, and therefore grateful. Prythee, Nan,
Use him with all thy loving'st courtesy.

Mis. Frank. As far as modesty may well extend,
It is my duty to receive your friend.

Frank. To dinner: come, sir, from this present day,
Welcome to me for ever: come, away.

        [*Exeunt Frankford, Mistress Frankford, and Wendoll.*

Nic. I do not like this fellow by no means:
I never see him but my heart still earns:
Zounds! I could fight with him, yet know not why:
The devil and he are all one in my eye.

Enter JENKIN

Jenk. O Nick, what gentleman is that comes to lie at our
house? My master allows him one to wait on him,
and I believe it will fall to thy lot.

Nic. I love my master, by these hilts I do:
But rather than I'll ever come to serve him,
I'll turn away my master.

Enter CICELY

Cicely. Nich'las, where are you, Nich'las? You must come
in, Nich'las, and help the young gentleman off with
his boots.

Nic. If I pluck off his boots, I'll eat the spurs,
And they shall stick fast in my throat like burs.

Cicely. Then, Jenkin, come you.

Jenk. 'Tis no boot for me to deny it. My master hath
given me a coat here, but he takes pains himself to
brush it once or twice a day with a holly-wand.

Cicely. Come, come, make haste, that you may wash your
hands again, and help to serve in dinner.

Jenk. You may see, my masters, though it be afternoon
with you, 'tis but early days with us, for we have not
dined yet: stay a little, I'll but go in and help to bear
up the first course, and come to you again presently.

[*Exeunt.*

ACT II, SCENE 2

Enter MALBY *and* CRANWELL

Mal. This is the sessions-day; pray can you tell me
How young Sir Charles hath sped? Is he acquit,
Or must he try the law's strict penalty?

Cran. He's cleared of all, spite of his enemies,
Whose earnest labour was to take his life:

But in this suit of pardon he hath spent
All the revenues that his father left him;
And he is now turned a plain countryman,
Reformed in all things. See, sir, here he comes.

Enter SIR CHARLES *and* KEEPER

Keep. Discharge your fees, and you are then at freedom.
Sir Char. Here, Master Keeper, take the poor remainder
Of all the wealth I have: my heavy foes
Have made my purse light; but, alas! to me
'Tis wealth enough that you have set me free.
Mal. God give you joy of your delivery!
I am glad to see you abroad, Sir Charles.
Sir Char. The poorest knight in England, Master
Malby;
My life hath cost me all my patrimony
My father left his son: well, God forgive them
That are the authors of my penury.

Enter SHAFTON

Shaf. Sir Charles! a hand, a hand, at liberty?
Now, by the faith I owe, I am glad to see it.
What want you? Wherein may I pleasure you?
Sir Char. O me! O most unhappy gentleman!
I am not worthy to have friends stirred up,
Whose hands may help me in this plunge of want.
I would I were in heaven, to inherit there
Th' immortal birth-right which my Saviour keeps,
And by no unthrift can be bought and sold;
For here on earth what pleasures should we trust?
Shaf. To rid you from these contemplations,
Three hundred pounds you shall receive of me:
Nay, five for fail. Come, sir; the sight of gold
Is the most sweet receipt for melancholy,
And will revive your spirits: you shall hold law
With your proud adversaries. Tush, let Frank Acton

Wage with his knighthood like expense with me,
And he will sink, he will. Nay, good Sir Charles,
Applaud your fortune, and your fair escape
From all these perils.

Sir Char.   O sir, they have undone me.
Two thousand and five hundred pounds a year
My father at his death possessed me of;
All of which the envious Acton made me spend.
And notwithstanding all this large expense
I had much ado to gain my liberty:
And I have now only a house of pleasure,
With some five hundred pounds, reserved
Both to maintain me and my loving sister.

Shaf. [*aside*]. That must I have, it lies convenient for me:
If I can fasten but one finger on him,
With my full hand I'll gripe him to the heart.
'Tis not for love I proffered him this coin,
But for my gain and pleasure. [*Aloud*] Come, Sir
      Charles,
I know you have need of money; take my offer.

Sir Char. Sir, I accept it, and remain indebted
Even to the best of my unable power.
Come, gentlemen, and see it tendered down.
                                        [*Exeunt.*

ACT II, SCENE 3

Enter WENDOLL *melancholy*

Wen. I am a villain if I apprehend
But such a thought: then, to attempt the deed –
Slave, thou art damned without redemption.
I'll drive away this passion with a song.
A song! ha, ha: a song! as if, fond man,
Thy eyes could swim in laughter, when thy soul
Lies drenched and drowned in red tears of blood.

I'll pray, and see if God within my heart
Plant better thoughts. Why, prayers are meditations;
And when I meditate (O God, forgive me!)
It is on her divine perfections.
I will forget her; I will arm myself
Not to entertain a thought of love to her:
And, when I come by chance into her presence,
I'll hale these balls until my eye-strings crack,
From being pulled and drawn to look that way.

Enter over the stage, FRANKFORD, *his* WIFE, *and*
NICHOLAS

O God! O God! with what a violence
I am hurried to my own destruction.
There goest thou, the most perfectest man
That ever England bred a gentleman;
And shall I wrong his bed? Thou God of thunder!
Stay in thy thoughts of vengeance and of wrath,
Thy great, almighty, and all-judging hand
From speedy execution on a villain:
A villain, and a traitor to his friend.

Enter JENKIN

Jenk. Did your worship call?
Wen. He doth maintain me, he allows me largely
  Money to spend —
Jenk. By my faith, so do not you me; I cannot get a cross
  of you.
Wen. My gelding, and my man —
Jenk. That's Sorrell and I.
Wen. This kindness grows of no alliance 'twixt us —
Jenk. Nor is my service of any great acquaintance.
Wen. I never bound him to me by desert:
  Of a mere stranger, a poor gentleman,
  A man by whom in no kind he could gain,
  He hath placed me in the height of all his thoughts,

Made me companion with the best and chiefest
In Yorkshire. He cannot eat without me,
Nor laugh without me: I am to his body
As necessary as his digestion,
And equally do make him whole or sick:
And shall I wrong this man? Base man, ingrate!
Hast thou the power straight with thy gory hands
To rip thy image from his bleeding heart?
To scratch thy name from out the holy book
Of his remembrance; and to wound his name
That holds thy name so dear, or rend his heart
To whom thy heart was knit and joined together?
And yet I must: then, Wendoll, be content;
Thus villains, when they would, cannot repent.

Jenk. What a strange humour is my new master in! Pray
God he be not mad: if he should be so, I should
never have any mind to serve him in Bedlam. It may
be he is mad for missing of me.

Wen. What, Jenkin, where's your mistress?

Jenk. Is your worship married?

Wen. Why dost thou ask?

Jenk. Because you are my master, and if I have a mistress,
I would be glad, like a good servant, to do my duty
to her.

Wen. I mean where's Mistress Frankford.

Jenk. Marry, sir, her husband is riding out of town, and
she went very lovingly to bring him on his way to
horse. Do you see, sir? Here she comes, and here I go.

Wen. Vanish.   [*Exit Jenkin.*

Enter MISTRESS FRANKFORD

Mis. Frank. You are well met, sir; now, in troth, my hus-
band,
Before he took horse, had a great desire
To speak with you: we sought about the house,
Hollaed into the fields, sent every way,

But could not meet you: therefore he enjoined me
To do unto you his most kind commends.
Nay, more; he wills you, as you prize his love,
Or hold in estimation his kind friendship,
To make bold in his absence, and command
Even as himself were present in the house:
For you must keep his table, use his servants,
And be a present Frankford in his absence.

Wen. I thank him for his love. –

Give me a name, you whose infectious tongues
Are tipped with gall and poison: as you would
Think on a man that had your father slain,
Murdered your children, made your wives base strum-
    pets,
So call me, call me so: print in my face
The most stigmatic title of a villain,
For hatching treason to so true a friend.   *[Aside.*

Mis. Frank. Sir, you are much beholding to my husband;
You are a man most dear in his regard.

Wen. I am bound unto your husband, and you too.
I will not speak to wrong a gentleman
Of that good estimation, my kind friend:
I will not; zounds! I will not. I may choose,
And I will choose. Shall I be so misled?
Or shall I purchase to my father's crest
The motto of a villain? If I say
I will not do it, what thing can enforce me?
What can compel me? What sad destiny
Hath such command upon my yielding thoughts?
I will not – Ha! some fury pricks me on,
The swift Fates drag me at their chariot-wheel,
And hurry me to mischief. Speak I must;
Injure myself, wrong her, deceive his trust.   *[Aside.*

Mis. Frank. Are you not well, sir, that you seem thus
    troubled?
There is sedition in your countenance.

Wen. And in my heart, fair angel, chaste and wise.
　I love you: start not, speak not, answer not.
　I love you: nay, let me speak the rest:
　Bid me to swear, and I will call to record
　The host of Heaven.

Mis. Frank.　　　　　The host of Heaven forbid
　Wendoll should hatch such a disloyal thought!

Wen. Such is my fate; to this suit I was born,
　To wear rich pleasure's crown, or fortune's scorn.

Mis. Frank. My husband loves you.

Wen.　　　　　　　　　I know it.

Mis. Frank.　　　　　　　　He esteems you
　Even as his brain, his eye-ball, or his heart.

Wen. I have tried it.

Mis. Frank. His purse is your exchequer, and his table
　Doth freely serve you.

Wen.　　　　　So I have found it.

Mis. Frank. O! with what face of brass, what brow of
　　steel,
　Can you, unblushing, speak this to the face
　Of the espoused wife of so dear a friend?
　It is my husband that maintains your state;
　Will you dishonour him that in your power
　Hath left his whole affairs? I am his wife,
　It is to me you speak.

Wen.　　　　　O speak no more!
　For more than this I know, and have recorded
　Within the red-leaved table of my heart.
　Fair, and of all beloved, I was not fearful
　Bluntly to give my life into your hand,
　And at one hazard all my earthly means.
　Go, tell your husband; he will turn me off,
　And I am then undone: I care not, I;
　'Twas for your sake. Perchance in rage he'll [kill
　　me:
　I care not, 'twas for you. Say I incur

The general name of villain through the world,
Of traitor to my friend: I care not, I.
Beggary, shame, death, scandal, and reproach,
For you I'll hazard all: why, what care I?
For you I'll live, and in your love I'll die.

Mis. Frank. You move me, sir, to passion and to pity.
The love I bear my husband is as precious
As my soul's health.

Wen.   I love your husband too,
And for his love I will engage my life;
Mistake me not, the augmentation
Of my sincere affection borne to you
Doth no whit lessen my regard of him.
I will be secret, lady, close as night;
And not the light of one small glorious star
Shall shine here in my forehead, to bewray
That act of night.

Mis. Frank.   What shall I say?
My soul is wandering and hath lost her way.
Oh, Master Wendoll! Oh!

Wen.   Sigh not, sweet saint;
For every sigh you breathe draws from my heart
A drop of blood.

Mis. Frank.   I ne'er offended yet:
My fault, I fear, will in my brow be writ.
Women that fall, not quite bereft of grace,
Have their offences noted in their face.
I blush and am ashamed. Oh, Master Wendoll,
Pray God I be not born to curse your tongue,
That hath enchanted me! This maze I am in
I fear will prove the labyrinth of sin.

Enter NICK

Wen. The path of pleasure, and the gate to bliss,
Which on your lips I knock at with a kiss.

Nic. [*aside.*] I'll kill the rogue.

Wen. Your husband is from home, your bed's no blab.
   Nay, look not down and blush.

                              [*Exeunt Wendoll and Mistress Frankford.*
Nic.   Zounds, I'll stab!
   Ay, Nick, was it thy chance to come just in the nick?
   I love my master, and I hate that slave;
   I love my mistress, but these tricks I like not.
   My master shall not pocket up this wrong;
   I'll eat my fingers first. What say'st thou, metal?
   Does not the rascal Wendoll go on legs
   That thou must cut off? Hath he not ham-strings
   That thou must hough? Nay, metal, thou shalt stand
   To all I say. I'll henceforth turn a spy,
   And watch them in their close conveyances.
   I never looked for better of that rascal,
   Since he came miching first into our house:
   It is that Satan hath corrupted her,
   For she was fair and chaste. I'll have an eye
   In all their gestures. Thus I think of them,
   If they proceed as they have done before:
   Wendoll's a knave, my mistress is a —   [*Exit.*

Enter Sir Charles Mountford *and* Susan

Sir Char. Sister, you see we are driven to hard shift
    To keep this poor house we have left unsold;
    I am now enforced to follow husbandry,
    And you to milk; and do we not live well?
    Well, I thank God.
Susan.   O brother, here's a change,
    Since old Sir Charles died, in our father's house!
Sir Char. All things on earth thus change, some up, some
        down;
    Content's a kingdom, and I wear that crown.

Enter Shafton *with a* Sergeant

Shaf. Good morrow, good morrow, Sir Charles: what,
    with your sister,
    Plying your husbandry? – Sergeant, stand off. –
    You have a pretty house here, and a garden,
    And goodly ground about it. Since it lies
    So near a lordship that I lately bought,
    I would fain buy it of you. I will give you —
Sir Char. O, pardon me: this house successively
    Hath 'longed to me and my progenitors
    Three hundred year. My great-great-grandfather,
    He in whom first our gentle style began,
    Dwelt here; and in this ground, increased this molehill
    Unto that mountain which my father left me.
    Where he the first of all our house began,
    I now the last will end, and keep this house,
    This virgin title, never yet deflowered
    By any unthrift of the Mountfords' line.
    In brief, I will not sell it for more gold
    Than you could hide or pave the ground withal.
Shaf. Ha, ha! a proud mind and beggar's purse!

Where's my three hundred pounds, beside the use?
I have brought it to an execution
By course of law: what, is my money ready?

Sir Char. An execution, sir, and never tell me
You put my bond in suit! you deal extremely.

Shaf. Sell me the land, and I'll acquit you straight.

Sir Char. Alas, alas! 'tis all trouble hath left me
To cherish me and my poor sister's life.
If this were sold, our names should then be quite
Razed from the bead-roll of gentility.
You see what hard shift we have made to keep it
Allied still to our own name. This palm, you see,
Labour hath glowed within; her silver brow,
That never tasted a rough winter's blast
Without a mask or fan, doth with a grace
Defy cold winter, and his storms outface.

Susan. Sir, we feed sparing, and we labour hard,
We lie uneasy, to reserve to us
And our succession this small plot of ground.

Sir Char. I have so bent my thoughts to husbandry,
That I protest I scarcely can remember
What a new fashion is; how silk or satin
Feels in my hand: why, pride is grown to us
A mere, mere stranger. I have quite forgot
The names of all that ever waited on me;
I cannot name ye any of my hounds,
Once from whose echoing mouths I heard all music
That e'er my heart desired. What should I say?
To keep this place I have changed myself away.

Shaf. Arrest him at my suit. Actions and actions
Shall keep thee in perpetual bondage fast.
Nay, more, I'll sue thee by a late appeal,
And call thy former life in question.
The keeper is my friend, thou shalt have irons,
And usage such as I'll deny to dogs:
Away with him!

Sir Char. [*to Susan*]. You are too timorous:
　　But trouble is my master,
　　And I will serve him truly. My kind sister,
　　Thy tears are of no force to mollify
　　This flinty man. Go to my father's brother,
　　My kinsmen and allies; entreat them for me,
　　To ransom me from this injurious man,
　　That seeks my ruin.
Shaf.　　　　　　　　Come, irons, irons! away;
　　I'll see thee lodged far from the sight of day. [*Exeunt.*
Susan. My heart's so hardened with the frost of grief,
　　Death cannot pierce it through. Tyrant too fell!
　　So lead the fiends condemned souls to hell.

Enter SIR FRANCIS ACTON *and* MALBY

Sir Fran. Again to prison! Malby, hast thou seen
　　A poor slave better tortured? Shall we hear
　　The music of his voice cry from the grate,
　　'Meat for the Lord sake?' No, no, yet I am not
　　Throughly revenged. They say he hath a pretty wench
　　Unto his sister: shall I in mercy sake
　　To him and to his kindred, bribe the fool
　　To shame herself by lewd dishonest lust?
　　I'll proffer largely but, the deed being done,
　　I'll smile to see her base confusion.
Mal. Methinks, Sir Francis, you are full revenged
　　For greater wrongs than he can proffer you.
　　See where the poor sad gentlewoman stands.
Sir Fran. Ha, ha! now will I flout her poverty,
　　Deride her fortunes, scoff her base estate;
　　My very soul the name of Mountford hates.
　　But stay, my heart! oh, what a look did fly
　　To strike my soul through with thy piercing eye!
　　I am enchanted, all my spirits are fled,
　　And with one glance my envious spleen struck dead.
Susan. Acton, that seeks our blood!　　　　　[*Runs away.*

Sir Fran.   O chaste and fair!

Mal. Sir Francis, why, Sir Francis! zounds, in a trance?
  Sir Francis, what cheer, man? Come, come, how is't?

Sir Fran. Was she not fair? Or else this judging eye
  Cannot distinguish beauty.

Mal.   She was fair.

Sir Fran. She was an angel in a mortal's shape,
  And ne'er descended from old Mountford's line.
  But soft, soft, let me call my wits together.
  A poor, poor wench, to my great adversary
  Sister, whose very souls denounce stern war,
  One against other. How now, Frank? turned fool
  Or madman, whether? But no; master of
  My perfect senses and directest wits.
  Then why should I be in this violent humour
  Of passion and of love; and with a person
  So different every way, and so opposed
  In all contractions, and still-warring actions?
  Fie, fie; how I dispute against my soul!
  Come, come; I'll gain her, or in her fair quest
  Purchase my soul free and immortal rest.   *[Exeunt.*

ACT III, SCENE 2

Enter three or four SERVING-MEN, *one with a voider and a
wooden knife to take away all, another the salt and bread,
another the table-cloth and napkins, another the carpet:*
JENKIN *with two lights after them*

Jenk. So, march in order, and retire in battle array. My
    master and the guests have supped already, all's
    taken away: here, now spread for the serving-men in
    the hall. Butler, it belongs to your office.

But. I know it, Jenkin. What do you call the gentleman
    that supped there to-night?

Jenk. Who, my master?

But. No, no; Master Wendoll, he is a daily guest; I mean
the gentleman that came but this afternoon.

Jenk. His name is Master Cranwell. God's light, hark,
within there, my master calls to lay more billets on
the fire. Come, come! Lord, how we that are in
office here in the house are troubled! One spread the
carpet in the parlour, and stand ready to snuff the
lights; the rest be ready to prepare their stomachs.
More light in the hall there. Come, Nich'las.

          [Exeunt all but Nicholas.

Nic. I cannot eat, but had I Wendoll's heart
 I would eat that; the rogue grows impudent.
 Oh, I have seen such vild notorious tricks,
 Ready to make my eyes dart from my head.
 I'll tell my master, by this air I will!
 Fall what may fall, I'll tell him. Here he comes.

Enter MASTER FRANKFORD, *brushing the crumbs from
his clothes with a napkin, as newly risen from supper*

Frank. Nicholas, what make you here? why are not you
 At supper in the hall there, with your fellows?

Nic. Master, I stayed your rising from the board,
 To speak with you.

Frank.   Be brief, then, gentle Nicholas;
 My wife and guests attend me in the parlour.
 Why dost thou pause? Now, Nicholas, you want
  money,
 And, unthrift-like, would eat into your wages
 Ere you have earned it: here's, sir, half a crown;
 Play the good husband, and away to supper.

Nic. By this hand, an honourable gentleman! I will not
 see him wronged. – Sir, I have served you long; you
 entertained me seven years before your beard. You
 knew me, sir, before you knew my mistress.

Frank. What of this, good Nicholas?

Nic. I never was a make-bate or a knave;
  I have no fault but one: I am given to quarrel,
  But not with women. I will tell you, master,
  That which will make your heart leap from your
    breast,
  Your hair to startle from your head, your ears to
    tingle.
Frank. What preparation's this to dismal news?
Nic. 'Sblood, sir! I love you better than your wife;
  I'll make it good.
Frank. Thou art a knave, and I have much ado
  With wonted patience to contain my rage,
  And not to break thy pate. Thou art a knave;
  I'll turn you, with your base comparisons,
  Out of my doors.
Nic.   Do, do; there is not room
  For Wendoll and me too, both in one house.
  Oh master, master, that Wendoll is a villain.
Frank. Ay, saucy!
Nic. Strike, strike; do, strike; yet hear me: I am no fool,
  I know a villain, when I see him act
  Deeds of a villain. Master, master, that base slave
  Enjoys my mistress, and dishonours you.
Frank. Thou hast killed me with a weapon whose sharp-
    ened point
  Hath pricked quite through and through my shivering
    heart:
  Drops of cold sweat sit dangling on my hairs,
  Like morning's dew upon the golden flowers,
  And I am plunged into strange agony.
  What didst thou say? If any word that touched
  His credit or her reputation,
  It is as hard to enter my belief
  As Dives into heaven.
Nic.   I can gain nothing;
  They are two that never wronged me. I knew before

'Twas but a thankless office, and perhaps
As much as is my service, or my life
Is worth. All this I know; but this and more,
More by a thousand dangers, could not hire me
To smother such a heinous wrong from you.
I saw, and I have said.

Frank. [*aside*]. 'Tis probable; though blunt, yet he is
    honest:
Though I durst pawn my life, and on their faith
Hazard the dear salvation of my soul,
Yet in my trust I may be too secure.
May this be true? O, may it, can it be?
Is it by any wonder possible?
Man, woman, what thing mortal may we trust,
When friends and bosom wives prove so unjust? —
What instance hast thou of this strange report?

Nic. Eyes, eyes.

Frank.   Thy eyes may be deceived, I tell thee:
For should an angel from the heavens drop down,
And preach this to me that thyself hast told,
He should have much ado to win belief;
In both their loves I am so confident.

Nic. Shall I discourse the same by circumstance?

Frank. No more! to supper, and command your fellows
To attend us and the strangers. Not a word,
I charge thee on thy life: be secret then,
For I know nothing.

Nic. I am dumb; and, now that I have eased my stom-
    ach,
I will go fill my stomach.

Frank.   Away; be gone. [*Exit Nicholas.*
She is well born, descended nobly;
Virtuous her education, her repute
Is in the general voice of all the country
Honest and fair; her carriage, her demeanour,
In all her actions that concern the love

To me her husband, modest, chaste, and godly.
Is all this seeming gold plain copper?
But he, that Judas that hath borne my purse,
And sold me for a sin! – O God! O God!
Shall I put up these wrongs? No. Shall I trust
The bare report of this suspicious groom,
Before the double-gilt, the well-hatched ore
Of their two hearts? No, I will lose these thoughts:
Distraction I will banish from my brow,
And from my looks exile sad discontent;
Their wonted favours in my tongue shall flow;
Till I know all, I'll nothing seem to know.
Lights and a table there! Wife, Master Wendoll,
And gentle Master Cranwell.

Enter MISTRESS FRANKFORD, MASTER WENDOLL,
MASTER CRANWELL, NICHOLAS, *and* JENKIN,
with cards, carpet, stools, and other necessaries

Frank. O, you are a stranger Master Cranwell, you,
And often baulk my house: faith, y'are a churl:
Now we have supped, a table, and to cards.
Jenk. A pair of cards, Nicholas, and a carpet to cover the
table. Where's Cicely with her counters and her box?
Candles and candlesticks there! Fie, we have such a
household of serving creatures! unless it be Nick and
I, there's not one amongst them all can say bo to a
goose. Well said, Nick.
      [*They spread a carpet, set down lights and cards.*
Mis. Frank. Come, Master Frankford, who shall take my
part?
Frank. Marry, that will I, sweet wife.
Wen. No, by my faith, sir; when you are together I sit
out; it must be Mistress Frankford and I, or else it is
no match.
Frank. I do not like that match.
Nic. – You have no reason, marry, knowing all.

Frank. 'Tis no great matter neither. Come, Master Cranwell, shall you and I take them up?

Cran. At your pleasure, sir.

Frank. I must look to you, Master Wendoll, for you will
be playing false; nay, so will my wife too.

Nic. – Ay, I will be sworn she will.

Mis. Frank. Let them that are taken playing false, forfeit
the set.

Frank. Content; it shall go hard but I'll take you.

Cran. Gentlemen, what shall our game be?

Wen. Master Frankford, you play best at noddy.

Frank. You shall not find it so; indeed you shall not.

Mis. Frank. I can play at nothing so well as double
ruff.

Frank. If Master Wendoll and my wife be together, there's
no playing against them at double hand.

Nic. I can tell you, sir, the game that Master Wendoll is
best at.

Wen. What game is that, Nick?

Nic. Marry, sir, knave out of doors.

Wen. She and I will take you at lodam.

Mis. Frank. Husband, shall we play at saint?

Frank. My saint's turned devil. – No, we'll none of saint:
You are best at new-cut, wife; you'll play at that.

Wen. If you play at new-cut, I am soonest hitter of any
here, for a wager.

Frank. 'Tis me they play on. Well, you may draw out.
For all your cunning, 'twill be to your shame;
I'll teach you, at your new-cut, a new game.
Come, come.

Cran. If you cannot agree upon the game, to post and
pair.

Wen. We shall be soonest pairs; and my good host,
When he comes late home, he must kiss the post.

Frank. Whoever wins, it shall be thy cost.

Cran. Faith, let it be vide-ruff, and let's make honours.

Frank. If you make honours, one thing let me crave:
  Honour the king and queen; except the knave.
Wen. Well, as you please for that. Lift who shall deal.
Mis. Frank. The least in sight: what are you, Master
    Wendoll?
Wen. I am a knave.
Nic. – I'll swear it.
Mis. Frank. I a queen.
Frank. – A quean thou shouldst say. – Well, the cards are
    mine;
  They are the grossest pair that e'er I felt.
Mis. Frank. Shuffle, I'll cut: would I had never dealt.
Frank. I have lost my dealing.
Wen.   Sir, the fault's in me:
  This queen I have more than my own, you see.
  Give me the stock.
Frank.   My mind's not on my game.
  Many a deal I have lost, the more's your shame.
  You have served me a bad trick, Master Wendoll.
Wen. Sir, you must take your lot. To end this strife,
  I know I have dealt better with your wife.
Frank. Thou hast dealt falsely then.
Mis. Frank. What's trumps?
Wen. Hearts: partner, I rub.
Frank. Thou robb'st me of my soul, of her chaste love;
  In thy false dealing thou hast robbed my heart.
  – Booty you play; I like a loser stand,
  Having no heart, or here or in my hand.
  I will give o'er the set; I am not well.
  Come, who will hold my cards?
Mis. Frank. Not well, sweet Master Frankford!
  Alas, what ails you? 'Tis some sudden qualm.
Wen. How long have you been so, Master Frankford?
Frank. Sir, I was lusty, and I had my health,
  But I grew ill when you began to deal.
  Take hence this table. Gentle Master Cranwell,

You are welcome; see your chamber at your pleasure.
I am sorry that this megrim takes me so,
I cannot sit and bear you company.
Jenkin, some lights, and show him to his chamber.

[Exeunt Cranwell and Jenkin.

Mis. Frank. A night-gown for my husband; quickly there:
It is some rheum or cold.

Wen. Now, in good faith, this illness you have got
By sitting late, without your gown.

Frank. I know it, Master Wendoll.
Go, go to bed, lest you complain like me.
Wife, prythee, wife, into my bed-chamber;
The night is raw and cold, and rheumatic:
Leave me my gown and light; I'll walk away my fit.

Wen. Sweet sir, good night.

Frank. Myself, good night.   *[Exit Wendoll.*

Mis. Frank.   Shall I attend you, husband?

Frank. No, gentle wife, thou'lt catch cold in thy head;
Prythee, be gone, sweet; I'll make haste to bed.

Mis. Frank. No sleep will fasten on mine eyes, you know,
Until you come.

Frank.   Sweet Nan, I prythee go. –

[Exit Mistress Frankford.

I have bethought me: get me, by degrees,
The keys of all my doors, which I will mould
In wax, and take their fair impression,
To have by them new keys. This being compassed,
At a set hour a letter shall be brought me,
And, when they think they may securely play,
They are nearest to danger. Nick, I must rely
Upon thy trust and faithful secrecy.

Nic. Build on my faith.

Frank.   To bed then, not to rest;
Care lodges in my brain, grief in my breast.

[Exeunt.

Enter SUSAN, OLD MOUNTFORD, SANDY, RODER, *and* TIDY

O. Mount. You say my nephew is in great distress:
  Who brought it to him, but his own lewd life?
  I cannot spare a cross. I must confess
  He was my brother's son: why, niece, what then?
  This is no world in which to pity men.

Susan. I was not born a beggar, though his extremes
  Enforce this language from me: I protest
  No fortune of mine own could lead my tongue
  To this base key. I do beseech you, uncle,
  For the name's sake, for Christianity,
  Nay, for God's sake, to pity his distress:
  He is denied the freedom of the prison,
  And in the Hole is laid with men condemned;
  Plenty he hath of nothing but of irons,
  And it remains in you to free him thence.

O. Mount. Money I cannot spare; men should take heed;
  He lost my kindred when he fell to need.   [*Exit.*

Susan. Gold is but earth, thou earth enough shalt have,
  When thou hast once took measure of thy grave.
  You know me, Master Sandy, and my suit.

Sandy. I knew you, lady, when the old man lived;
  I knew you ere your brother sold his land;
  Then you were Mistress Sue, tricked up in jewels;
  Then you sung well, played sweetly on the flute;
  But now I neither know you nor your suit.   [*Exit.*

Susan. You, Master Roder, were my brother's tenant,
  Rent-free he placed you in that wealthy farm
  Of which you are possessed.

Roder.   True, he did;
  And have I not there dwelt still for his sake?
  I have some business now; but without doubt,

They that have hurled him in will help him out.

                                             [Exit.

Susan. Cold comfort still: what say you, cousin Tidy?

Tidy. I say this comes of roysting, swaggering.

   Call me not cousin: each man for himself.

   Some men are born to mirth, and some to sorrow.

   I am no cousin unto them that borrow.   *[Exit.*

Susan. O charity! why art thou fled to heaven,

   And left all things upon this earth uneven?

   Their scoffing answers I will ne'er return;

   But to myself his grief in silence mourn.

Enter SIR FRANCIS ACTON *and* MALBY

Sir Fran. She is poor, I'll therefore tempt her with this
    gold.

   Go, Malby, in my name deliver it,

   And I will stay thy answer.

Mal. Fair mistress, as I understand, your grief

   Doth grow from want, so I have here in store

   A means to furnish you, a bag of gold,

   Which to your hands I freely tender you.

Susan. I thank you, Heavens! I thank you, gentle sir:

   God make me able to requite this favour!

Mal. This gold Sir Francis Acton sends by me,

   And prays you —

Susan. Acton! O God! that name I'm born to curse:

   Hence, bawd! hence, broker! see, I spurn his gold;

   My honour never shall for gain be sold.

Sir Fran. Stay, lady, stay.

Susan.   From you I'll posting hie,

   Even as the doves from feathered eagles fly.   *[Exit.*

Sir Fran. She hates my name, my face: how should I woo?

   I am disgraced in every thing I do.

   The more she hates me, and disdains my love,

   The more I am rapt in admiration

   Of her divine and chaste perfections.

Woo her with gifts I cannot, for all gifts
Sent in my name she spurns; with looks I cannot,
For she abhors my sight; nor yet with letters,
For none she will receive. How then, how then?
Well, I will fasten such a kindness on her
As shall o'ercome her hate and conquer it.
Sir Charles, her brother, lies in execution
For a great sum of money: and, besides,
The appeal is sued still for my huntsman's death,
Which only I have power to reverse:
In her I'll bury all my hate of him.
Go seek the keeper, Malby, bring me to him:
To save his body, I his debts will pay;
To save his life, I his appeal will stay.   [*Exeunt.*

———

ACT IV, SCENE 2

Enter SIR CHARLES MOUNTFORD *in prison, with
irons, his feet bare, his garments all ragged and torn*

Sir Char. Of all on the earth's face most miserable,
Breathe in this hellish dungeon thy laments:
Thus like a slave ragged, like a felon gyved.
What hurls thee headlong to this base estate?
O unkind uncle! O my friends ingrate!
Unthankful kinsmen! Mountford all too base,
To let thy name lie fettered in disgrace!
A thousand deaths here in this grave I die;
Fear, hunger, sorrow, cold, all threat my death,
And join together to deprive my breath.
But that which most torments me, my dear sister
Hath left to visit me, and from my friends
Hath brought no hopeful answer: therefore I
Divine they will not help my misery.

If it be so, shame, scandal, and contempt
Attend their covetous thoughts; need make their graves!
Userers they live, and may they die like slaves!

Enter KEEPER

Keep. Knight, be of comfort, for I bring thee freedom
　From all thy troubles.
Sir Char.　　　　　　　Then I am doomed to die;
　Death is the end of all calamity.
Keep. Live: your appeal is stayed; the execution
　Of all your debts discharged; your creditors
　Even to the utmost penny satisfied.
　In sign whereof, your shackles I knock off;
　You are not left so much indebted to us
　As for your fees; all is discharged, all paid:
　Go freely to your house, or where you please,
　After long miseries, embrace your ease.
Sir Char. Thou grumblest out the sweetest music to me
　That ever organ played. Is this a dream
　Or do my waking senses apprehend
　The pleasing taste of these applausive news?
　Slave that I was, to wrong such honest friends,
　My loving kinsmen, and my near allies.
　Tongue, I will bite thee for the scandal breathed
　Against such faithful kinsmen: they are all
　Composed of pity and compassion,
　Of melting charity, and of moving ruth.
　That which I spake before was in my rage;
　They are my friends, the mirrors of this age,
　Bounteous and free. The noble Mountford's race,
　Ne'er bred a covetous thought, or humour base.

Enter SUSAN

Susan. I can no longer stay from visiting
　My woeful brother: while I could, I kept
　My hapless tidings from his hopeful ear.

Sir Char. Sister, how much am I indebted to thee,
  And to thy travail!
Susan.   What, at liberty?
Sir Char. Thou seest I am, thanks to thy industry:
  O, unto which of all my courteous friends
  Am I thus bound? My uncle Mountford, he
  Even of an infant loved me: was it he?
  So did my cousin Tidy; was it he?
  So Master Roder, Master Sandy too:
  Which of all these did this high kindness do?
Susan. Charles, can you mock me in your poverty,
  Knowing your friends deride your misery?
  Now, I protest I stand so much amazed
  To see your bonds free, and your irons knocked off,
  That I am rapt into a maze of wonder:
  The rather for I know not by what means
  This happiness hath chanced.
Sir Char.   Why, by my uncle,
  My cousins, and my friends; who else, I pray,
  Would take upon them all my debts to pay?
Susan. O brother, they are men all of flint,
  Pictures of marble, and as void of pity
  As chased bears. I begged, I sued, I kneeled,
  Laid open all your griefs and miseries,
  Which they derided; more than that, denied us
  A part in their alliance; but, in pride,
  Said that our kindred with our plenty died.
Sir Char. Drudges too much – what did they? O, known
    evil!
  Rich fly the poor, as good men shun the devil.
  Whence should my freedom come? Of whom alive,
  Saving of those, have I deserved so well?
  Guess, sister, call to mind, remember me:
  These I have raised, these follow the world's guise;
  Whom rich in honour, they in woe despise.
Susan. My wits have lost themselves, let's ask the keeper.

Sir Char. Gaoler!

Keep. At hand, sir.

Sir Char. Of courtesy resolve me one demand.
What was he took the burthen of my debts
From off my back, stayed my appeal to death,
Discharged my fees, and brought me liberty?

Keep. A courteous knight, one called Sir Francis Acton.

Susan. Acton!

Sir Char.   Ha! Acton! O me, more distressed
In this than all my troubles! hale me back,
Double my irons, and my sparing meals
Put into halves, and lodge me in a dungeon
More deep, more dark, more cold, more comfortless.
By Acton freed! not all thy manacles
Could fetter so my heels as this one word
Hath thralled my heart; and it must now lie bound
In more strict prison than thy stony gaol.
I am not free, I go but under bail.

Keep. My charge is done, sir, now I have my fees;
As we get little, we will nothing leese.   [*Exit.*

Sir Char. By Acton freed, my dangerous opposite!
Why, to what end? on what occasion? Ha!
Let me forget the name of enemy,
And with indifference balance this high favour:
Ha!

Susan. His love to me, upon my soul 'tis so!
That is the root from whence these strange things grow.
        [*Aside.*

Sir Char. Had this proceeded from my father, he
That by the law of nature is most bound
In offices of love, it had deserved
My best employment to requite that grace:
Had it proceeded from my friends or him,
From them this action had deserved my life;
And from a stranger more, because from such
There is less expectation of good deeds.

But he, nor father, nor ally, nor friend,
More than a stranger, both remote in blood,
And in his heart opposed my enemy –
That this high bounty should proceed from him!
Oh, there I lose myself! What should I say,
What think, what do, his bounty to repay?

Susan. You wonder, I am sure, whence this strange kind-
ness
Proceeds in Acton. I will tell you, brother:
He dotes on me, and oft hath sent me gifts,
Letters and tokens: I refused them all.

Sir Char. I have enough; though poor, my heart is set,
In one rich gift to pay back all my debt.   [*Exeunt.*

━━━

ACT IV, SCENE 3

Enter FRANKFORD, *and* NICHOLAS *with keys, and a
letter in his hand*

Frank. This is the night that I must play my part
To try two seeming angels. Where's my keys?

Nic. They are made according to your mould in wax:
I bade the smith be secret, gave him money,
And here they are. The letter, sir.

Frank. True, take it, there it is;   [*Gives him letter.*
And when thou seest me in my pleasantest vein,
Ready to sit to supper, bring it me.

Nic. I'll do't, make no more question but I'll do't.
[*Exit.*

Enter MISTRESS FRANKFORD, CRANWELL,
WENDOLL, *and* JENKIN

Mis. Frank. Sirrah, 'tis six o'clock already struck!
Go bid them spread the cloth and serve in supper.

Jenk. It shall be done, forsooth, mistress. Where is Spigot,
the butler, to give us out salt and trenchers? [*Exit.*

Wen. We that have been a-hunting all the day
  Come with prepared stomachs. Master Frankford,
  We wished you at our sport.
Frank. My heart was with you, and my mind was on you.
  Fie, Master Cranwell! you are still thus sad?
  A stool, a stool. Where's Jenkin, and where's Nick?
  'Tis supper-time at least an hour ago.
  What's the best news abroad?
Wen.   I know none good.
Frank. But I know too much bad.   [*Aside.*

Enter BUTLER *and* JENKIN *with a table-cloth, bread,*
trenchers, and salt

Cran. Methinks, sir, you might have that interest
  In your wife's brother, to be more remiss
  In his hard dealing against poor Sir Charles,
  Who, as I hear, lies in York Castle, needy,
  And in great want.   [*Exeunt Butler and Jenkin.*
Frank. Did not more weighty business of my own
  Hold me away, I would have laboured peace
  Betwixt them, with all care; indeed I would, sir.
Mis. Frank. I'll write unto my brother earnestly
  In that behalf.
Wen.   A charitable deed,
  And will beget the good opinion
  Of all your friends that love you, Mistress Frankford.
Frank. That's you for one; I know you love Sir Charles,
  And my wife too, well.
Wen.   He deserves the love
  Of all true gentlemen; be yourselves judge.
Frank. But supper, ho! Now as thou lov'st me, Wendoll,
  Which I am sure thou dost, be merry pleasant,
  And frolic it to-night. Sweet Master Cranwell,
  Do you the like. Wife, I protest my heart
  Was ne'er more bent on sweet alacrity.
  Where be those lazy knaves to serve in supper?

Enter NICHOLAS

Nic. Sir, here's a letter.

Frank. Whence comes it? and who brought it?

Nic. A stripling that below attends your answer,
  And, as he tells me, it is sent from York.

Frank. Have him into the cellar; let him taste
  A cup of our March beer: go, make him drink.
                                          [*Reads the letter.*

Nic. I'll make him drunk, if he be a Trojan.

Frank. My boots and spurs! where's Jenkin? God forgive
    me,
  How I neglect my business! Wife, look here;
  I have a matter to be tried to-morrow
  By eight o'clock, and my attorney writes me,
  I must be there betimes with evidence,
  Or it will go against me. Where's my boots?

Enter JENKIN *with boots and spurs*

Mis. Frank. I hope your business craves no such despatch
  That you must ride to-night.

Wen. I hope it doth.   [*Aside.*

Frank.   God's me! no such despatch!
  Jenkin, my boots. Where's Nick? Saddle my roan,
  And the grey dapple for himself. Content ye,
  It much conerns me. Gentle Master Cranwell,
  And Master Wendoll, in my absence use
  The very ripest pleasure of my house.

Wen. Lord! Master Frankford, will you ride to-night?
  The ways are dangerous.

Frank.   Therefore will I ride
  Appointed well; and so shall Nick my man.

Mis. Frank. I'll call you up by five o'clock to-morrow.

Frank. No, by my faith, wife, I'll not trust to that;
  'Tis not such easy rising in a morning
  From one I love so dearly: no, by my faith,
  I shall not leave so sweet a bedfellow,

But with much pain. You have made me a sluggard
Since I first knew you.

Mis. Frank.   Then, if you needs will go
This dangerous evening, Master Wendoll,
Let me entreat you bear him company.

Wen. With all my heart, sweet mistress. My boots there!

Frank. Fie, fie, that for my private business
I should disease my friend, and be a trouble
To the whole house! Nick!

Nic. Anon, sir.

Frank. Bring forth my gelding. –   [*Exit Nicholas.*
                    As you love me, sir,
Use no more words: a hand, good Master Cranwell.

Cran. Sir, God be your good speed!

Frank. Good night, sweet Nan; nay, nay, a kiss and part.
[*Aside*]. Dissembling lips, you suit not with my heart.
                                    [*Exit.*

Wen. How business, time, and hours, all gracious prove,
And are the furthers to my new-born love!
I am husband now in Master Frankford's place,
And must command the house. My pleasure is
We will not sup abroad so publicly,
But in your private chamber, Mistress Frankford.

Mis. Frank. O, sir, you are too public in your love,
And Master Frankford's wife —

Cran.   Might I crave favour,
I would entreat you I might see my chamber;
I am on the sudden grown exceeding ill,
And would be spared from supper.

Wen.   Light there, ho!
See you want nothing, sir; for if you do,
You injure that good man, and wrong me too.

Cran. I will make bold: good night.   [*Exit.*

Wen.   How all conspire
To make our bosom sweet, and full entire!
Come, Nan, I prythee let us sup within.

Mis. Frank. Oh, what a clog unto the soul is sin!
  We pale offenders are still full of fear;
  Every suspicious eye brings danger near,
  When they whose clear hearts from offence are free
  Despise report, base scandals do outface,
  And stand at mere defiance with disgrace.
Wen. Fie, fie! you talk too like a puritan.
Mis. Frank. You have tempted me to mischief, Master
    Wendoll:
  I have done I know not what. Well, you plead custom;
  That which for want of wit I granted erst,
  I now must yield through fear. Come, come, let's in;
  Once o'er shoes, we are straight o'er head in sin.
Wen. My jocund soul is joyful above measure;
  I'll be profuse in Frankford's richest treasure.

                                          [*Exeunt.*

ACT IV, SCENE 4

Enter CICELY, JENKIN, *and* BUTLER *and other*
SERVING-MEN

Jenk. My mistress and Master Wendoll, my master, sup in
  her chamber to-night. Cicely, you are preferred
  from being the cook to be chambermaid: of all the
  loves betwixt thee and me, tell me what thou think'st
  of this!
Cicely. Mum; there's an old proverb, – when the cat's
  away, the mouse may play.
Jenk. Now you talk of a cat, Cicely, I smell a rat.
Cicely. Good words, Jenkin, lest you be called to answer
  them.
Jenk. Why, God make my mistress an honest woman! are
  not these good words? Pray God my new master play
  not the knave with my old master! is there any hurt in
  this? God send no villainy intended! and, if they do

sup together, pray God they do not lie together! God make my mistress chaste, and make us all His servants! what harm is there in all this? Nay, more; here is my hand, thou shalt never have my heart unless thou say Amen.

Cicely. Amen, I pray God, I say.

Enter SERVING-MAN

Serv. My mistress sends that you should make less noise, to lock up the doors, and see the household all got to bed: you, Jenkin, for this night are made the porter to see the gates shut in.

Jenk. Thus, by little and little, I creep into office. Come, to kennel, my masters, to kennel; 'tis eleven o'clock, already.

Serv. When you have locked the gates in, you must send up the keys to my mistress.

Cicely. Quickly, for God's sake, Jenkin, for I must carry them. I am neither pillow nor bolster, but I know more than both.

Jenk. To bed, good Spigot; to bed, good honest serving-creatures; and let us sleep as snug as pigs in pease-straw.   [*Exeunt.*

ACT IV, SCENE 5

Enter FRANKFORD *and* NICHOLAS

Frank. Soft, soft; we have tied our geldings to a tree,
Two flight-shot off, lest by their thundering hoofs
They blab our coming back. Hear'st thou no noise?

Nic. Hear! I hear nothing but the owl and you.

Frank. So; now my watch's hand points upon twelve,
And it is dead midnight. Where are my keys?

Nic. Here, sir.

Frank. This is the key that opes my outward gate;
  This is the hall-door; this my withdrawing chamber;
  But this, that door that's bawd unto my shame,
  Fountain and spring of all my bleeding thoughts,
  Where the most hallowed order and true knot
  Of nuptial sanctity hath been profaned;
  It leads to my polluted bed-chamber,
  Once my terrestrial heaven, now my earth's hell,
  The place where sins in all their ripeness dwell.
  But I forget myself: now to my gate.

Nic. It must ope with far less noise than Cripple-gate, or
  your plot's dashed.

Frank. So, reach me my dark lanthorn to the rest;
  Tread softly, softly.

Nic. I will walk on eggs this pace.

Frank. A general silence hath surprised the house,
  And this is the last door. Astonishment,
  Fear, and amazement play against my heart,
  Even as a madman beats upon a drum.
  Oh, keep my eyes, you Heavens, before I enter,
  From any sight that may transfix my soul;
  Or, if there be so black a spectacle,
  Oh, strike mine eyes stark blind; or, if not so,
  Lend me such patience to digest my grief
  That I may keep this white and virgin hand
  From any violent outrage or red murther!
  And with that prayer I enter.   [*Exit.*

Nic.   Here's a circumstance.
  A man may be made cuckold in the time
  That he's about it. An the case were mine,
  As 'tis my master's, – 'sblood that he makes me swear! –
  I would have placed his action, entered there;
  I would, I would —

Enter FRANKFORD

Frank. Oh! oh!

Nic. Master, 'sblood! master! master!

Frank. O me unhappy! I have found them lying
Close in each other's arms, and fast asleep.
But that I would not damn two precious souls,
Bought with my Saviour's blood, and send them, laden
With all their scarlet sins upon their backs,
Unto a fearful judgment, their two lives
Had met upon my rapier.

Nic. 'Sblood, master, have you left them sleeping still?
Let me go wake them.

Frank.   Stay, let me pause a while.
O God! O God! that it were possible
To undo things done; to call back yesterday!
That Time could turn up his swift sandy glass,
To untell the days, and to redeem these hours!
Or that the sun
Could, rising from the west, draw his coach backward,
Take from th' account of time so many minutes,
Till he had all these seasons called again,
Those minutes, and those actions done in them,
Even from her first offence; that I might take her
As spotless as an angel in my arms!
But, oh! I talk of things impossible,
And cast beyond the moon. God give me patience!
For I will in and wake them.   [*Exit.*

Nic.   Here's patience perforce;
He needs must trot afoot that tires his horse.

Enter WENDOLL, *running over the stage in a night-gown, he
after him with his sword drawn; the maid in her smock stays
his hand, and claps hold on him. He pauses for a while.*

Frank. I thank thee, maid; thou, like the angel's hand,
Hast stayed me from a bloody sacrifice.
                              [*Exit Maidservant.*
Go, villain, and my wrongs sit on thy soul

As heavy as this grief doth upon mine!
When thou record'st my many courtesies,
And shalt compare them with thy treacherous heart,
Lay them together, weigh them equally,
'Twill be revenge enough. Go, to thy friend
A Judas: pray, pray, lest I live to see
Thee, Judas-like, hanged on an elder-tree.

Enter MISTRESS FRANKFORD *in her smock, night-
gown, and night attire*

Mis. Frank. Oh, by what word, what title, or what
  name,
  Shall I entreat your pardon? Pardon! oh!
  I am as far from hoping such sweet grace
  As Lucifer from heaven. To call you husband –
  O me, most wretched! I have lost that name,
  I am no more your wife.
Nic.   'Sblood, sir, she swoons.
Frank. Spare thou thy tears, for I will weep for thee;
  And keep thy countenance, for I'll blush for thee.
  Now, I protest, I think 'tis I am tainted,
  For I am most ashamed; and 'tis more hard
  For me to look upon thy guilty face,
  Than on the sun's clear brow. What wouldst thou
  speak?
Mis. Frank. I would I had no tongue, no ears, no eyes,
  No apprehension, no capacity.
  When do you spurn me like a dog? when tread me
  Under your feet? when drag me by the hair?
  Though I deserve a thousand thousand fold
  More than you can inflict: yet, once my husband,
  For womanhood, to which I am a shame,
  Though once an ornament – even for His sake
  That hath redeemed our souls, mark not my face
  Nor hack me with your sword: but let me go
  Perfect and undeformed to my tomb.

I am not worthy that I should prevail
In the least suit; no, not to speak to you,
Nor look on you; nor to be in your presence.
Yet, as an abject, this one suit I crave;
This granted, I am ready for my grave.   [*Kneels*.
Frank. My God, with patience arm me! Rise, nay, rise,
And I'll debate with thee. Was it for want
Thou play'dst the strumpet? Wast thou not supplied
With every pleasure, fashion, and new toy
Nay, even beyond my calling?
Mis. Frank.   I was.
Frank. Was it then disability in me?
Or in thine eye seemed he a properer man?
Mis. Frank. Oh, no.
Frank. Did I not lodge thee in my bosom? wear thee
Here in my heart?
Mis. Frank.   You did.
Frank.   I did, indeed;
Witness my tears I did.
Go, bring my infants hither.

Enter SERVANT *with two* CHILDREN

                    O Nan! O Nan!
If neither fear of shame, regard of honour,
The blemish of my house, nor my dear love
Could have withheld thee from so lewd a fact,
Yet for these infants, these young harmless souls,
On whose white brows thy shame is charactered,
And grows in greatness as they wax in years, —
Look but on them, and melt away in tears.
Away with them! lest, as her spotted body
Hath stained their names with stripe of bastardy,
So her adulterous breath may blast their spirits
With her infectious thoughts. Away with them!
                    [*Exeunt Servant and Children*.
Mis. Frank. In this one life I die ten thousand deaths.

Frank. Stand up, stand up; I will do nothing rashly;
  I will retire a while into my study,
  And thou shalt hear thy sentence presently.   [*Exit.*
Mis. Frank. 'Tis welcome, be it death. O me, base
      strumpet,
  That, having such a husband, such sweet children,
  Must enjoy neither! Oh, to redeem my honour,
  I would have this hand cut off, these my breasts seared,
  Be racked, strappadoed, put to any torment:
  Nay, to whip but this scandal out, I would hazard
  The rich and dear redemption of my soul.
  He cannot be so base as to forgive me;
  Nor I so shameless to accept his pardon.
  O women, women, you that have yet kept
  Your holy matrimonial vow unstained,
  Make me your instance: when you tread awry,
  Your sins, like mine, will on your conscience lie.

Enter CICELY, SPIGOT, *all the* SERVING-MEN, *and*
    JENKIN, *as newly come out of bed*

All. O mistress, mistress, what have you done, mistress?
Nic. 'Sblood, what a caterwauling keep you here!
Jenk. O Lord, mistress, how comes this to pass? My
    master is run away in his shirt, and never so much as
    called me to bring his clothes after him.
Mis. Frank. See what guilt is! here stand I in this place
  Ashamed to look my servants in the face.

Enter MASTER FRANKFORD *and* CRANWELL; *whom*
    seeing she falls on her knees

Frank. My words are registered in Heaven already,
  With patience hear me. I'll not martyr thee,
  Nor mark thee for a strumpet; but with usage
  Of more humility torment thy soul,
  And kill thee even with kindness.
Cran.   Master Frankford —

Frank. Good Master Cranwell! – Woman, hear thy judge-
　　ment.

　　Go make thee ready in thy best attire;
　　Take with thee all thy gowns, all thy apparel;
　　Leave nothing that did ever call thee mistress,
　　Or by whose sight, being left here in the house,
　　I may remember such a woman by.
　　Choose thee a bed and hangings for thy chamber;
　　Take with thee every thing that hath thy mark;
　　And get thee to my manor seven mile off,
　　Where live; 'tis thine; I freely give it thee.
　　My tenants by shall furnish thee with wains
　　To carry all thy stuff, within two hours, –
　　No longer will I limit thee my sight.
　　Choose which of all my servants thou likest best,
　　And they are thine to attend thee.

Mis. Frank.　　　　　　　　A mild sentence.

Frank. But, as thou hop'st for Heaven, as thou believest
　　Thy names recorded in the book of life,
　　I charge thee never after this sad day
　　To see me, or to meet me, or to send
　　By word or writing, gift, or otherwise,
　　To move me, by thyself, or by thy friends;
　　Nor challenge any part in my two children.
　　So farewell, Nan! for we will henceforth be
　　As we had never seen, ne'er more shall see.

Mis. Frank. How full my heart is, in my eyes appears;
　　What wants in words, I will supply in tears.

Frank. Come, take your coach, your stuff; all must along;
　　Servants and all, make ready; all be gone.
　　It was thy hand cut two hearts out of one.

　　　　　　　　　　　　　　　　　[*Exeunt.*

Enter Sir Charles Mountford, *gentleman-like,*
and Susan, *gentlewoman-like*

Susan. Brother, why have you tricked me like a bride,
   Bought me this gay attire, these ornaments?
   Forget you our estate, our poverty?
Sir Char. Call me not brother, but imagine me
   Some barbarous outlaw, or uncivil kern;
   For if thou shutt'st thy eye, and only hearest
   The words that I shall utter, thou shalt judge me
   Some staring ruffian, not thy brother Charles.
   O Susan! —
Susan. O brother, what doth this strange language mean?
Sir Char. Dost love me, sister? Wouldst thou see me live
   A bankrupt beggar in the world's disgrace,
   And die indebted to my enemies?
   Wouldst thou behold me stand like a huge beam
   In the world's eye, a bye-word and a scorn?
   It lies in thee of these to acquit me free,
   And all my debt I may out-strip by thee.
Susan. By me! why, I have nothing, nothing left;
   I owe even for the clothes upon my back;
   I am not worth —
Sir Char.   O sister, say not so;
   It lies in you my downcast state to raise,
   To make me stand on even points with the world.
   Come, sister, you are rich; indeed you are;
   And in your power you have, without delay,
   Acton's five hundred pounds back to repay.
Susan. Till now I had thought you loved me. By mine
     honour
   (Which I have kept as spotless as the moon),
   I ne'er was mistress of that single doit
   Which I reserved not to supply your wants;

And do you think that I would hoard from you?
Now, by my hopes in Heaven, knew I the means
To buy from the slavery of your debts
(Especially from Acton, whom I hate),
I would redeem it with my life or blood.

Sir Char. I challenge it; and, kindred set apart,
Thus, ruffian-like, I lay siege to your heart.
What do I owe to Acton?

Susan. Why some five hundred pounds; towards which, I
swear,
In all the world I have not one denier.

Sir Char. It will not prove so. Sister, now resolve me:
What do you think (and speak your conscience)
Would Acton give, might he enjoy your bed?

Susan. He would not shrink to spend a thousand pounds,
To give the Mountfords' name so deep a wound.

Sir Char. A thousand pounds! I but five hundred owe;
Grant him your bed, he's paid with interest so.

Susan. O brother!

Sir Char.　　　　　O sister! only this one way,
With that rich jewel you my debts may pay:
In speaking this my cold heart shakes with shame,
Nor do I woo you in a brother's name,
But in a stranger's. Shall I die in debt
To Acton, my grand foe, and you still wear
The precious jewel that he holds so dear?

Susan. My honour I esteem as dear and precious
As my redemption.

Sir Char.　　　　　I esteem you, sister,
As dear, for so dear prizing it.

Susan.　　　　　　　Will Charles
Have me cut off my hands, and send them Acton?
Rip up my breast, and with my bleeding heart
Present him, as a token?

Sir Char.　　　　　Neither, sister:
But hear me in my strange assertion.

Thy honour and my soul are equal in my regard;
Nor will thy brother Charles survive thy shame.
His kindness, like a burthen hath surcharged me,
And under his good deeds I stooping go,
Not with an upright soul. Had I remained
In prison still, there doubtless I had died:
Then, unto him that freed me from that prison,
Still do I owe this life. What moved my foe
To enfranchise me? 'Twas, sister, for your love.
With full five hundred pounds he bought your love,
And shall he not enjoy it? Shall the weight
Of all this heavy burthen lean on me,
And will not you bear part? You did partake
The joy of my release, will you not stand
In joint-bond bound to satisfy the debt?
Shall I be only charged?

Susan.   But that I know
These arguments come from an honoured mind,
As in your most extremity of need
Scorning to stand in debt to one you hate, –
Nay, rather would engage your unstained honour
Than to be held ingrate, – I should condemn you.
I see your resolution, and assent;
So Charles will have me, and I am content.

Sir Char. For this I tricked you up.

Susan.   But here's a knife,
To save mine honour, shall slice out my life.

Sir Char. Ay, now thou pleasest me a thousand time
More in that resolution than thy grant. –
Observe her love; to soothe it to my suit,
Her honour she will hazard, though not lose:
To bring me out of debt, her rigorous hand
Will pierce her heart. O wonder! that will choose,
Rather than stain her blood, her life to lose. –
Come, you sad sister to a woeful brother,
This is the gate: I'll bear him such a present,

Such an acquittance for the knight to seal,
As will amaze his senses, and surprise
With admiration all his fantasies.

Enter SIR FRANCIS ACTON *and* MALBY

Susan. Before his unchaste thoughts shall seize on me,
  'Tis here shall my imprisoned soul set free.
Sir Fran. How! Mountford with his sister, hand in hand!
  What miracle's afoot?
Mal.   It is a sight
  Begets in me much admiration.
Sir Char. Stand not amazed to see me thus attended:
  Acton, I owe thee money, and being unable
  To bring thee the full sum in ready coin,
  Lo! for thy assurance, here's a pawn:
  My sister, my dear sister, whose chaste honour
  I prize above a million: here, nay, take her;
  She's worth your money, man; do not forsake her.
Sir Fran. I would he were in earnest!
Susan. Impute it not to my immodesty,
  My brother being rich in nothing else
  But in his interest that he hath in me,
  According to his poverty hath brought you
  Me, all his store; whom howsoe'er you prize
  As forfeit to your hand, he values highly
  And would not sell, but to acquit your debt,
  For any emperor's ransom.
Sir Fran.   Stern heart, relent;
  Thy former cruelty at length repent.
  Was ever known, in any former age,
  Such honourable wrested courtesy?
  Lands, honours, life, and all the world forego,
  Rather than stand engaged to such a foe.
Sir Char. Acton, she is too poor to be thy bride,
  And I too much opposed to be thy brother.
  There, take her to thee: if thou hast the heart

To seize her as a rape, or lustful prey;
To blur our house, that never yet was stained;
To murther her that never meant thee harm;
To kill me now, whom once thou sav'dst from death;
Do them at once: on her all these rely,
And perish with her spotted chastity.

Sir Fran. You overcome me in your love, Sir Charles;
I cannot be so cruel to a lady
I love so dearly. Since you have not spared
To engage your reputation to the world,
Your sister's honour, which you prize so dear,
Nay, all the comforts which you hold on earth,
To grow out of my debt, being your foe,
Your honoured thoughts, lo! thus I recompense:
Your metamorphosed foe receives your gift
In satisfaction of all former wrongs.
This jewel I will wear here in my heart;
And, where before I thought her for her wants
Too base to be my bride, to end all strife,
I seal you my dear brother, her my wife.

Susan. You still exceed us: I will yield to fate,
And learn to love, where I till now did hate.

Sir Char. With that enchantment you have charmed my
   soul,
And made me rich even in those very words:
I pay no debt, but am indebted more;
Rich in your love, I never can be poor.

Sir Fran. All's mine is yours; we are alike in state,
Let's knit in love what was opposed in hate.
Come, for our nuptials we will straight provide,
Blest only in our brother and fair bride.   [*Exeunt.*

F.T —6

Enter CRANWELL, FRANKFORD, *and* NICHOLAS

Cran. Why do you search each room about your house,
  Now that you have despatched your wife away?
Frank. O sir, to see that nothing may be left
  That ever was my wife's. I loved her dearly,
  And when I do but think of her unkindness,
  My thoughts are all in hell; to avoid which torment.
  I would not have a bodkin or a cuff,
  A bracelet, necklace, or rebato wire,
  Nor any thing that ever was called hers,
  Left me, by which I might remember her.
  Seek round about.
Nic. 'Sblood, master! here's her lute flung in a corner.
Frank. Her lute! O God! upon this instrument
  Her fingers have run quick division,
  Sweeter than that which now divides our hearts.
  These frets have made me pleasant, that have now
  Frets of my heart-strings made. O Master Cranwell,
  Oft hath she made this melancholy wood,
  Now mute and dumb for her disastrous chance,
  Speak sweetly many a note, sound many a strain
  To her own ravishing voice, which being well strung,
  What pleasant strange airs have they jointly sung!
  Post with it after her. Now nothing's left;
  Of her and hers I am at once bereft.
Nic. I'll ride and overtake her; do my message,
  And come back again.   [*Exit.*
Cran.   Mean time, sir, if you please,
  I'll to Sir Francis Acton, and inform him
  Of what hath passed betwixt you and his sister.
Frank. Do as you please. How ill am I bested,
  To be a widower ere my wife be dead!   [*Exeunt.*

ACT V, SCENE 3

Enter MISTRESS FRANKFORD, *with* JENKIN, *her maid*
CICELY, *her* COACHMAN, *and three* CARTERS

Mis. Frank. Bid my coach stay: why should I ride in
state,
 Being hurled so low down by the hand of fate?
 A seat like to my fortunes let me have;
 Earth for my chair, and for my bed a grave.

Jenk. Comfort, good mistress; you have watered your
coach with tears already: you have but two mile now
to go to your manor. A man cannot say by my old
master Frankford as he may say by me, that he wants
manors, for he hath three or four; of which this is
one that we are going to now.

Cicely. Good mistress, be of good cheer; sorrow, you see,
hurts you, but helps you not: we all mourn to see
you so sad.

Carter. Mistress, I spy one of my landlord's men
 Come riding post: 'tis like he brings some news.

Mis. Frank. Comes he from Master Frankford, he is welcome;
 So are his news because they come from him.

Enter NICHOLAS

Nic. There!

Mis. Frank. I know the lute; oft have I sung to thee:
 We both are out of tune, both out of time.

Nic. Would that had been the worst instrument that e'er
you played on. My master commends him to ye;
there's all he can find that was ever yours: he hath
nothing left that ever you could lay claim to but his
own heart, an he could afford you that. All that I
have to deliver you is this: he prays you to forget
him, and so he bids you farewell.

Mis. Frank. I thank him; he is kind, and ever was.
　　All you that have true feeling of my grief,
　　That know my loss, and have relenting hearts,
　　Gird me about, and help me with your tears
　　To wash my spotted sins: my lute shall groan;
　　It cannot weep, but shall lament my moan.

Enter WENDOLL, *apart*

Wen. Pursued with horror of a guilty soul,
　　And with the sharp scourge of repentance lashed,
　　I fly from my own shadow. O my stars!
　　What have my parents in their lives deserved,
　　That you should lay this penance on their son?
　　When I but think of Master Frankford's love,
　　And lay it to my treason, or compare
　　My murthering him for his relieving me,
　　It strikes a terror like a lightning's flash
　　To scorch my blood up. Thus I, like the owl,
　　Ashamed of day, live in these shadowy woods,
　　Afraid of every leaf or murmuring blast,
　　Yet longing to receive some perfect knowledge
　　How he hath dealt with her.

　　　　　　　　　　　　　[Sees Mistress Frankford.
　　　　　　　　　　　O my sad fate!
　　Here, and so far from home, and thus attended!
　　O God! I have divorced the truest turtles
　　That ever lived together, and being divided
　　In several places, make their several moan;
　　She in the fields laments, and he at home.
　　So poets write that Orpheus made the trees
　　And stones to dance to his melodious harp,
　　Meaning the rustic and the barbarous hinds,
　　That had no understanding part in them:
　　So she from these rude carters tears extracts,
　　Making their flinty hearts with grief to rise,
　　And draw down rivers from their rocky eyes. –

Mis. Frank. If you return unto your master, say
    (Though not from me; for I am all unworthy
    To blast his name so with a strumpet's tongue)
    That you have seen me weep, wish myself dead:
    Nay, you may say too, for my vow is passed,
    Last night you saw me eat and drink my last.
    This to your master you may say and swear;
    For it is writ in Heaven, and decreed here.

Nic. I'll say you wept: I'll swear you made me sad.
    Why how now, eyes? what now? what's here to do?
    I am gone, or I shall straight turn baby, too.

Wen. I cannot weep, my heart is all on fire:
    Curst be the fruits of my unchaste desire!

Mis. Frank. Go, break this lute upon my coach's wheel,
    As the last music that I e'er shall make;
    Not as my husband's gift, but my farewell
    To all earth's joy; and so your master tell.

Nic. If I can for crying.

Wen.   Grief, have done,
    Or like a madman I shall frantic run.

Mis. Frank. You have beheld the woefullest wretch on
    earth;
    A woman made of tears: would you had words
    To express but what you see! My inward grief
    No tongue can utter; yet unto your power
    You may describe my sorrow, and disclose
    To thy sad master my abundant woes.

Nic. I'll do your commendations.

Mis. Frank.   O no:
    I dare not so presume; nor to my children:
    I am disclaimed in both; alas, I am.
    Oh, never teach them, when they come to speak,
    To name the name of mother: chide their tongue,
    If they by chance light on that hated word;
    Tell them 'tis naught; for, when that word they name,
    Poor pretty souls! they harp on their own shame.

Wen. To recompense her wrongs, what canst thou do?
Thou hast made her husbandless and childless too.

Mis. Frank. I have no more to say. Speak not for me;
Yet you may tell your master what you see.

Nic. I'll do't.   [*Exit.*

Wen. I'll speak to her, and comfort her in grief.
Oh! but her wound cannot be cured with words.
No matter though, I'll do my best good-will
To work a cure on her whom I did kill.

Mis. Frank. So, now unto my coach, then to my home,
So to my death-bed; for from this sad hour
I never will nor eat, nor drink, nor taste
Of any cates that may preserve my life:
I never will nor smile, nor sleep, nor rest;
But when my tears have washed my black soul
    white,
Sweet Saviour, to Thy hands I yield my sprite.

Wen. O Mistress Frankford —

Mis. Frank.   Oh, for God's sake fly!
The devil doth come to tempt me ere I die.
My coach! This fiend, that with an angel's face
Courted mine honour, till he sought my wrack,
In my repentant eyes seems ugly black.

           [*Exeunt all, except Wendoll and Jenkin, the Carters
                             whistling.*

Jenk. What, my young master that fled in his shirt! How
    come you by your clothes again? You have made
    our house in a sweet pickle, have you not, think
    you? What, shall I serve you still, or cleave to the
    old house!

Wen. Hence, slave! away with thy unseasoned mirth!
Unless thou canst shed tears, and sigh, and howl,
Curse thy sad fortunes, and exclaim on fate,
Thou art not for my turn.

Jenk. Marry, an you will not, another will: farewell, and
    be hanged! Would you had never come to have kept

  this coil within our doors; we shall ha' you run away
  like a sprite again.   [*Exit.*

Wen. She's gone to death; I live to want and woe;
  Her life, her sins, and all upon my head.
  And I must now go wander, like a Cain,
  In foreign countries and remoted climes,
  Where the report of my ingratitude
  Cannot be heard. I'll over first to France,
  And so to Germany and Italy;
  Where when I have recovered, and by travel
  Gotten those perfect tongues, and that these rumours
  May in their height abate, I will return:
  And I divine (however now dejected)
  My worth and parts being by some great man praised,
  At my return I may in court be raised.   [*Exit.*

———

ACT V, SCENE 4

Enter SIR FRANCIS ACTON, SIR CHARLES MOUNT-
FORD, CRANWELL, MALBY, *and* SUSAN

Sir Fran. Brother, and now my wife, I think these troubles
  Fall on my head by justice of the Heavens,
  For being so strict to you in your extremities:
  But we are now atoned. I would my sister
  Could with like happiness o'ercome her griefs,
  As we have ours.
Susan. You tell us, Master Cranwell, wondrous things,
  Touching the patience of that gentleman,
  With what strange virtue he demeans his grief.
Cran. I told you what I was a witness of;
  It was my fortune to lodge there that night.
Sir Fran. O that same villain Wendoll! 'twas his tongue
  That did corrupt her; she was of herself
  Chaste, and devoted well. Is this the house?

Cran. Yes, sir, I take it, here your sister lies.

Sir Fran. My brother Frankford showed too mild a spirit
In the revenge of such a loathed crime;
Less than he did, no man of spirit could do:
I am so far from blaming his revenge,
That I commend it. Had it been my case,
Their souls at once had from their breasts been freed:
Death to such deeds of shame is the due meed.

Enter JENKIN *and* CICELY

Jenk. O my mistress, my mistress, my poor mistress.

Cicely. Alas that ever I was born! what shall I do for my
poor mistress?

Sir Char. Why, what of her?

Jenk. O Lord, sir, she no sooner heard that her brother
and his friends were come to see how she did, but she,
for very shame of her guilty conscience, fell into such
a swoon, that we had much ado to get life into her.

Susan. Alas that she should bear so hard a fate!
Pity it is repentance comes too late.

Sir Fran. Is she so weak in body?

Jenk. O sir, I can assure you there's no hope of life in her,
for she will take no sustenance: she hath plainly
starved herself, and now she's as lean as a lath. She
ever looks for the good hour. Many gentlemen and
gentlewomen of the country are come to comfort her.

Enter MISTRESS FRANKFORD, *in her bed*

Mal. How fare you, Mistress Frankford?

Mis. Frank. Sick, sick, oh, sick. Give me some air, I pray
you.
Tell me, oh, tell me where is Master Frankford?
Will not he deign to see me ere I die?

Mal. Yes, Mistress Frankford: divers gentlemen,
Your loving neighbours, with that just request
Have moved, and told him of your weak estate:

Who, though with much ado to get belief,
Examining of the general circumstance,
Seeing your sorrow and your penitence,
And hearing therewithal the great desire
You have to see him ere you left the world,
He gave to us his faith to follow us,
And sure he will be here immediately.

Mis. Frank. You have half revived me with those pleasing
    news;
Raise me a little higher in my bed.
Blush I not, brother Acton? Blush I not, Sir Charles?
Can you not read my fault writ in my cheek?
Is not my crime there, tell me, gentlemen?

Sir Char. Alas, good mistress, sickness hath not left you
Blood in your face enough to make you blush.

Mis. Frank. Then sickness, like a friend, my fault would
    hide.
Is my husband come? My soul but tarries
His arrive, and I am fit for Heaven.

Sir Fran. I came to chide you, but my words of hate
Are turned to pity and compassionate grief.
I came to rate you; but my brawls, you see,
Melt into tears, and I must weep by thee.
Here's Master Frankford now.

Enter FRANKFORD

Frank. Good-morrow, brother; good-morrow, gentlemen:
God, that hath laid this cross upon our heads,
Might (had He pleased) have made our cause of
    meeting
On a more fair and more contented ground;
But He that made us, made us to this woe.

Mis. Frank. And is he come? Methinks that voice I know.

Frank. How do you, woman?

Mis. Frank. Well, Master Frankford, well; but shall be
    better,

I hope, within this hour. Will you vouchsafe,
Out of your grace and your humanity,
To take a spotted strumpet by the hand?

Frank. This hand once held my heart in faster bonds
Than now 'tis gripped by me. God pardon them
That made us first break hold!

Mis. Frank.   Amen, amen.
Out of my zeal to Heaven, whither I am now bound,
I was so impudent to wish you here;
And once more beg your pardon. O good man,
And father to my children, pardon me,
Pardon, oh, pardon me! My fault so heinous is,
That if you in this world forgive it not,
Heaven will not clear it in the world to come.
Faintness hath so usurped upon my knees
That kneel I cannot, but on my heart's knees
My prostrate soul lies thrown down at your feet
To beg your gracious pardon. Pardon, oh, pardon
   me!

Frank. As freely, from the low depth of my soul,
As my Redeemer hath forgiven His death,
I pardon thee; I will shed tears for thee,
Pray with thee; and, in mere pity
Of thy weak state, I'll wish to die with thee.

All. So do we all.

Nic.   So will not I;
I'll sigh and sob, but, by my faith, not die.

Sir Fran. O Master Frankford, all the near alliance
I lose by her shall be supplied in thee:
You are my brother by the nearest way;
Her kindred hath fallen off, but yours doth stay.

Frank. Even as I hope for pardon at that day
When the great Judge of Heaven in scarlet sits,
So be thou pardoned. Though thy rash offence
Divorced our bodies, thy repentant tears
Unite our souls.

Sir Char.   Then comfort, Mistress Frankford;
  You see your husband hath forgiven your fall;
  Then rouse your spirits, and cheer your fainting soul.
Susan. How is it with you?
Sir Fran.   How do you feel yourself?
Mis. Frank. Not of this world.
Frank. I see you are not, and I weep to see it.
  My wife, the mother to my pretty babes!
  Both those lost names I do restore thee back,
  And with this kiss I wed thee once again:
  Though thou art wounded in thy honoured name,
  And with that grief upon thy death-bed liest,
  Honest in heart, upon my soul, thou diest.
Mis. Frank. Pardoned on earth, soul, thou in Heaven art
    free.
  Once more thy wife dies, thus embracing thee. [*Dies.*
Frank. New married, and new widowed. O! she's dead,
  And a cold grave must be her nuptial bed.
Sir Char. Sir, be of good comfort; and your heavy sorrow
  Part equally amongst us: storms divided
  Abate their force, and with less rage are guided.
Cran. Do, Master Frankford; he that hath least part
  Will find enough to drown one troubled heart.
Sir Fran. Peace with thee, Nan. Brothers, and gentlemen,
  All we that can plead interest in her grief,
  Bestow upon her body funeral tears.
  Brother, had you with threats and usage bad
  Punished her sin, the grief of her offence
  Had not with such true sorrow touched her heart.
Frank. I see it had not: therefore on her grave
  Will I bestow this funeral epitaph,
  Which on her marble tomb shall be engraved.
  In golden letters shall these words be filled,
  Here lies she whom her husband's kindness killed.

THE EPILOGUE

An honest crew, disposed to be merry,
Came to a tavern by, and called for wine:
The drawer brought it, smiling like a cherry,
And told them it was pleasant, neat, and fine.
'Taste it,' quoth one. He did so. 'Fie!' quoth he,
'This wine was good; now't runs too near the lee.'

Another sipped, to give the wine his due,
And said unto the rest it drunk too flat;
The third said, it was old; the fourth, too new;
'Nay,' quoth the fifth, 'the sharpness likes me not.'
Thus, gentlemen, you see how in one hour
The wine was new, old, flat, sharp, sweet, and sour.

Unto this wine we do allude our play;
Which some will judge too trivial, some too grave;
You as our guests we entertain this day,
And bid you welcome to the best we have.
Excuse us then; good wine may be disgraced,
When every several mouth hath sundry taste.

John Webster

—

THE DUCHESS OF MALFY

TO THE

RIGHT HONOURABLE GEORGE HARDING, BARON BERKELEY, OF BERKELEY CASTLE, AND KNIGHT OF THE ORDER OF THE BATH TO THE ILLUSTRIOUS PRINCE CHARLES

My noble lord,

That I may present my excuse why, being a stranger to your lordship, I offer this poem to your patronage, I plead this warrant: men who never saw the sea yet desire to behold that regiment of waters, choose some eminent river to guide them thither, and make that, as it were, their conduct or postilion: by the like ingenious means has your fame arrived at my knowledge, receiving it from some of worth, who both in contemplation and practice owe to your honour their clearest service. I do not altogether look up at your title; the ancientest nobility being but a relic of time past, and the truest honour indeed being for a man to confer honour on himself, which your learning strives to propagate, and shall make you arrive at the dignity of a great example. I am confident this work is not unworthy your honour's perusal; for by such poems as this poets have kissed the hands of great princes, and drawn their gentle eyes to look down upon their sheets of paper when the poets themselves were bound up in their winding-sheets. The like courtesy from your lordship shall make you live in your grave, and laurel spring out of it, when the ignorant scorners of the Muses, that like worms in libraries seem to live only to destroy learning, shall wither neglected and forgotten. This work and myself I humbly present to your approved censure, it being the utmost of my wishes to have your honourable self my weighty and perspicuous comment; which grace so done me shall ever be acknowledged

By your lordship's

in all duty and observance

John Webster.

DRAMATIS PERSONAE

FERDINAND, *Duke of Calabria*

CARDINAL, *his brother*

ANTONIO BOLOGNA, *steward of the household to the Duchess*

DELIO, *his friend*

DANIEL DE BOSOLA, *gentleman of the horse to the Duchess*

CASTRUCCIO

MARQUIS OF PESCARA

COUNT MALATESTE

RODERIGO

SILVIO

GRISOLAN

DOCTOR

The several MADMEN

DUCHESS OF MALFY

CARIOLA, *her woman*

JULIA, *Castruccio's wife, and the Cardinal's mistress*

OLD LADY

LADIES, CHILDREN, PILGRIMS, EXECUTIONERS, OFFICERS, *and* ATTENDANTS, *etc.*

THE DUCHESS OF MALFY

—

ACT I, SCENE 1

Enter ANTONIO *and* DELIO

Delio. You are welcome to your country, dear Antonio;
    You have been long in France, and you return
    A very formal Frenchman in your habit:
    How do you like the French court?
Ant. I admire it:
    In seeking to reduce both state and people
    To a fixed order, their judicious king
    Begins at home; quits first his royal palace
    Of flattering sycophants, of dissolute
    And infamous persons – which he sweetly terms
    His master's masterpiece, the work of Heaven;
    Considering duly that a prince's court
    Is like a common fountain, whence should flow
    Pure silver drops in general, but if 't chance
    Some cursed example poison 't near the head,
    Death and diseases through the whole land spread.
    And what is 't makes this blessed government
    But a most provident council, who dare freely
    Inform him the corruption of the times?
    Though some o' the court hold it presumption
    To instruct princes what they ought to do,
    It is a noble duty to inform them
    What they ought to foresee. – Here comes Bosola,
    The only court-gall; yet I observe his railing
    Is not for simple love of piety:
    Indeed, he rails at those things which he wants;
    Would be as lecherous, covetous, or proud,
    Bloody, or envious, as any man,
    If he had means to be so. – Here's the cardinal.

Enter CARDINAL *and* BOSOLA

Bos. I do haunt you still.

Card. So.

Bos. I have done you better service than to be slighted thus. Miserable age, where only the reward of doing well is the doing of it!

Card. You enforce your merit too much.

Bos. I fell into the galleys in your service; where, for two years together, I wore two towels instead of a shirt, with a knot on the shoulder, after the fashion of a Roman mantle. Slighted thus! I will thrive some way: blackbirds fatten best in hard weather; why not I in these dog-days?

Card. Would you could become honest!

Bos. With all your divinity do but direct me the way to it. I have known many travel far for it, and yet return as arrant knaves as they went forth, because they carried themselves always along with them. [*Exit Cardinal.*] Are you gone? Some fellows, they say, are possessed with the devil, but this great fellow were able to possess the greatest devil, and make him worse.

Ant. He hath denied thee some suit?

Bos. He and his brother are like plum-trees that grow crooked over standing-pools; they are rich and o'er-laden with fruit, but none but crows, pies, and cater-pillars feed on them. Could I be one of their flatter-ing panders, I would hang on their ears like a horse-leech, till I were full, and then drop off. I pray, leave me. Who would rely upon these miserable depen-dencies, in expectation to be advanced to-morrow? What creature ever fed worse than hoping Tantalus? nor ever died any man more fearfully than he that hoped for a pardon. There are rewards for hawks and dogs when they have done us service; but for a

soldier that hazards his limbs in a battle, nothing
but a kind of geometry is his last supportation.

Delio. Geometry!

Bos. Ay, to hang in a fair pair of slings, take his latter
swing in the world upon an honourable pair of
crutches, from hospital to hospital. Fare ye well, sir:
and yet do not you scorn us; for places in the court
are but like beds in the hospital, where this man's
head lies at that man's foot, and so lower and lower.

[*Exit.*

Delio. I knew this fellow seven years in the galleys
For a notorious murder; and 'twas thought
The cardinal suborned it: he was released
By the French general, Gaston de Foix,
When he recovered Naples.

Ant. 'Tis great pity
He should be thus neglected: I have heard
He's very valiant. This foul melancholy
Will poison all his goodness; for, I'll tell you,
If too immoderate sleep be truly said
To be an inward rust unto the soul,
It then doth follow want of action
Breeds all black malcontents; and their close rearing,
Like moths in cloth, do hurt for want of wearing.

Delio. The presence 'gins to fill: you promised me
To make me the partaker of the natures
Of some of your great courtiers.

Ant. The lord cardinal's,
And other strangers' that are now in court?
I shall. – Here comes the great Calabrian duke.

Enter FERDINAND, CASTRUCCIO, SILVIO,
RODERIGO, GRISOLAN, *and* ATTENDANTS

Ferd. Who took the ring oftenest?

Sil. Antonio Bologna, my lord.

Ferd. Our sister duchess' great-master of her household?

Give him the jewel. – When shall we leave this sportive action, and fall to action indeed?

Cast. Methinks, my lord, you should not desire to go to war in person.

Ferd. Now for some gravity: why, my lord?

Cast. It is fitting a soldier arise to be a prince, but not necessary a prince descend to be a captain.

Ferd. No?

Cast. No, my lord, he were far better do it by a deputy.

Ferd. Why should he not as well sleep or eat by a deputy? This might take idle, offensive, and base office from him, whereas the other deprives him of honour.

Cast. Believe my experience, that realm is never long in quiet where the ruler is a soldier.

Ferd. Thou toldest me thy wife could not endure fighting.

Cast. True, my lord.

Ferd. And of a jest she broke of a captain she met full of wounds: I have forgot it.

Cast. She told him, my lord, he was a pitiful fellow, to lie, like the children of Ishmael, all in tents.

Ferd. Why, there's a wit were able to undo all the chirurgeons o' the city; for although gallants should quarrel, and had drawn their weapons, and were ready to go to it, yet her persuasions would make them put up.

Cast. That she would, my lord. – How do you like my Spanish gennet?

Rod. He is all fire.

Ferd. I am of Pliny's opinion, I think he was begot by the wind; he runs as if he were ballasted with quicksilver.

Sil. True, my lord, he reels from the tilt often.

Rod., Gris. Ha, ha, ha!

Ferd. Why do you laugh? Methinks you that are courtiers should be my touchwood, take fire when I give fire;

that is, laugh when I laugh, were the subject never
so witty.

Cast. True, my lord: I myself have heard a very good jest,
and have scorned to seem to have so silly a wit as to
understand it.

Ferd. But I can laugh at your fool, my lord.

Cast. He cannot speak, you know, but he makes faces: my
lady cannot abide him.

Ferd. No?

Cast. Nor endure to be in merry company; for she says
too much laughing, and too much company, fills her
too full of the wrinkle.

Ferd. I would, then, have a mathematical instrument
made for her face, that she might not laugh out of
compass. – I shall shortly visit you at Milan, Lord
Silvio.

Sil. Your grace shall arrive most welcome.

Ferd. You are a good horseman, Antonio: you have excellent riders in France: what do you think of good
horsemanship?

Ant. Nobly, my lord: as out of the Grecian horse issued
many famous princes, so out of brave horsemanship
arise the first sparks of growing resolution, that raise
the mind to noble action.

Ferd. You have bespoke it worthily.

Sil. Your brother, the lord cardinal, and sister duchess.

Re-enter CARDINAL, *with* DUCHESS, CARIOLA,
and JULIA

Card. Are the galleys come about?

Gris. They are, my lord.

Ferd. Here 's the Lord Silvio is come to take his leave.

Delio. Now, sir, your promise: what's that cardinal?
I mean his temper? They say he 's a brave fellow,
Will play his five thousand crowns at tennis, dance,
Court ladies, and one that hath fought single combats.

Ant. Some such flashes superficially hang on him for form;
but observe his inward character: he is a melancholy
churchman; the spring in his face is nothing but the
engendering of toads; where he is jealous of any man,
he lays worse plots for them than ever was imposed on
Hercules, for he strews in his way flatterers, panders, intelligencers, atheists, and a thousand such
political monsters. He should have been Pope; but
instead of coming to it by the primitive decency of
the Church, he did bestow bribes so largely and so
impudently as if he would have carried it away without Heaven's knowledge. Some good he hath done —

Delio. You have given too much of him. What 's his
brother?

Ant. The duke there? a most perverse and turbulent
nature:
What appears in him mirth is merely outside;
If he laugh heartily, it is to laugh
All honesty out of fashion.

Delio. Twins?

Ant. In quality.
He speaks with others' tongues, and hears men's
suits
With others' ear; will seem to sleep o' the bench
Only to entrap offenders in their answers;
Dooms men to death by information;
Rewards by hearsay.

Delio. Then the law to him
Is like a foul black cobweb to a spider —
He makes it his dwelling and a prison
To entangle those shall feed him.

Ant. Most true:
He never pays debts unless they be shrewd turns,
And those he will confess that he doth owe.
Last, for his brother there, the cardinal,
They that do flatter him most say oracles

Hang at his lips; and verily I believe them,
For the devil speaks in them.
But for their sister, the right noble duchess,
You never fixed your eye on three fair medals
Cast in one figure, of so different temper.
For her discourse, it is so full of rapture,
You only will begin then to be sorry
When she doth end her speech, and wish, in wonder,
She held it less vainglory to talk much,
Than your penance to hear her: whilst she speaks,
She throws upon a man so sweet a look,
That it were able to raise one to a galliard
That lay in a dead palsy, and to dote
On that sweet countenance; but in that look
There speaketh so divine a continence
As cuts off all lascivious and vain hope.
Her days are practised in such noble virtue,
That sure her nights, nay, more, her very sleeps,
Are more in heaven than other ladies' shrifts.
Let all sweet ladies break their flattering glasses,
And dress themselves in her.

Delio. Fie, Antonio,
    You play the wire-drawer with her commendations.

Ant. I 'll case the picture up: only thus much;
    All her particular worth grows to this sum, —
    She stains the time past, lights the time to come.

Cari. You must attend my lady in the gallery,
    Some half an hour hence.

Ant. I shall.   [*Exeunt Antonio and Delio.*

Ferd. Sister, I have a suit to you.

Duch. To me, sir?

Ferd. A gentleman here, Daniel de Bosola,
    One that was in the galleys —

Duch. Yes, I know him.

Ferd. A worthy fellow he is: pray, let me entreat for
    The provisorship of your horse.

Duch. Your knowledge of him.
　　Commends him and prefers him.
Ferd. Call him hither.   [*Exit Attendant.*
　　We are now upon parting. Good Lord Silvio,
　　Do us commend to all our noble friends
　　At the leaguer.
Silvio. Sir, I shall.
Ferd. You are for Milan?
Silvio. I am.
Duch. Bring the caroches. – We 'll bring you down to the
　　haven.
　　　　　[*Exeunt Duchess, Silvio, Castruccio, Roderigo, Grisolan,*
　　　　　　　　　　　Cariola, Julia, and Attendants.
Card. Be sure you entertain that Bosola
　　For your intelligence: I would not be seen in 't;
　　And therefore many times I have slighted him
　　When he did court our furtherance, as this morning.
Ferd. Antonio, the great-master of her household,
　　Had been far fitter.
Card. You are deceived in him:
　　His nature is too honest for such business. –
　　He comes: I 'll leave you.   [*Exit.*

Re-enter BOSOLA

Bos. I was lured to you.
Ferd. My brother, here, the cardinal could never
　　Abide you.
Bos. Never since he was in my debt.
Ferd. May be some oblique character in your face
　　Made him suspect you.
Bos. Doth he study physiognomy?
　　There 's no more credit to be given to the face
　　Than to a sick man's urine, which some call
　　The physician's whore because she cozens him.
　　He did suspect me wrongfully.
Ferd. For that

You must give great men leave to take their times.
Distrust doth cause us seldom be deceived:
You see the oft shaking of the cedar-tree
Fastens it more at root.

Bos. Yet, take heed;
For to suspect a friend unworthily
Instructs him the next way to suspect you,
And prompts him to deceive you.

Ferd. There 's gold.

Bos. So:
What follows? never rained such showers as these
Without thunderbolts i' the tail of them: whose throat
   must I cut?

Ferd. Your inclination to shed blood rides post
Before my occasion to use you. I give you that
To live i' the court here, and observe the duchess;
To note all the particulars of her haviour,
What suitors do solicit her for marriage,
And whom she best affects. She 's a young widow:
I would not have her marry again.

Bos. No, sir?

Ferd. Do not you ask the reason; but be satisfied
I say I would not.

Bos. It seems you would create me
One of your familiars.

Ferd. Familiar! what 's that?

Bos. Why, a very quaint invisible devil in flesh,
An intelligencer.

Ferd. Such a kind of thriving thing
I would wish thee; and ere long thou mayst arrive
At a higher place by 't.

Bos. Take your devils,
Which hell calls angels: these cursed gifts would make
You a corrupter, me an impudent traitor;
And should I take these, they 'd take me to hell.

Ferd. Sir, I 'll take nothing from you that I have given:

There is a place that I procured for you
This morning, the provisorship o' the horse;
Have you heard on 't?

Bos. No.

Ferd. 'Tis yours: is 't not worth thanks?

Bos. I would have you curse yourself now, that your bounty
(Which makes men truly noble) e'er should make me
A villain. Oh, that to avoid ingratitude
For the good deed you have done me, I must do
All the ill man can invent! Thus the devil
Candies all sins o'er; and what heaven terms vile,
That names he complimental.

Ferd. Be yourself;
Keep your old garb of melancholy; 'twill express
You envy those that stand above your reach,
Yet strive not to come near 'em: this will gain
Access to private lodgings, where yourself
May, like a politic dormouse —

Bos. As I have seen some
Feed in a lord's dish, half asleep, not seeming
To listen to any talk; and yet these rogues
Have cut his throat in a dream. What 's my place?
The provisorship o' the horse? say, then, my corruption
Grew out of horse-dung: I am your creature.

Ferd. Away!

Bos. Let good men, for good deeds, covet good fame,
Since place and riches oft are bribes of shame:
Sometimes the devil doth preach.   [*Exit.*

Re-enter DUCHESS, CARDINAL, *and* CARIOLA

Card. We are to part from you; and your own discretion
Must now be your director.

Ferd. You are a widow:
You know already what man is; and therefore
Let not youth, high promotion, eloquence —

Card. No,
    Nor anything without the addition, honour,
    Sway your high blood.

Ferd. Marry! they are most luxurious
    Will wed twice.

Card. Oh, fie!

Ferd. Their livers are more spotted
    Than Laban's sheep.

Duch. Diamonds are of most value,
    They say, that have passed through most jewellers'
      hands.

Ferd. Whores by that rule are precious.

Duch. Will you hear me?
    I 'll never marry.

Card. So most widows say;
    But commonly that motion lasts no longer
    Than the turning of an hour-glass: the funeral sermon
    And it end both together.

Ferd. Now hear me:
    You live in a rank pasture, here, i' the court;
    There is a kind of honey-dew that 's deadly;
    'Twill poison your fame; look to 't: be not cunning;
    For they whose faces do belie their hearts
    Are witches ere they arrive at twenty years,
    Ay, and give the devil suck.

Duch. This is terrible good counsel.

Ferd. Hypocrisy is woven of a fine small thread,
    Subtler than Vulcan's engine: yet, believe 't,
    Your darkest actions, nay, your privatest thoughts,
    Will come to light.

Card. You may flatter yourself,
    And take your own choice; privately be married
    Under the eves of night —

Ferd. Think 't the best voyage
    The e'er you made; like the irregular crab,
    Which, though 't goes backward, thinks that it goes right

Because it goes its own way: but observe,
Such weddings may more properly be said
To be executed than celebrated.

Card. The marriage night
Is the entrance into some prison.

Ferd. And those joys,
Those lustful pleasures, are like heavy sleeps
Which do forerun man's mischief.

Card. Fare you well.
Wisdom begins at the end: remember it.   [*Exit.*

Duch. I think this speech between you both was studied,
It came so roundly off.

Ferd. You are my sister;
This was my father's poniard, do you see?
I 'd be loth to see 't look rusty, 'cause 'twas his.
I would have you give o'er these chargeable revels:
A visor and a mask are whispering-rooms
That were never built for goodness; fare ye well;
And women like that part which, like the lamprey,
Hath never a bone in 't.

Duch. Fie, sir!

Ferd. Nay,
I mean the tongue; variety of courtship:
What cannot a neat knave with a smooth tale
Make a woman believe? Farewell, lusty widow.

[*Exit.*

Duch. Shall this move me? If all my royal kindred
Lay in my way unto this marriage,
I 'd make them my low footsteps: and even now,
Even in this hate, as men in some great battles,
By apprehending danger, have achieved
Almost impossible actions (I have heard soldiers say
    so),
So I through frights and threatenings will assay
This dangerous venture. Let old wives report
I winked and chose a husband. – Cariola,

    To thy known secrecy I have given up
    More than my life – my fame.

Cari. Both shall be safe;
    For I 'll conceal this secret from the world
    As warily as those that trade in poison
    Keep poison from their children.

Duch. Thy protestation
    Is ingenious and hearty: I believe it.
    Is Antonio come?

Cari. He attends you.

Duch. Good dear soul,
    Leave me; but place thyself behind the arras,
    Where thou mayst overhear us. Wish me good speed;
    For I am going into a wilderness
    Where I shall find nor path nor friendly clue
    To be my guide.   *[Cariola goes behind the arras.*

Enter ANTONIO

    I sent for you: sit down;
    Take pen and ink, and write: are you ready?

Ant. Yes.

Duch. What did I say?

Ant. That I should write somewhat.

Duch. Oh, I remember.
    After these triumphs and this large expense,
    It 's fit, like thrifty husbands, we inquire
    What 's laid up for to-morrow.

Ant. So please your beauteous excellence.

Duch. Beauteous!
    Indeed, I thank you: I look young for your sake;
    You have ta'en my cares upon you.

Ant. I 'll fetch your grace
    The particulars of your revenue and expense.

Duch. Oh, you are
    An upright treasurer: but you mistook:
    For when I said I meant to make inquiry

What's laid up for to-morrow, I did mean
What's laid up yonder for me.

Ant. Where?

Duch. In heaven.
I am making my will (as 'tis fit princes should,
In perfect memory), and, I pray, sir, tell me,
Were not one better make it smiling, thus,
Than in deep groans and terrible ghastly looks,
As if the gifts we parted with procured
That violent distraction?

Ant. Oh, much better.

Duch. If I had a husband now, this care were quit:
But I intend to make you overseer.
What good deed shall we first remember? say.

Ant. Begin with that first good deed began i' the world
After man's creation, the sacrament of marriage:
I'd have you first provide for a good husband;
Give him all.

Duch. All!

Ant. Yes, your excellent self.

Duch. In a winding-sheet?

Ant. In a couple.

Duch. Saint Winifred, that were a strange will!

Ant. 'Twere stranger if there were no will in you
To marry again.

Duch. What do you think of marriage?

Ant. I take 't, as those that deny purgatory,
It locally contains or heaven or hell;
There's no third place in 't.

Duch. How do you affect it?

Ant. My banishment, feeding my melancholy,
Would often reason thus.

Duch. Pray, let's hear it.

Ant. Say a man never marry, nor have children,
What takes that from him? only the bare name
Of being a father, or the weak delight

To see the little wanton ride a-cock-horse
Upon a painted stick, or hear him chatter
Like a taught starling.
Duch. Fie, fie, what 's all this?
One of your eyes is bloodshot; use my ring to 't,
They say 'tis very sovereign: 'twas my wedding-ring,
And I did vow never to part with it
But to my second husband.
Ant. You have parted with it now.
Duch. Yes, to help your eyesight.
Ant. You have made me stark blind.
Duch. How?
Ant. There is a saucy and ambitious devil
Is dancing in this circle.
Duch. Remove him.
Ant. How?
Duch. There needs small conjuration, when your finger
May do it: thus; is it fit?
                    [*She puts the ring upon his finger: he kneels.*
Ant. What said you?
Duch. Sir,
This goodly roof of yours is too low built;
I cannot stand upright in 't nor discourse,
Without I raise it higher: raise yourself;
Or, if you please, my hand to help you: so.
                                    [*Raises him.*
Ant. Ambition, madam, is a great man's madness,
That is not kept in chains and close-pent rooms,
But in fair lightsome lodgings, and is girt
With the wild noise of prattling visitants,
Which makes it lunatic beyond all cure.
Conceive not I am so stupid but I aim
Whereto your favours tend: but he 's a fool
That, being a-cold, would thrust his hands i' the fire
To warm them.
Duch. So, now the ground 's broke,

    You may discover what a wealthy mine
    I make you lord of.
Ant. Oh, my unworthiness!
Duch. You were ill to sell yourself:
    This darkening of your worth is not like that
    Which tradesmen use i' the city; their false lights
    Are to rid bad wares off: and I must tell you,
    If you will know where breathes a complete man
    (I speak it without flattery), turn your eyes,
    And progress through yourself.
Ant. Were there nor heaven nor hell,
    I should be honest: I have long served virtue,
    And ne'er ta'en wages of her.
Duch. Now she pays it.
    The misery of us that are born great!
    We are forced to woo, because none dare woo us;
    And as a tyrant doubles with his words,
    And fearfully equivocates, so we
    Are forced to express our violent passions
    In riddles and in dreams, and leave the path
    Of simple virtue, which was never made
    To seem the thing it is not. Go, go brag
    You have left me heartless; mine is in your bosom:
    I hope 'twill multiply love there. You do tremble:
    Make not your heart so dead a piece of flesh,
    To fear more than to love me. Sir, be confident:
    What is 't distracts you? This is flesh and blood, sir;
    'Tis not the figure cut in alabaster
    Kneels at my husband's tomb. Awake, awake, man!
    I do here put off all vain ceremony,
    And only do appear to you a young widow
    That claims you for her husband, and, like a widow,
    I use but half a blush in 't.
Ant. Truth speak for me;
    I will remain the constant sanctuary
    Of your good name.

Duch. I thank you, gentle love:
And cause you shall not come to me in debt,
Being now my steward, here upon your lips
I sign your *Quietus est*. This you should have begged
    now:
I have seen children oft eat sweetmeats thus,
As fearful to devour them too soon.

Ant. But for your brothers?

Duch. Do not think of them:
All discord without this circumference
Is only to be pitied, and not feared:
Yet, should they know it, time will easily
Scatter the tempest.

Ant. These words should be mine,
And all the parts you have spoke, if some part of it
Would not have savoured flattery.

Duch. Kneel.   [*Cariola comes from behind the arras.*

Ant. Ha!

Duch. Be not amazed; this woman's of my counsel:
I have heard lawyers say, a contract in a chamber
Per verba presenti is absolute marriage.

                            [*She and Antonio kneel.*
Bless, Heaven, this sacred gordian, which let violence
Never untwine!

Ant. And may our sweet affections, like the spheres,
Be still in motion!

Duch. Quickening, and make
The like soft music!

Ant. That we may imitate the loving palms,
Best emblem of a peaceful marriage,
That never bore fruit, divided!

Duch. What can the Church force more?

Ant. That fortune may not know an accident,
Either of joy or sorrow, to divide
Our fixed wishes!

Duch. How can the Church build faster?

We now are man and wife, and 'tis the Church
That must but echo this. – Maid, stand apart:
I now am blind.

Ant. What 's your conceit in this?

Duch. I would have you lead your fortune by the hand
Unto your marriage-bed:
(You speak in me this, for we now are one:)
We 'll only lie, and talk together, and plot
To appease my humorous kindred; and if you please,
Like the old tale in Alexander and Lodowick,
Lay a naked sword between us, keep us chaste.
Oh, let me shroud my blushes in your bosom,
Since 'tis the treasury of all my secrets!

> [*Exeunt Duchess and Antonio.*

Cari. Whether the spirit of greatness or of woman
Reign most in her, I know not; but it shows
A fearful madness: I owe her much of pity.　　[*Exit.*

Enter BOSOLA *and* CASTRUCCIO

Bos. You say you would fain be taken for an eminent courtier?

Cast. 'Tis the very main of my ambition.

Bos. Let me see: you have a reasonable good ace for 't already, and your night-cap expresses your ears sufficient largely. I would have you learn to twirl the strings of your band with a good grace, and in a set speech, at the end of every sentence, to hum three or our times, or blow your nose till it smart again, to recover your memory. When you come to be a president in criminal causes, if you smile upon a prisoner, hang him; but if you frown upon him and threaten him, let him be sure to scape the gallows.

Cast. I would be a very merry president.

Bos. Do not sup o' nights; 'twill beget you an admirable wit.

Cast. Rather it would make me have a good stomach to quarrel; for they say, your roaring boys eat meat seldom, and that makes them so valiant. But how shall I know whether the people take me for an eminent fellow?

Bos. I will teach a trick to know it: give out you lie a-dying, and if you hear the common people curse you, be sure you are taken for one of the prime night-caps.

Enter an OLD LADY

You come from painting now.

Old Lady. From what?

Bos. Why, from your scurvy face-physic. To behold thee not painted inclines somewhat near a miracle: these in thy face here were deep ruts and foul sloughs the last progress. There was a lady in France that, having

had the smallpox, flayed the skin off her face to make
it more level; and whereas before she looked like a
nutmeg-grater, after she resembled an abortive
hedgehog.

Old Lady. Do you call this painting?

Bos. No, no, but you call it careening of an old mor-
phewed lady, to make her disembogue again: there's
rough-cast phrase to your plastic.

Old Lady. It seems you are well acquainted with my
closet.

Bos. One would suspect it for a shop of witchcraft, to find
in it the fat of serpents, spawn of snakes, Jews' spittle,
and their young children's ordure; and all these for
the face. I would sooner eat a dead pigeon taken
from the soles of the feet of one sick of the plague,
than kiss one of you fasting. Here are two of you,
whose sin of your youth is the very patrimony of the
physician; makes him renew his foot-cloth with the
spring, and change his high-priced courtesan with
the fall of the leaf. I do wonder you do not loathe
yourselves. Observe my meditation now.

What thing is in this outward form of man
To be beloved? We account it ominous,
If nature do produce a colt, or lamb,
A fawn, or goat, in any limb resembling
A man, and fly from 't as a prodigy:
Man stands amazed to see his deformity
In any other creature but himself.
But in our own flesh though we bear diseases
Which have their true names only ta'en from beasts, –
As the most ulcerous wolf and swinish measle, –
Though we are eaten up of lice and worms,
And though continually we bear about us
A rotten and dead body, we delight
To hide it in rich tissue: all our fear,
Nay, all our terror, is, lest our physician

Should put us in the ground to be made sweet. –
Your wife's gone to Rome: you two couple, and get
    you to the wells at Lucca to recover your aches. I have
    other work on foot.   [*Exeunt Castruccio and Old Lady.*
I observe our duchess
Is sick a-days, she pukes, her stomach seethes,
The fins of her eyelids look most teeming blue,
She wanes i' the cheek, and waxes fat i' the flank,
And, contrary to our Italian fashion,
Wears a loose-bodied gown: there 's somewhat in 't.
I have a trick may chance discover it,
A pretty one; I have bought some apricots,
The first our spring yields.

Enter ANTONIO *and* DELIO

Delio. And so long since married!
    You amaze me.
Ant. Let me seal your lips for ever:
    For did I think that anything but the air
    Could carry these words from you, I should wish
    You had no breath at all. – Now, sir, in your con-
        templation?
    You are studying to become a great wise fellow.
Bos. Oh, sir, the opinion of wisdom is a foul tetter that
    runs all over a man's body: if simplicity direct us to
    have no evil, it directs us to a happy being; for the
    subtlest folly proceeds from the subtlest wisdom: let
    me be simply honest.
Ant. I do understand your inside.
Bos. Do you so?
Ant. Because you would not seem to appear to the world
    Puffed up with your preferment, you continue
    This out-of-fashion melancholy: leave it, leave it.
Bos. Give me leave to be honest in any phrase, in any
    compliment whatsoever. Shall I confess myself to
    you? I look no higher than I can reach: they are the

gods that must ride on winged horses. A lawyer's
mule of a slow pace will both suit my disposition and
business; for, mark me, when a man's mind rides
faster than his horse can gallop, they quickly both
tire.

Ant. You would look up to heaven, but I think
   The devil, that rules i' the air, stands in your light.

Bos. Oh, sir, you are lord of the ascendant, chief man with
   the duchess; a duke was your cousin-german removed. Say you were lineally descended from King
   Pepin, or he himself, what of this? Search the heads
   of the greatest rivers in the world, you shall find them
   but bubbles of water. Some would think the souls of
   princes were brought forth by some more weighty
   cause than those of meaner persons: they are deceived, there 's the same hand to them; the like
   passions sway them; the same reason that makes a
   vicar to go to law for a tithe-pig and undo his
   neighbours, makes them spoil a whole province, and
   batter down goodly cities with the cannon.

Enter DUCHESS *and* LADIES

Duch. Your arm, Antonio: do I not grow fat?
   I am exceeding short-winded. – Bosola,
   I would have you, sir, provide for me a litter;
   Such a one as the duchess of Florence rode in.

Bos. The duchess used one when she was great with child.

Duch. I think she did. – Come hither, mend my ruff:
   Here, when? thou art such a tedious lady; and
   Thy breath smells of lemon-pills: would thou hadst
      done!
   Shall I swoon under thy fingers? I am
   So troubled with the mother!

Bos. [*aside*]. I fear too much.

Duch. I have heard you say that the French courtiers
   Wear their hats on 'fore the king.

Ant. I have seen it.

Duch. In the presence?

Ant. Yes.

Duch. Why should not we bring up that fashion?
 'Tis ceremony more than duty that consists
 In the removing of a piece of felt:
 Be you the example to the rest o' the court;
 Put on your hat first.

Ant. You must pardon me:
 I have seen, in colder countries than in France,
 Nobles stand bare to the prince; and the distinction
 Methought showed reverently.

Bos. I have a present for your grace.

Duch. For me, sir?

Bos. Apricots, madam.

Duch. Oh, sir, where are they?
 I have heard of none to-year.

Bos. [*aside*]. Good; her colour rises.

Duch. Indeed, I thank you: they are wondrous fair ones.
 What an unskilful fellow is our gardener!
 We shall have none this month.

Bos. Will not your grace pare them?

Duch. No: they taste of musk, methinks; indeed they
  do.

Bos. I know not: yet I wish your grace had pared 'em.

Duch. Why?

Bos. I forgot to tell you, the knave gardener,
 Only to raise his profit by them the sooner,
 Did ripen them in horse-dung.

Duch. Oh, you jest. –
 You shall judge: pray taste one.

Ant. Indeed, madam,
 I do not love the fruit.

Duch. Sir, you are loth
 To rob us of our dainties: 'tis a delicate fruit;
 They say they are restorative.

Bos. 'Tis a pretty art,
   This grafting.
Duch. 'Tis so; bettering of nature.
Bos. To make a pippin grow upon a crab.
   A damson on a blackthorn. – [*Aside.*] How greedily she
      eats them!
   A whirlwind strike off these bawd farthingales!
   For, but for that and the loose-bodied gown,
   I should have discovered apparently
   The young springal cutting a caper in her belly.
Duch. I thank you, Bosola: they were right good ones,
   If they do not make me sick.
Ant. How now, madam!
Duch. This green fruit and my stomach are not friends:
   How they swell me!
Bos. [*aside*]. Nay, you are too much swelled already.
Duch. Oh, I am in an extreme cold sweat!
Bos. I am very sorry.
Duch. Lights to my chamber! – Oh, good Antonio,
   I fear I am undone!
Delio. Lights there, lights!
      [*Exeunt Duchess and Ladies. – Exit, on the other side, Bosola.*
Ant. Oh, my most trusty Delio, we are lost!
   I fear she 's fallen in labour; and there 's left
   No time for her remove.
Delio. Have you prepared
   Those ladies to attend her? and procured
   That politic safe conveyance for the midwife
   Your duchess plotted?
Ant. I have.
Delio. Make use, then, of this forced occasion:
   Give out that Bosola hath poisoned her
   With these apricots; that will give some colour
   For her keeping close.
Ant. Fie, fie, the physicians
   Will then flock to her.

Delio. For that you may pretend
　She 'll use some prepared antidote of her own,
　Lest the physicians should re-poison her.
Ant. I am lost in amazement: I know not what to think
　　on 't.　　　　　　　　　　　　　　　　[*Exeunt.*

———

ACT II, SCENE 2

Enter BOSOLA

Bos. So, so, there 's no question but her techiness and
　most vulturous eating of the apricots are apparent
　signs of breeding.

Enter an OLD LADY

　Now?
Old Lady. I am in haste, sir.
Bos. There was a young waiting-woman had a monstrous
　desire to see the glass-house —
Old Lady. Nay, pray, let me go.
Bos. And it was only to know what strange instrument it
　was should swell up a glass to the fashion of a
　woman's belly.
Old Lady. I will hear no more of the glass-house. You are
　still abusing women?
Bos. Who, I? no; only, by the way now and then, mention
　your frailties. The orange-tree bears ripe and green
　fruit and blossoms all together; and some of you give
　entertainment for pure love, but more for more
　precious reward. The lusty spring smells well; but
　drooping autumn tastes well. If we have the same
　golden showers that rained in the time of Jupiter the
　thunderer, you have the same Danaës still, to hold
　up their laps to receive them. Didst thou never study
　the mathematics?

Old Lady. What 's that, sir?

Bos. Why, to know the trick how to make a many lines meet in one centre. Go, go, give your foster-daughters good counsel: tell them, that the devil takes delight to hang at a woman's girdle, like a false rusty watch, that she cannot discern how the time passes.

[*Exit Old Lady.*

Enter ANTONIO, RODERIGO, *and* GRISOLAN

Ant. Shut up the court-gates.

Rod. Why, sir? what 's the danger?

Ant. Shut up the posterns presently, and call
  All the officers o' the court.

Gris. I shall instantly.   [*Exit.*

Ant. Who keeps the key o' the park-gate?

Rod. Forobosco.

Ant. Let him bring 't presently.

Re-enter GRISOLAN *with* SERVANTS

First Serv. Oh, gentlemen o' the court, the foulest treason!

Bos. [*aside*]. If that these apricots should be poisoned now,
  Without my knowledge!

First Serv. There was taken even now a Switzer in the duchess' bed-chamber —

Second Serv. A Switzer!

First Serv. With a pistol in his great cod-piece.

Bos. Ha, ha, ha!

First Serv. The cod-piece was the case for 't.

Second Serv. There was a cunning traitor: who would have searched his cod-piece?

First Serv. True, if he had kept out of the ladies' chambers: and all the moulds of his buttons were leaden bullets.

Second Serv. O wicked cannibal! a fire-lock in 's cod-piece!

First Serv. 'Twas a French plot, upon my life.

Second Serv. To see what the devil can do!

Ant. Are all the officers here?

Serv. We are.

Ant. Gentlemen,
   We have lost much plate you know; and but this
      evening
   Jewels, to the value of four thousand ducats,
   Are missing in the duchess' cabinet.
   Are the gates shut?

Serv. Yes.

Ant. 'Tis the duchess' pleasure.
   Each officer be locked into his chamber
   Till the sun-rising; and to send the keys
   Of all their chests and of their outward doors
   Into her bed-chamber. She is very sick.

Rod. At her pleasure.

Ant. She entreats you take 't not ill; the innocent
   Shall be the more approved by it.

Bos. Gentleman o' the wood-yard, where 's your Switzer
      now?

First Serv. By this hand, 'twas credibly reported by one o'
      the black guard.   [*Exeunt all except Antonio and Delio.*

Delio. How fares it with the duchess?

Ant. She 's exposed
   Unto the worst of torture, pain, and fear.

Delio. Speak to her all happy comfort.

Ant. How I do play the fool with mine own danger!
   You are this night, dear friend, to post to Rome:
   My life lies in your service.

Delio. Do not doubt me.

Ant. Oh, 'tis far from me: and yet fear presents me
   Somewhat that looks like danger.

Delio. Believe it,
   'Tis but the shadow of your fear, no more:
   How superstitiously we mind our evils!
   The throwing down salt, or crossing of a hare
   Bleeding at nose, the stumbling of a horse,

    Or singing of a cricket, are of power
    To daunt whole man in us. Sir, fare you well:
    I wish you all the joys of a blessed father;
    And, for my faith, lay this unto your breast, —
    Old friends, like old swords, still are trusted best.

                               [Exit.

Enter CARIOLA

Cari. Sir, you are the happy father of a son:
    Your wife commends him to you.
Ant. Blessed comfort! —
    For heaven's sake tend her well: I 'll presently
    Go set a figure for 's nativity.   *[Exeunt.*

ACT II, SCENE 3

Enter BOSOLA, *with a dark lantern*

Bos. Sure I did hear a woman shriek: list, ha!
    And the sound came, if I received it right,
    From the duchess' lodgings. There 's some stratagem
    In the confining all our courtiers
    To their several wards: I must have part of it;
    My intelligence will freeze else. List, again!
    It may be 'twas the melancholy bird,
    Best friend of silence and of solitariness,
    The owl, that screamed so. — Ha! Antonio!

Enter ANTONIO

Ant. I heard some noise. — Who 's there? what art thou?
    speak.
Bos. Antonio, put not your face nor body
    To such a forced expression of fear:
    I am Bosola, your friend.

Ant. Bosola! –

[*Aside.*] This mole does undermine me. – Heard you not

A noise even now?

Bos. From whence?

Ant. From the duchess' lodging.

Bos. Not I: did you?

Ant. I did, or else I dreamed.

Bos. Let 's walk towards it.

Ant. No: it may be 'twas

But the rising of the wind.

Bos. Very likely.

Methinks 'tis very cold, and yet you sweat:

You look wildly.

Ant. I have been setting a figure

For the duchess' jewels.

Bos. Ah, and how falls your question?

Do you find it radical?

Ant. What 's that to you?

'Tis rather to be questioned what design,

When all men were commanded to their lodgings,

Makes you a night-walker.

Bos. In sooth, I 'll tell you:

Now all the court 's asleep, I thought the devil

Had least to do here; I came to say my prayers;

And if it do offend you I do so,

You are a fine courtier.

Ant. [*aside*]. This fellow will undo me. –

You gave the duchess apricots to-day:

Pray heaven they were not poisoned!

Bos. Poisoned! a Spanish fig

For the imputation.

Ant. Traitors are ever confident

Till they are discovered. There were jewels stol'n too.

In my conceit, none are to be suspected

More than yourself.

Bos. You are a false steward.

Ant. Saucy slave, I'll pull thee up by the roots.

Bos. Maybe the ruin will crush you to pieces.

Ant. You are an impudent snake indeed, sir:

Are you scarce warm, and do you show your sting?
You libel well, sir.

Bos. No, sir: copy it out,

And I will set my hand to 't.

Ant. [*aside*]. My nose bleeds.

One that were superstitious would count
This ominous, when it merely comes by chance:
Two letters, that are wrote here for my name,
Are drowned in blood!
Mere accident. – For you, sir, I 'll take order
I' the morn you shall be safe: – [*Aside.*] 'tis that must
      colour
Her lying-in: – sir, this door you pass not:
I do not hold it fit that you come near
The duchess' lodgings, till you have quit yourself. –
[*Aside.*] The great are like the base, nay, they are the
      same,
When they seek shameful ways to avoid shame. [*Exit.*

Bos. Antonio hereabout did drop a paper:

Some of your help, false friend: – Oh, here it is.
What 's here? a child's nativity calculated!   [*Reads.*

 '*The duchess was delivered of a son,* '*tween the hours twelve*
and one in the night, Anno Dom. 1504', – that 's this year –
'*decimo nono Decembris,*' – that 's this night, – '*taken*
according to the meridian of Malfy,' – that 's our duchess:
happy discovery! – '*The lord of the first house being combust*
in the ascendant, signifies short life; and Mars being in a
human sign, joined to the tail of the Dragon, in the eighth
house, doth threaten a violent death. Caetera non scrutantur.'

Why, now 'tis most apparent: this precise fellow
Is the duchess' bawd: – I have it to my wish!

This is a parcel of intelligency
Our courtiers were cased up for: it needs must follow
That I must be committed on pretence
Of poisoning her: which I 'll endure, and laugh at.
If one could find the father now! but that
Time will discover. Old Castruccio
I' the morning posts to Rome: by him I'll send
A letter that shall make her brothers' galls
O'erflow their livers. This was a thrifty way.
Though lust do mask in ne'er so strange disguise,
She 's oft found witty, but is never wise.   [*Exit.*

——

ACT II, SCENE 4

Enter CARDINAL *and* JULIA

Card. Sit: thou art my best of wishes. Prithee, tell me
   What trick didst thou invent to come to Rome
   Without thy husband?
Julia. Why, my lord, I told him
   I came to visit an old anchorite
   Here for devotion.
Card. Thou art a witty false one, —
   I mean, to him.
Julia. You have prevailed with me
   Beyond my strongest thoughts: I would not now
   Find you inconstant.
Card. Do not put thyself
   To such a voluntary torture, which proceeds
   Out of your own guilt.
Julia. How, my lord!
Card. You fear
   My constancy, because you have approved
   Those giddy and wild turnings in yourself.
Julia. Did you e'er find them?

Card. Sooth, generally for women,
　　A man might strive to make glass malleable,
　　Ere he should make them fixed.

Julia. So, my lord.

Card. We had need go borrow that fantastic glass
　　Invented by Galileo the Florentine
　　To view another spacious world i' the moon,
　　And look to find a constant woman there.

Julia. This is very well, my lord.

Card. Why do you weep?
　　Are tears your justification? The self-same tears
　　Will fall into your husband's bosom, lady,
　　With a loud protestation that you love him
　　Above the world. Come, I 'll love you wisely,
　　That 's jealously; since I am very certain
　　You cannot make me cuckold.

Julia. I 'll go home
　　To my husband.

Card. You may thank me, lady,
　　I have taken you off your melancholy perch,
　　Bore you upon my fist, and showed you game,
　　And let you fly at it. – I pray thee, kiss me. –
　　When thou wast with thy husband, thou wast watched
　　Like a tame elephant – still you are to thank me –
　　Thou hadst only kisses from him and high feeding:
　　But what delight was that? 'Twas just like one
　　That hath a little fingering on the lute,
　　Yet cannot tune it – still you are to thank me.

Julia. You told me of a piteous wound i' the heart
　　And a sick liver, when you wooed me first,
　　And spake like one in physic.

Card. Who 's that? –

Enter SERVANT

　　Rest firm, for my affection to thee,
　　Lightning moves slow to 't.

Serv. Madam, a gentleman,
That 's come post from Malfy, desires to see you.
Card. Let him enter: I 'll withdraw.   [*Exit.*
Serv. He says
Your husband, old Castruccio, is come to Rome,
Most pitifully tired with riding post.   [*Exit.*

Enter DELIO

Julia [*aside*]. Signior Delio! 'tis one of my old suitors.
Delio. I was bold to come and see you.
Julia. Sir, you are welcome.
Delio. Do you lie here?
Julia. Sure, your own experience
Will satisfy you no: our Roman prelates
Do not keep lodging for ladies.
Delio. Very well:
I have brought you no commendations from your
husband,
For I know none by him.
Julia. I hear he 's come to Rome.
Delio. I never knew man and beast, of a horse and a
knight,
So weary of each other: if he had had a good back,
He would have undertook to have borne his horse,
His breech was so pitifully sore.
Julia. Your laughter
Is my pity.
Delio. Lady, I know not whether
You want money, but I have brought you some.
Julia. From my husband?
Delio. No, from mine own allowance.
Julia. I must hear the condition, ere I be bound to take
it.
Delio. Look on 't, 'tis gold: hath it not a fine colour?
Julia. I have a bird more beautiful.
Delio. Try the sound on 't.

Julia. A lute-string far exceeds it:
  It hath no smell, like cassia or civet;
  Nor is it physical, though some fond doctors
  Persuade us seethe 't in cullises. I 'll tell you,
  This is a creature bred by —

Re-enter SERVANT

Serv. Your husband 's come,
  Hath delivered a letter to the Duke of Calabria
  That, to my thinking, hath put him out of his wits.
                                                    [*Exit.*

Julia. Sir, you hear;
  Pray, let me know your business and your suit
  As briefly as can be.
Delio. With good speed: I would wish you,
  At such time as you are non-resident
  With your husband, my mistress.
Julia. Sir, I 'll go ask my husband if I shall,
  And straight return your answer.   [*Exit.*
Delio. Very fine!
  Is this her wit, or honesty, that speaks thus?
  I heard one say the duke was highly moved
  With a letter sent from Malfy. I do fear
  Antonio is betrayed: how fearfully
  Shows his ambition now! unfortunate fortune!
  They pass through whirlpools, and deep woes do shun,
  Who the event weigh ere the action 's done.   [*Exit.*

———

ACT II, SCENE 5

Enter CARDINAL, *and* FERDINAND *with a letter*

Ferd. I have this night digged up a mandrake.
Card. Say you?
Ferd. And I am grown mad with 't.
Card. What 's the prodigy?

Ferd. Read there – a sister damned: she 's loose i' the
   hilts;
  Grown a notorious strumpet.

Card. Speak lower.

Ferd. Lower!
  Rogues do not whisper 't now, but seek to publish 't
  (As servants do the bounty of their lords)
  Aloud; and with a covetous searching eye,
  To mark who note them. Oh, confusion seize her!
  She hath had most cunning bawds to serve her turn,
  And more secure conveyances for lust
  Than towns of garrison for service.

Card. Is 't possible?
  Can this be certain?

Ferd. Rhubarb, oh, for rhubarb
  To purge this choler! here 's the cursed day
  To prompt my memory; and here 't shall stick
  Till of her bleeding heart I make a sponge
  To wipe it out.

Card. Why do you make yourself
  So wild a tempest?

Ferd. Would I could be one,
  That I might toss her palace 'bout her ears,
  Root up her goodly forests, blast her meads,
  And lay her general territory as waste
  As she hath done her honours.

Card. Shall our blood,
  The royal blood of Arragon and Castile,
  Be thus attainted?

Ferd. Apply desperate physic:
  We must not now use balsamum, but fire,
  The smarting cupping-glass, for that 's the mean
  To purge infected blood, such blood as hers.
  There is a kind of pity in mine eye –
  I 'll give it to my handkercher; and now 'tis here,
  I 'll bequeath this to her bastard.

Card. What to do?

Ferd. Why, to make soft lint for his mother's wounds,
   When I have hewed her to pieces.

Card. Cursed creature!
   Unequal nature, to place women's hearts
   So far upon the left side!

Ferd. Foolish men,
   That e'er will trust their honour in a bark
   Made of so slight weak bulrush as is woman,
   Apt every minute to sink it!

Card. Thus
   Ignorance, when it hath purchased honour,
   It cannot wield it.

Ferd. Methinks I see her laughing, –
   Excellent hyena! Talk to me somewhat quickly,
   Or my imagination will carry me
   To see her in the shameful act of sin.

Card. With whom?

Ferd. Happily with some strong-thighed bargeman,
   Or one o' the wood-yard that can quoit the sledge
   Or toss the bar, or else some lovely squire
   That carries coals up to her privy lodgings.

Card. You fly beyond your reason.

Ferd. Go to, mistress!
   'Tis not your whore's milk that shall quench my wild
      fire,
   But your whore's blood.

Card. How idly shows this rage, which carries you,
   As men conveyed by witches through the air,
   On violent whirlwinds! This intemperate noise
   Fitly resembles deaf men's shrill discourse,
   Who talk aloud, thinking all other men
   To have their imperfection.

Ferd. Have not you
   My palsy?

Card. Yes, but I can be angry

Without this rupture: there is not in nature
A thing that makes man so deformed, so beastly,
As doth intemperate anger. Chide yourself.
You have divers men who never yet expressed
Their strong desire of rest but by unrest,
By vexing of themselves. Come, put yourself
In tune.

Ferd. So I will only study to seem
The thing I am not. I could kill her now,
In you, or in myself; for I do think
It is some sin in us heaven doth revenge
By her.

Card. Are you stark mad?

Ferd. I would have their bodies
Burnt in a coal-pit with the ventage stopped,
That their cursed smoke might not ascend to heaven;
Or dip the sheets they lie in in pitch or sulphur,
Wrap them in 't, and then light them like a match;
Or else to-boil their bastard to a cullis,
And give 't his lecherous father to renew
The sin of his back.

Card. I 'll leave you.

Ferd. Nay, I have done.
I am confident, had I been damned in hell,
And should have heard of this, it would have put me
Into a cold sweat. In, in; I 'll go sleep.
Till I know who leaps my sister, I 'll not stir:
That known, I 'll find scorpions to string my whips,
And fix her in a general eclipse.   [*Exeunt.*

Enter ANTONIO *and* DELIO

Ant. Our noble friend, my most beloved Delio!
  Oh, you have been a stranger long at court:
  Came you along with the Lord Ferdinand?

Delio. I did, sir: and how fares your noble duchess?

Ant. Right fortunately well: she 's an excellent
  Feeder of pedigrees; since you last saw her,
  She hath had two children more, a son and daughter.

Delio. Methinks 'twas yesterday: let me but wink,
  And not behold your face, which to mine eye
  Is somewhat leaner, verily I should dream
  It were within this half-hour.

Ant. You have not been in law, friend Delio,
  Nor in prison, nor a suitor at the court,
  Nor begged the reversion of some great man's place,
  Nor troubled with an old wife, which doth make
  Your time so insensibly hasten.

Delio. Pray, sir, tell me,
  Hath not this news arrived yet to the ear
  Of the lord cardinal?

Ant. I fear it hath:
  The Lord Ferdinand, that 's newly come to court,
  Doth bear himself right dangerously.

Delio. Pray, why?

Ant. He is so quiet that he seems to sleep
  The tempest out, as dormice do in winter:
  Those houses that are haunted are most still
  Till the devil be up.

Delio. What say the common people?

Ant. The common rabble do directly say
  She is a strumpet.

Delio. And your graver heads
  Which would be politic, what censure they?

Ant. They do observe I grow to infinite purchase,
   The left-hand way; and all suppose the duchess
   Would amend it, if she could; for, say they,
   Great princes, though they grudge their officers
   Should have such large and unconfined means
   To get wealth under them, will not complain,
   Lest thereby they should make them odious
   Unto the people: for other obligation
   Of love or marriage between her and me
   They never dream of.
Delio. The Lord Ferdinand
   Is going to bed.

   Enter DUCHESS, FERDINAND, *and* ATTENDANTS

Ferd. I 'll instantly to bed,
   For I am weary. – I am to bespeak
   A husband for you.
Duch. For me, sir! pray, who is 't?
Ferd. The great Count Malateste.
Duch. Fie upon him!
   A count! he 's a mere stick of sugar-candy;
   You may look quite thorough him. When I choose
   A husband, I will marry for your honour.
Ferd. You shall do well in 't. – How is 't, worthy Antonio?
Duch. But, sir, I am to have private conference with
      you
   About a scandalous report is spread
   Touching mine honour.
Ferd. Let me be ever deaf to 't;
   One of Pasquil's paper-bullets, court-calumny,
   A pestilent air, which princes' palaces
   Are seldom purged of. Yet say that it were true,
   I pour it in your bosom, my fixed love
   Would strongly excuse, extenuate, nay, deny
   Faults, were they apparent in you. Go, be safe
   In your own innocency.

Duch. [*aside*]. O blessed comfort!
  This deadly air is purged.
        [*Exeunt Duchess, Antonio, Delio, and Attendants.*
Ferd. Her guilt treads on
  Hot-burning coulters.

Enter BOSOLA

  Now, Bosola, how thrives our intelligence?
Bos. Sir, uncertainly:
  'Tis rumoured she hath had three bastards, but
  By whom we may go read i' the stars.
Ferd. Why, some
  Hold opinion all things are written there.
Bos. Yes, if we could find spectacles to read them.
  I do suspect there hath been some sorcery
  Used on the duchess.
Ferd. Sorcery! to what purpose?
Bos. To make her dote on some desertless fellow
  She shames to acknowledge.
Ferd. Can your faith give way
  To think there's power in potions or in charms,
  To make us love whether we will or no?
Bos. Most certainly.
Ferd. Away! these are mere gulleries, horrid things,
  Invented by some cheating mountebanks
  To abuse us. Do you think that herbs or charms
  Can force the will? Some trials have been made
  In this foolish practice, but the ingredients
  Were lenitive poisons, such as are of force
  To make the patient mad; and straight the witch
  Swears by equivocation they are in love.
  The witchcraft lies in her rank blood. This night
  I will force confession from her. You told me
  You had got, within these two days, a false key
  Into her bed-chamber.
Bos. I have.

Ferd. As I would wish.

Bos. What do you intend to do?

Ferd. Can you guess?

Bos. No.

Ferd. Do not ask, then:
  He that can compass me, and know my drifts,
  May say he hath put a girdle 'bout the world,
  And sounded all her quicksands.

Bos. I do not
  Think so.

Ferd.   What do you think, then, pray?

Bos. That you
  Are your own chronicle too much, and grossly
  Flatter yourself.

Ferd. Give me thy hand; I thank thee:
  I never gave pension but to flatterers,
  Till I entertained thee. Farewell.
  That friend a great man's ruin strongly checks,
  Who rails into his belief all his defects.   [*Exeunt.*

―――

ACT III, SCENE 2

Enter DUCHESS, ANTONIO, *and* CARIOLA

Duch. Bring me the casket hither, and the glass. –
  You get no lodging here to-night, my lord.

Ant. Indeed, I must persuade one.

Duch. Very good:
  I hope in time 'twill grow into a custom,
  That nobleman shall come with cap and knee
  To purchase a night's lodging of their wives.

Ant. I must lie here.

Duch. Must! you are a lord of misrule.

Ant. Indeed, my rule is only in the night.

Duch. To what use will you put me?

Ant. We 'll sleep together.

Duch. Alas,
What pleasure can two lovers find in sleep!

Cari. My lord, I lie with her often; and I know
She 'll much disquiet you.

Ant. See, you are complained of.

Cari. For she's the sprawling'st bedfellow.

Ant. I shall like her the better for that.

Cari. Sir, shall I ask you a question?

Ant. Ay, pray thee, Cariola.

Cari. Wherefore still, when you lie with my lady,
Do you rise so early?

Ant. Labouring men
Count the clock oftenest, Cariola,
Are glad when their task 's ended.

Duch. I 'll stop your mouth.   [*Kisses him.*

Ant. Nay, that 's but one; Venus had two soft doves
To draw her chariot; I must have another. –
                              [*She kisses him again.*
When wilt thou marry, Cariola?

Cari. Never, my lord.

Ant. Oh, fie upon this single life! forgo it.
We read how Daphne, for her peevish flight,
Became a fruitless bay-tree; Syrinx turned
To the pale empty reed; Anaxarete
Was frozen into marble: whereas those
Which married, or proved kind unto their friends,
Were by a gracious influence transhaped
Into the olive, pomegranate, mulberry,
Became flowers, precious stones, or eminent stars.

Cari. This is a vain poetry: but I pray you, tell me,
If there were proposed me, wisdom riches, and beauty,
In three several young men, which should I choose?

Ant. 'Tis a hard question: this was Paris' case,
And he was blind in 't, and there was great cause;
For how was 't possible he could judge right,

Having three amorous goddesses in view,
And they stark naked? 'Twas a motion
Were able to benight the apprehension
Of the severest counsellor of Europe.
Now I look on both your faces so well formed,
It puts me in mind of a question I would ask.

Cari. What is 't?

Ant. I do wonder why hard-favoured ladies,
  For the most part, keep worse-favoured waiting-women
  To attend them, and cannot endure fair ones.

Duch. Oh, that 's soon answered.
  Did you ever in your life know an ill painter
  Desire to have his dwelling next door to the shop
  Of an excellent picture-maker? 'twould disgrace
  His face-making, and undo him. I pray thee,
  When were we so merry? – My hair tangles.

Ant. Pray thee, Cariola, let 's steal forth the room,
  And let her talk to herself: I have divers times
  Served her the like, when she hath chafed extremely.
  I love to see her angry. Softly, Cariola.

[Exeunt Antonio and Cariola.

Duch. Doth not the colour of my hair 'gin to change?
  When I wax grey, I shall have all the court
  Powder their hair with arras, to be like me.
  You have cause to love me; I entered you into my
    heart
  Before you would vouchsafe to call for the keys.

Enter FERDINAND *behind*

We shall one day have my brothers take you napping:
  Methinks his presence, being now in court,
  Should make you keep your own bed; but you 'll say
  Love mixed with fear is sweetest. I 'll assure you,
  You shall get no more children till my brothers
  Consent to be your gossips. Have you lost your tongue?
  'Tis welcome:

For know, whether I am doomed to live or die,
I can do both like a prince.

Ferd. Die, then, quickly!   [*Giving her a poniard.*
Virtue, where art thou hid? What hideous thing
Is it that doth eclipse thee?

Duch. Pray, sir, hear me.

Ferd. Or is it true thou art but a bare name,
And no essential thing?

Duch. Sir, —

Ferd. Do not speak.

Duch. No, sir:
I will plant my soul in mine ears, to hear you.

Ferd. O most imperfect light of human reason,
That mak'st us so unhappy to foresee
What we can least prevent! Pursue thy wishes,
And glory in them: there 's in shame no comfort
But to be past all bounds and sense of shame.

Duch. I pray, sir, hear me: I am married.

Ferd. So!

Duch. Happily, not to your liking: but for that,
Alas, your shears do come untimely now
To clip the bird's wings that 's already flown!
Will you see my husband?

Ferd. Yes, if I could change
Eyes with a basilisk.

Duch. Sure, you came hither
By his confederacy.

Ferd. The howling of a wolf.
Is music to thee, screech-owl: prithee, peace. —
Whate'er thou art that hast enjoyed my sister,
For I am sure thou hear'st me, for thine own sake
Let me not know thee. I came hither prepared
To work thy discovery; yet am now persuaded
It would beget such violent effects
As would damn us both. I would not for ten millions
I had beheld thee: therefore use all means

I never may have knowledge of thy name;
Enjoy thy lust still, and a wretched life,
On that condition. – And for thee, vile woman,
If thou do wish thy lecher may grow old
In thy embracements, I would have thee build
Such a room for him as our anchorites
To holier use inhabit. Let not the sun
Shine on him till he's dead– let dogs and monkeys
Only converse with him, and such dumb things
To whom nature denies use to sound his name;
Do not keep a paraquito, lest she learn it;
If thou do love him, cut out thine own tongue,
Lest it bewray him.

Duch. Why might not I marry?
  I have not gone about in this to create
  Any new world or custom.

Ferd. Thou art undone;
  And thou hast ta'en that massy sheet of lead
  That hid thy husband's bones, and folded it
  About my heart.

Duch. Mine bleeds for 't.

Ferd. Thine! thy heart!
  What should I name 't unless a hollow bullet
  Filled with unquenchable wildfire?

Duch. You are in this
  Too strict; and were you not my princely brother,
  I would say, too wilful: my reputation
  Is safe.

Ferd. Dost thou know what reputation is?
  I 'll tell thee – to small purpose, since the instruction
  Comes now too late.
  Upon a time Reputation, Love, and Death
  Would travel o'er the world; and it was concluded
  That they should part, and take three several ways.
  Death told them they should find him in great battles,
  Or cities plagued with plagues: Love gives them counsel

To inquire for him 'mongst unambitious shepherds,
Where dowries were not talked of, and sometimes
'Mongst quiet kindred that had nothing left
By their dead parents: 'Stay,' quoth Reputation,
'Do not forsake me; for it is my nature,
If once I part from any man I meet,
I am never found again.' And so for you:
You have shook hands with Reputation,
And made him invisible. So, fare you well:
I will never see you more.

Duch. Why should only I,
Of all the other princes of the world,
Be cased up, like a holy relic? I have youth
And a little beauty.

Ferd. So you have some virgins
That are witches. I will never see thee more.   [*Exit.*

Re-enter ANTONIO *with a pistol, and* CARIOLA

Duch. You saw this apparition?

Ant. Yes: we are
Betrayed. How came he hither? I should turn
This to thee, for that.

Cari. Pray, sir, do; and when
That you have cleft my heart, you shall read there
Mine innocence.

Duch. That gallery gave him entrance.

Ant. I would this terrible thing would come again,
That, standing on my guard, I might relate
My warrantable love. —   [*She shows the poniard.*
Ha! what means this?

Duch. He left this with me.

Ant. And it seems did wish
You would use it on yourself.

Duch. His action
Seemed to intend so much.

Ant. This hath a handle to 't,

As well as a point: turn it towards him,
And so fasten the keen edge in his rank gall.

> [*Knocking within.*

How now! who knocks? more earthquakes?

Duch. I stand
As if a mine beneath my feet were ready
To be blown up.

Cari. 'Tis Bosola.

Duch. Away!
O misery! methinks unjust actions
Should wear these masks and curtains, and not we.
You must instantly part hence: I have fashioned it
  already.   [*Exit Antonio.*

Enter BOSOLA

Bos. The duke your brother is ta'en up in a whirlwind;
Hath took horse, and 's rid post to Rome.

Duch. So late?

Bos. He told me, as he mounted into the saddle,
You were undone.

Duch. Indeed, I am very near it.

Bos. What 's the matter?

Duch. Antonio, the master of our household,
Hath dealt so falsely with me in 's accounts:
My brother stood engaged with me for money
Ta'en up of certain Neapolitan Jews,
And Antonio lets the bonds be forfeit.

Bos. Strange! – [*Aside.*] This is cunning.

Duch. And hereupon
My brother's bills at Naples are protested
Against. – Call up our officers.

Bos. I shall.   [*Exit.*

Re-enter ANTONIO

Duch. The place that you must fly to is Ancona:
Hire a house there; I 'll send after you

My treasure and my jewels. Our weak safety
Runs upon enginous wheels: short syllables
Must stand for periods. I must now accuse you
Of such a feigned crime as Tasso calls
Magnanima menzogna, a noble lie,
'Cause it must shield our honours. – Hark! they are
  coming.

Re-enter BOSOLA *and* OFFICERS

Ant. Will your grace hear me?
Duch. I have got well by you: you have yielded me
  A million of loss: I am like to inherit
  The people's curses for your stewardship.
  You had the trick in audit-time to be sick,
  Till I had signed your quietus; and that cured you
  Without help of a doctor. – Gentlemen,
  I would have this man be an example to you all;
  So shall you hold my favour; I pray, let him;
  For h' as done that, alas, you would not think of,
  And, because I intend to be rid of him,
  I mean not to publish. – Use your fortune elsewhere.
Ant. I am strongly armed to brook my overthrow,
  As commonly men bear with a hard year:
  I will not blame the cause on 't; but do think
  The necessity of my malevolent star
  Procures this, not her humour. O, the inconstant
  And rotten ground of service! You may see,
  'Tis even like him, that in a winter night,
  Takes a long slumber o'er a dying fire,
  A-loath to part from 't; yet parts thence as cold
  As when he first sat down.
Duch. We do confiscate,
  Towards the satisfying of your accounts,
  All that you have.
Ant. I am all yours; and 'tis very fit
  All mine should be so.

Would needs down with thee, it cannot be said yet
That any ill happened unto thee, considering thy
   fall
Was accompanied with virtue.

Duch. O, you render me excellent music!

Bos. Say you?

Duch. This good one that you speak of is my husband.

Bos. Do I not dream? Can this ambitious age
Have so much goodness in 't as to prefer
A man merely for worth, without these shadows
Of wealth and painted honours? possible?

Duch. I have had three children by him.

Bos. Fortunate lady!
For you have made your private nuptial bed
The humble and fair seminary of peace.
No question but many an unbeneficed scholar
Shall pray for you for this deed, and rejoice
That some preferment in the world can yet
Arise from merit. The virgins of your land
That have no dowries shall hope your example
Will raise them to rich husbands. Should you want
Soldiers, 'twould make the very Turks and Moors
Turn Christians, and serve you for this act.
Last, the neglected poets of your time,
In honour of this trophy of a man,
Raised by that curious engine, your white hand,
Shall thank you, in your grave for 't; and make that
More reverend than all the cabinets
Of living princes. For Antonio,
His fame shall likewise flow from many a pen,
When heralds shall want coats to sell to men.

Duch. As I taste comfort in this friendly speech,
So would I find concealment.

Bos. O, the secret of my prince,
Which I will wear on the inside of my heart!

Duch. You shall take charge of all my coin and jewels,

And follow him; for he retires himself
To Ancona.

Bos. So.

Duch. Whither, within few days,
I mean to follow thee.

Bos. Let me think:
I would wish your grace to feign a pilgrimage
To our Lady of Loretto, scarce seven leagues
From fair Ancona; so may you depart
Your country with more honour, and your flight
Will seem a princely progress, retaining
Your usual train about you.

Duch. Sir, your direction
Shall lead me by the hand.

Cari. In my opinion,
She were better progress to the baths at Lucca,
Or go visit the Spa
In Germany; for, if you will believe me,
I do not like this jesting with religion,
This feigned pilgrimage.

Duch. Thou art a superstitious fool:
Prepare us instantly for our departure.
Past sorrows, let us moderately lament them,
For those to come, seek wisely to prevent them.
                [*Exeunt Duchess and Cariola.*

Bos. A politician is the devil's quilted anvil;
He fashions all sins on him, and the blows
Are never heard: he may work in a lady's chamber,
As here for proof. What rests but I reveal
All to my lord? O, this base quality
Of intelligencer! Why, every quality i' the world
Prefers but gain or commendation:
Now, for this act I am certain to be raised,
And men that paint weeds to the life are praised.
                [*Exit.*

Enter CARDINAL, FERDINAND, MALATESTE,
PESCARA, DELIO, *and* SILVIO

Card. Must we turn soldier, then?
Mal. The emperor,
 Hearing your worth that way, ere you attained
 This reverend garment, joins you in commission
 With the right fortunate soldier the Marquis of
  Pescara,
 And the famous Lannoy.
Card. He that had the honour
 Of taking the French king prisoner?
Mal. The same.
 Here 's a plot drawn for a new fortification
 At Naples.
Ferd. This great Count Malateste, I perceive,
 Hath got employment?
Delio. No employment, my lord;
 A marginal note in the muster-book, that he is
 A voluntary lord.
Ferd. He 's no soldier.
Delio. He has worn gunpowder in 's hollow tooth for the
  toothache.
Sil. He comes to the leaguer with a full intent
 To eat fresh beef and garlic, means to stay
 Till the scent be gone, and straight return to court.
Delio. He hath read all the late service
 As the city chronicle relates it;
 And keeps two pewterers going, only to express
 Battles in model.
Sil. Then he 'll fight by the book.
Delio. By the almanac, I think,
 To choose good days and shun the critical;
 That 's his mistress' scarf.

Sil. Yes, he protests
  He would do much for that taffeta.
Delio. I think he would run away from a battle,
  To save it from taking prisoner.
Sil. He is horribly afraid
  Gunpowder will spoil the perfume on 't.
Delio. I saw a Dutchman break his pate once
  For calling him pot-gun; he made his head
  Have a bore in 't like a musket.
Sil. I would he had made a touch-hole to 't.
  He is indeed a guarded sumpter-cloth,
  Only for the remove of the court.

Enter BOSOLA

Pes. Bosola arrived! What should be the business?
  Some falling-out amongst the cardinals.
  These factions amongst great men, they are like
  Foxes, when their heads are divided,
  They carry fire in their tails, and all the country
  About them goes to wreck for 't.
Sil. What 's that Bosola?
Delio. I knew him in Padua – a fantastical scholar, like
  such who study to know how many knots was in
  Hercules' club, of what colour Achilles' beard was,
  or whether Hector were not troubled with the tooth-
  ache. He hath studied himself half blear-eyed to
  know the true symmetry of Caesar's nose by a shoe-
  ing-horn; and this he did to gain the name of a
  speculative man.
Pes. Mark Prince Ferdinand:
  A very salamander lives in 's eye,
  To mock the eager violence of fire.
Sil. That cardinal hath made more bad faces with his
  oppression than ever Michael Angelo made good
  ones: he lifts up 's nose, like a foul porpoise before a
  storm.

Pes. The Lord Ferdinand laughs.

Delio. Like a deadly cannon
  That lightens ere it smokes.

Pes. These are your true pangs of death,
  The pangs of life, that struggle with great statesmen.

Delio. In such a deformed silence witches whisper their
    charms.

Card. Doth she make religion her riding-hood
  To keep her from the sun and tempest?

Ferd. That,
  That damns her. Methinks her fault and beauty,
  Blended together, show like leprosy,
  The whiter, the fouler. I make it a question
  Whether her beggarly brats were ever christened.

Card. I will instantly solicit the state of Ancona
  To have them banished.

Ferd. You are for Loretto:
  I shall not be at your ceremony; fare you well. —
  Write to the Duke of Malfy, my young nephew
  She had by her first husband, and acquaint him
  With 's mother's honesty.

Bos. I will.

Ferd. Antonio!
  A slave that only smelled of ink and counters,
  And never in 's life looked like a gentleman,
  But in the audit-time. — Go, go presently,
  Draw me out an hundred and fifty of our horse,
  And meet me at the fort-bridge.   [*Exeunt.*

ACT III, SCENE 4

Enter Two Pilgrims *to the Shrine of our Lady of Loretto*

First Pil. I have not seen a goodlier shrine than this;
  Yet I have visited many.
Sec. Pil. The Cardinal of Arragon
  Is this day to resign his cardinal's hat:
  His sister duchess likewise is arrived
  To pay her vow of pilgrimage. I expect
  A noble ceremony.
First Pil. No question. – They come.

> [*Here the ceremony of the Cardinal's instalment, in the habit*
>   *of a soldier, performed in delivering up his cross, hat,*
>   *robes, and ring, at the shrine, and investing him with*
>   *sword, helmet, shield, and spurs; then Antonio, the*
>   *Duchess, and their children, having presented themselves*
>   *at the shrine, are, by a form of banishment in dumb-*
>   *show expressed towards them by the Cardinal and the*
>   *state of Ancona, banished: during all which ceremony,*
>   *this ditty is sung, to very solemn music, by divers*
>   *churchmen: and then exeunt.*

Arms and honours deck thy story,
To thy fame's eternal glory!
Adverse fortune ever fly thee;
No disastrous fate come nigh thee!
I alone will sing thy praises,
Whom to honour virtue raises;
And thy study, that divine is,
Bent to martial discipline is.
Lay aside all those robes lie by thee;
Crown thy arts with arms, they 'll beautify thee.
O worthy of worthiest name, adorned in this manner,
Lead bravely thy forces on under war's warlike banner!
O mayst thou prove fortunate in all martial courses!

Guide thou still by skill in arts and forces!
Victory attend thee nigh, whilst fame sings loud thy powers;
Triumphant conquest crown thy head, and blessings pour
  down showers!

First Pil. Here 's a strange turn of state! Who would have
    thought
  So great a lady would have matched herself
  Unto so mean a person? Yet the cardinal
  Bears himself much too cruel.
Sec. Pil. They are banished.
First Pil. But I would ask what power hath this state
  Of Ancona to determine of a free prince?
Sec. Pil. They are a free state, sir, and her brother showed
  How that the Pope, fore-hearing of her looseness,
  Hath seized into the protection of the church
  The dukedom which she held as dowager.
First Pil. But by what justice?
Sec. Pil. Sure I think by none,
  Only her brother's instigation.
First Pil. What was it with such violence he took
  Off from her finger?
Sec. Pil. 'Twas her wedding-ring;
  Which he vowed shortly he would sacrifice
  To his revenge.
First Pil. Alas, Antonio!
  If that a man be thrust into a well,
  No matter who sets hand to 't, his own weight
  Will bring him sooner to the bottom. Come, let 's
    hence.
  Fortune makes this conclusion general,
  All things do help the unhappy man to fall.   [*Exeunt.*

ACT III, SCENE 5

Enter DUCHESS, ANTONIO, CHILDREN, CARIOLA,
and SERVANTS

Duch. Banished Ancona!
Ant. Yes, you see what power
    Lightens in great men's breath.
Duch. Is all our train
    Shrunk to this poor remainder?
Ant. These poor men,
    Which have got little in your service, vow
    To take your fortune: but your wiser buntings,
    Now they are fledged, are gone.
Duch. They have done wisely.
    This puts me in mind of death: physicians thus,
    With their hands full of money, use to give o'er
    Their patients.
Ant. Right the fashion of the world:
    From decayed fortunes every flatterer shrinks;
    Men cease to build where the foundation sinks.
Duch. I had a very strange dream to-night.
Ant. What was 't?
Duch. Methought I wore my coronet of state,
    And on a sudden all the diamonds
    Were changed to pearls.
Ant. My interpretation
    Is, you 'll weep shortly; for to me the pearls
    Do signify your tears.
Duch. The birds that live i' the field
    On the wild benefit of nature live
    Happier than we; for they may choose their mates,
    And carol their sweet pleasures to the spring.

Enter BOSOLA *with a letter*

Bos. You are happily o'erta'en.

Duch. From my brother?

Bos. Yes, from the Lord Ferdinand your brother
All love and safety.

Duch. Thou dost blanch mischief,
Wouldst make it white. See, see, like to calm weather
At sea before a tempest, false hearts speak fair
To those they intend most mischief.   [*Reads.*

'Send Antonio to me; I want his head in a business.'

A politic equivocation!
He doth not want your counsel, but your head:
This is, he cannot sleep till you be dead.
And here 's another pitfall that 's strewed o'er
With roses; mark it, 'tis a cunning one: [*Reads.*

'I stand engaged for your husband for several debts at
   Naples: let not that trouble him; I had rather
   have his heart than his money: –'

And I believe so too.

Bos. What do you believe?

Duch. That he so much distrusts my husband's love,
He will by no means believe his heart is with him
Until he see it: the devil is not cunning enough
To circumvent us in riddles.

Bos. Will you reject that noble and free league
Of amity and love which I present you?

Duch. Their league is like that of some politic kings,
Only to make themselves of strength and power
To be our after-ruin: tell them so.

Bos. And what from you?

Ant. Thus tell him; I will not come.

Bos. And what of this?

Ant. My brothers have dispersed
Bloodhounds abroad; which till I hear are muzzled,
No truce, though hatched with ne'er such politic skill,

Is safe, that hangs upon our enemies' will.
I 'll not come at them.

Bos. This proclaims your breeding:
Every small thing draws a base mind to fear,
As the adamant draws iron. Fare you well, sir:
You shall shortly hear from 's.   [*Exit.*

Duch. I suspect some ambush:
Therefore by all my love I do conjure you
To take your eldest son, and fly towards Milan.
Let us not venture all this poor remainder
In one unlucky bottom.

Ant. You counsel safely.
Best of my life, farewell, since we must part:
Heaven hath a hand in 't; but no otherwise
Than as some curious artist takes in sunder
A clock or watch, when it is out of frame,
To bring 't in better order.

Duch. I know not which is best,
To see you dead, or part with you. — Farewell, boy:
Thou art happy that thou hast not understanding
To know thy misery; for all our wit
And reading brings us to a truer sense
Of sorrow. — In the eternal church, sir,
I do hope we shall not part thus.

Ant. Oh, be of comfort!
Make patience a noble fortitude,
And think not how unkindly we are used:
Man, like to cassia, is proved best, being bruised.

Duch. Must I, like to a slave-born Russian,
Account it praise to suffer tyranny?
And yet, O Heaven, thy heavy hand is in 't!
I have seen my little boy oft scourge his top,
And compared myself to 't: naught made me e'er
Go right but heaven's scourge-stick.

Ant. Do not weep:
Heaven fashioned us of nothing; and we strive

To bring ourselves to nothing. – Farewell, Cariola,
And thy sweet armful. – If I do never see thee more,
Be a good mother to your little ones,
And save them from the tiger: fare you well.

Duch. Let me look upon you once more, for that speech
Came from a dying father: your kiss is colder
Than that I have seen an holy anchorite
Give to a dead man's skull.

Ant. My heart is turned to a heavy lump of lead,
With which I sound my danger: fare you well.

> [*Exeunt Antonio and his son.*

Duch. My laurel is all withered.

Cari. Look, madam, what a troop of armed men
Make toward us.

Duch. Oh, they are very welcome:
When Fortune's wheel is overcharged with princes,
The weight makes it move swift: I would have my ruin
Be sudden.

Re-enter BOSOLA *vizarded, with a Guard.*

I am your adventure, am I not?

Bos. You are: you must see your husband no more.

Duch. What devil art thou that counterfeit'st heaven's
thunder?

Bos. Is that terrible? I would have you tell me whether
Is that note worse that frights the silly birds
Out of the corn, or that which doth allure them
To the nets? You have hearkened to the last too much.

Duch. O misery! like to a rusty o'ercharged cannon,
Shall I never fly in pieces? – Come, to what prison?

Bos. To none.

Duch. Whither, then?

Bos. To your palace.

Duch. I have heard
That Charon's boat serves to convey all o'er
The dismal lake, but brings none back again.

Bos. Your brothers mean you safety and pity.

Duch. Pity!
  With such a pity men preserve alive
  Pheasants and quails, when they are not fat enough
  To be eaten.

Bos. These are your children?

Duch. Yes.

Bos. Can they prattle?

Duch. No:
  But I intend, since they were born accursed,
  Curses shall be their first language.

Bos. Fie, madam!
  Forget this base, low fellow —

Duch. Were I a man,
  I 'd beat that counterfeit face into thy other.

Bos. One of no birth.

Duch. Say that he was born mean,
  Man is most happy when 's own actions
  Be arguments and examples of his virtue.

Bos. A barren, beggarly virtue.

Duch. I prithee, who is greatest? Can you tell?
  Sad tales befit my woe: I 'll tell you one.
  A salmon, as she swam unto the sea,
  Met with a dog-fish, who encounters her
  With this rough language: 'Why art thou so bold
  To mix thyself with our high state of floods,
  Being no eminent courtier, but one
  That for the calmest and fresh time o' the year
  Dost live in shallow rivers, rank'st thyself
  With silly smelts and shrimps? and darest thou
  Pass by our dogship without reverence?'
  'O,' quoth the salmon, 'sister, be at peace:
  Thank Jupiter we both have passed the net!
  Our value never can be truly known,
  Till in the fisher's basket we be shown:
  I' the market then my price may be the higher,

Even when I am nearest to the cook and fire.'
So to great men the moral may be stretched;
Men oft are valued high, when they 're most wretched. –
But come, whither you please. I am armed 'gainst
   misery;
Bent to all sways of the oppressor's will:
There 's no deep valley but near some great hill.

                               [*Exeunt.*

Enter FERDINAND *and* BOSOLA

Ferd. How doth our sister duchess bear herself
   In her imprisonment?
Bos. Nobly: I 'll describe her.
   She 's sad as one long used to 't, and she seems
   Rather to welcome the end of misery
   Than shun it; a behaviour so noble
   As gives a majesty to adversity:
   You may discern the shape of loveliness
   More perfect in her tears than in her smiles:
   She will muse four hours together; and her silence,
   Methinks, expresseth more than if she spake.
Ferd. Her melancholy seems to be fortified
   With a strange disdain.
Bos.   'Tis so; and this restraint,
   Like English mastiffs that grow fierce with tying,
   Makes her too passionately apprehend
   Those pleasures she 's kept from.
Ferd.   Curse upon her!
   I will no longer study in the book
   Of another's heart. Inform her what I told you. [*Exit.*

Enter DUCHESS

Bos. All comfort to your grace!
Duch. I will have none.
   Pray thee, why dost thou wrap thy poisoned pills
   In gold and sugar?
Bos. Your elder brother, the Lord Ferdinand,
   Is come to visit you, and sends you word,
   'Cause once he rashly made a solemn vow
   Never to see you more, he comes i' the night;
   And prays you gently neither torch nor taper
   Shine in your chamber: he will kiss your hand,

And reconcile himself; but for his vow
He dares not see you.
Duch. At his pleasure. –
Take hence the lights. – He 's come.

Enter FERDINAND

Ferd. Where are you?
Duch. Here, sir.
Ferd. This darkness suits you well.
Duch. I would ask you pardon.
Ferd. You have it;
For I account it the honourabl'st revenge,
Where I may kill, to pardon. – Where are your cubs?
Duch. Whom?
Ferd. Call them your children;
For though our national law distinguish bastards
From true legitimate issue, compassionate nature
Makes them all equal.
Duch. Do you visit me for this?
You violate a sacrament o' the Church
Shall make you howl in hell for 't.
Ferd. It had been well,
Could you have lived thus always; for, indeed,
You were too much i' the light: but no more –
I come to seal my peace with you. Here 's a hand
                    [*Gives her a dead man's hand.*
To which you have vowed much love; the ring upon 't
You gave.
Duch. I affectionately kiss it.
Ferd. Pray, do, and bury the print of it in your heart.
I will leave this ring with you for a love token;
And the hand as sure as the ring; and do not doubt
But you shall have the heart too: when you need a
    friend,
Send it to him that owned it; you shall see
Whether he can aid you.

Duch. You are very cold:
  I fear you are not well after your travel. —
  Ha! lights! — O horrible!
Ferd. Let her have lights enough.   [*Exit.*
Duch. What witchcraft doth he practise, that he hath left
  A dead man's hand here?
    [*Here is discovered, behind a traverse, the artificial figures
      of Antonio and his children, appearing as if they were
      dead.*
Bos. Look you, here 's the piece from which 'twas ta'en.
  He doth present you this sad spectacle,
  That, now you know directly they are dead,
  Hereafter you may wisely cease to grieve
  For that which cannot be recovered.
Duch. There is not between heaven and earth one wish
  I stay for after this: it wastes me more
  Than were 't my picture, fashioned out of wax,
  Stuck with a magical needle, and then buried
  In some foul dunghill; and yond 's an excellent property
  For a tyrant, which I would account mercy.
Bos. What 's that?
Duch. If they would bind me to that lifeless trunk,
  And let me freeze to death.
Bos. Come, you must live.
Duch. That 's the greatest torture souls feel in hell,
  In hell, that they must live, and cannot die.
  Portia, I 'll new kindle thy coals again,
  And revive the rare and almost dead example
  Of a loving wife.
Bos. Oh, fie! despair? Remember
  You are a Christian.
Duch. The Church enjoins fasting:
  I 'll starve myself to death.
Bos. Leave this vain sorrow.
  Things being at the worst begin to mend: the bee

When he hath shot his sting into your hand,
May then play with your eyelid.
Duch. Good comfortable fellow,
  Persuade a wretch that 's broke upon the wheel
  To have all his bones new set; entreat him live
  To be executed again. Who must dispatch me?
  I account this world a tedious theatre,
  For I do play a part in 't 'gainst my will.
Bos. Come, be of comfort; I will save your life.
Duch. Indeed, I have not leisure to tend
  So small a business.
Bos. Now, by my life, I pity you.
Duch. Thou art a fool, then,
  To waste thy pity on a thing so wretched
  As cannot pity itself. I am full of daggers.
  Puff, let me blow these vipers from me.

Enter SERVANT

  What are you?
Serv. One that wishes you long life.
Duch. I would thou wert hanged for the horrible curse
  Thou hast given me: I shall shortly grow one
  Of the miracles of pity. I 'll go pray;
  No, I 'll go curse.
Bos. Oh, fie!
Duch. I could curse the stars.
Bos. Oh, fearful!
Duch. And those three smiling seasons of the year
  Into a Russian winter: nay, the world
  To its first chaos.
Bos. Look you, the stars shine still.
Duch. O, but you must
  Remember, my curse hath a great way to go. –
  Plagues, that make lanes through largest families,
  Consume them! –
Bos. Fie, lady!

Duch. Let them, like tyrants,
   Never be remembered but for the ill they have done;
   Let all the zealous prayers of mortified
   Churchmen forget them! –
Bos. O, uncharitable!
Duch. Let heaven a little while cease crowning martyrs,
   To punish them! –
   Go, howl them this, and say, I long to bleed:
   It is some mercy when men kill with speed.   [*Exit.*

Re-enter FERDINAND

Ferd. Excellent, as I would wish; she 's plagued in art:
   These presentations are but framed in wax
   By the curious master in that quality,
   Vincentio Lauriola, and she takes them
   For true substantial bodies.
Bos. Why do you do this?
Ferd. To bring her to despair.
Bos. Faith, end here,
   And go no farther in your cruelty:
   Send her a penitential garment to put on
   Next to her delicate skin, and furnish her
   With beads and prayer-books.
Ferd. Damn her! that body of hers,
   While that my blood ran pure in 't, was more worth
   Than that which thou wouldst comfort, called a soul.
   I will send her masks of common courtesans,
   Have her meat served up by bawds and ruffians,
   And, 'cause she 'll needs be mad, I am resolved
   To remove forth the common hospital
   All the mad folk, and place them near her lodging;
   There let them practise together, sing and dance,
   And act their gambols to the full o' the moon:
   If she can sleep the better for it, let her.
   Your work is almost ended.
Bos. Must I see her again?

Ferd. Yes.

Bos. Never.

Ferd. You must.

Bos. Never in mine own shape;
   That 's forfeited by my intelligence
   And this last cruel lie: when you send me next,
   The business shall be comfort.

Ferd. Very likely;
   Thy pity is nothing of kin to thee. Antonio
   Lurks about Milan: thou shalt shortly thither,
   To feed a fire as great as my revenge,
   Which never will slack till it have spent his fuel:
   Intemperate agues make physicians cruel.   [*Exeunt.*

ACT IV, SCENE 2

Enter DUCHESS *and* CARIOLA

Duch. What hideous noise was that?

Cari. 'Tis the wild consort
   Of madmen, lady, which your tyrant brother
   Hath placed about your lodging: this tyranny,
   I think, was never practised till this hour.

Duch. Indeed, I thank him: nothing but noise and folly
   Can keep me in my right wits; whereas reason
   And silence make me stark mad. Sit down;
   Discourse to me some dismal tragedy.

Cari. O, 'twill increase your melancholy.

Duch. Thou art deceived:
   To hear of greater grief would lessen mine.
   This is a prison?

Cari. Yes, but you shall live
   To shake this durance off.

Duch. Thou art a fool:

The robin-redbreast and the nightingale
Never live long in cages.

Cari. Pray, dry your eyes.
What think you of, madam?

Duch. Of nothing;
When I muse thus, I sleep.

Cari. Like a madman, with your eyes open?

Duch. Dost thou think we shall know one another
In the other world?

Cari. Yes, out of question.

Duch. O, that it were possible we might
But hold some two days' conference with the dead!
From them I should learn somewhat, I am sure,
I never shall know here. I 'll tell thee a miracle;
I am not mad yet, to my cause of sorrow:
The heaven o'er my head seems made of molten brass,
The earth of flaming sulphur, yet I am not mad.
I am acquainted with sad misery
As the tanned galley-slave is with his oar;
Necessity makes me suffer constantly,
And custom makes it easy. Who do I look like now?

Cari. Like to your picture in the gallery,
A deal of life in show, but none in practice;
Or rather like some reverend monument
Whose ruins are even pitied.

Duch. Very proper;
And Fortune seems only to have her eyesight
To behold my tragedy. – How now!
What noise is that?

Enter SERVANT

Serv. I am come to tell you
Your brother hath intended you some sport.
A great physician, when the Pope was sick
Of a deep melancholy, presented him
With several sorts of madmen, which wild object

Being full of change and sport, forced him to laugh,
And so the imposthume broke: the selfsame cure
The duke intends on you.

Duch. Let them come in.

Serv. There 's a mad lawyer; and a secular priest;
A doctor that hath forfeited his wits
By jealousy; an astrologian
That in his works said such a day o' the month
Should be the day of doom, and failing of 't,
Ran mad; an English tailor crazed in the brain
With the study of new fashions; a gentleman-usher
Quite beside himself with care to keep in mind
The number of his lady's salutations
Or 'How do you' she employed him in each morning;
A farmer, too, an excellent knave in grain,
Mad 'cause he was hindered transportation:
And let one broker that 's mad loose to these,
You 'd think the devil were among them.

Duch. Sit, Cariola. – Let them loose when you please,
For I am chained to endure all your tyranny.

Enter MADMEN

[*Here by a Madman this song is sung to a dismal kind of
    music.*

> *Oh, let us howl some heavy note,*
>   *Some deadly dogged howl,*
> *Sounding as from the threatening throat*
>   *Of beasts and fatal fowl!*
> *As ravens, screech-owls, bulls, and bears,*
>   *We 'll bell, and bawl our parts,*
> *Till irksome noise have cloyed your ears*
>   *And corrosived your hearts.*
> *At last, whenas our choir wants breath,*
>   *Our bodies being blest,*
> *We 'll sing, like swans, to welcome death,*
>   *And die in love and rest.*

First Madman. Doomsday not come yet! I 'll draw it nearer by a perspective, or make a glass that shall set all the world on fire upon an instant. I cannot sleep; my pillow is stuffed with a litter of porcupines.

Second Madman. Hell is a mere glass-house, where the devils are continually blowing up women's souls on hollow irons, and the fire never goes out.

Third Madman. I will lie with every woman in my parish the tenth night; I will tithe them over like hay-cocks.

Fourth Madman. Shall my pothecary outgo me because I am a cuckold? I have found out his roguery; he makes alum of his wife's urine, and sells it to Puritans that have sore throats with over-straining.

First Madman. I have skill in heraldry.

Second Madman. Hast?

First Madman. You do give for your crest a woodcock's head with the brains picked out on 't; you are a very ancient gentleman.

Third Madman. Greek is turned Turk: we are only to be saved by the Helvetian translation.

First Madman. Come on, sir, I will lay the law to you.

Second Madman. Oh, rather lay a corrosive: the law will eat to the bone.

Third Madman. He that drinks but to satisfy nature is damned.

Fourth Madman. If I had my glass here, I would show a sight should make all the women here call me mad doctor.

First Madman. What 's he? a rope-maker?

Second Madman. No, no, no, a snuffling knave that, while he shows the tombs, will have his hand in a wench's placket.

Third Madman. Woe to the caroche that brought home my wife from the masque at three o'clock in the morning! It had a large feather-bed in it.

Fourth Madman. I have pared the devil's nails forty times, roasted them in raven's eggs, and cured agues with them.

Third Madman. Get me three hundred milch-bats, to make possets to procure sleep.

Fourth Madman. All the college may throw their caps at me: I have made a soap-boiler costive; it was my masterpiece.

> [*Here the dance, consisting of Eight Madmen, with music answerable thereunto; after which, Bosola, like an old man, enters.*

Duch. Is he mad too?

Serv. Pray, question him. I 'll leave you.

> [*Exeunt Servant and Madmen.*

Bos. I am come to make thy tomb.

Duch. Ha! my tomb!
Thou speak'st as if I lay upon my death-bed,
Gasping for breath: dost thou perceive me sick?

Bos. Yes, and the more dangerously, since thy sickness is insensible.

Duch. Thou art not mad, sure: dost know me?

Bos. Yes.

Duch. Who am I?

Bos. Thou art a box of worm-seed, at best but a salvatory of green mummy. What 's this flesh? a little crudded milk, fantastical puff-paste. Our bodies are weaker than those paper-prisons boys use to keep flies in; more contemptible, since ours is to preserve earth-worms. Didst thou ever see a lark in a cage? Such is the soul in the body: this world is like her little turf of grass, and the heaven o'er our heads like her looking-glass, only gives us a miserable knowledge of the small compass of our prison.

Duch. Am not I thy duchess?

Bos. Thou art some great woman, sure, for riot begins to sit on thy forehead (clad in grey hairs) twenty years

sooner than on a merry milkmaid's. Thou sleepest
worse than if a mouse should be forced to take up
her lodging in a cat's ear: a little infant that breeds
its teeth, should it lie with thee, would cry out, as if
thou wert the more unquiet bedfellow.

Duch. I am Duchess of Malfy still.

Bos. That makes thy sleeps so broken:
   Glories, like glow-worms, afar off shine bright,
   But, looked to near, have neither heat nor light.

Duch. Thou art very plain.

Bos. My trade is to flatter the dead, not the living; I am a
tomb-maker.

Duch. And thou comest to make my tomb?

Bos. Yes.

Duch. Let me be a little merry: of what stuff wilt thou
make it?

Bos. Nay, resolve me first, of what fashion?

Duch. Why, do we grow fantastical in our death-bed? do
we affect fashion in the grave?

Bos. Most ambitiously. Princes' images on their tombs do
not lie, as they were wont, seeming to pray up to
heaven; but with their hands under their cheeks, as
if they died of the toothache: they are not carved
with their eyes fixed upon the stars; but as their
minds were wholly bent upon the world, the self-
same way they seem to turn their faces.

Duch. Let me know fully therefore the effect
   Of this thy dismal preparation,
   This talk fit for a charnel.

Bos. Now I shall: —

Enter EXECUTIONERS, *with a coffin, cords, and a bell.*

   Here is a present from your princely brothers;
   And may it arrive welcome, for it brings
   Last benefit, last sorrow.

Duch. Let me see it:

I have so much obedience in my blood,
I wish it in their veins to do them good.

Bos. This is your last presence-chamber.

Cari. O, my sweet lady!

Duch. Peace; it affrights not me.

Bos. I am the common bellman,
That usually is sent to condemned persons
The night before they suffer.

Duch. Even now thou said'st
Thou wast a tomb-maker.

Bos. 'Twas to bring you
By degrees to mortification. Listen:

> Hark, now everything is still,
> The screech-owl and the whistler shrill
> Call upon our dame aloud,
> And bid her quickly don her shroud!
> Much you had of land and rent;
> Your length in clay 's now competent:
> A long war disturbed your mind;
> Here your perfect peace is signed.
> Of what is 't fools make such vain keeping?
> Sin their conception, their birth weeping,
> Their life a general mist of error,
> Their death a hideous storm of terror.
> Strew your hair with powders sweet,
> Don clean linen, bathe your feet,
> And (the foul fiend more to check)
> A crucifix let bless your neck:
> 'Tis now full tide 'tween night and day;
> End your groan, and come away.

Cari. Hence, villains, tyrants, murderers! alas!
What will you do with my lady? — Call for help.

Duch. To whom? to our next neighbours? they are mad-
folks.

Bos. Remove that noise.

Duch. Farewell, Cariola.
   In my last will I have not much to give:
   A many hungry guests have fed upon me;
   Thine will be a poor reversion.
Cari. I will die with her.
Duch. I pray thee, look thou giv'st my little boy
   Some syrup for his cold, and let the girl
   Say her prayers ere she sleep.   [*Cariola is forced off.*
   Now what you please:
   What death?
Bos. Strangling; here are your executioners.
Duch. I forgive them:
   The apoplexy, catarrh, or cough o' the lungs,
   Would do as much as they do.
Bos. Doth not death fright you?
Duch. Who would be afraid on 't,
   Knowing to meet such excellent company
   In the other world?
Bos. Yet, methinks,
   The manner of your death should much afflict you:
   This cord should terrify you.
Duch. Not a whit:
   What would it pleasure me to have my throat cut
   With diamonds? or to be smothered
   With cassia? or to be shot to death with pearls?
   I know death hath ten thousand several doors
   For men to take their exits; and 'tis found
   They go on such strange geometrical hinges,
   You may open them both ways: any way, for heaven
      sake,
   So I were out of your whispering. Tell my brothers
   That I perceive death, now I am well awake,
   Best gift is they can give or I can take.
   I would fain put off my last woman's fault,
   I 'd not be tedious to you.
First Execut. We are ready.

Duch. Dispose my breath how please you; but my body
   Bestow upon my women, will you?

First Execut. Yes.

Duch. Pull, and pull strongly, for your able strength
   Must pull down heaven upon me:
   Yet stay; heaven gates are not so highly arched
   As princes' palaces; they that enter there
   Must go upon their knees. [*Kneels.*] – Come, violent
     death,
   Serve for mandragora to make me sleep! –
   Go tell my brothers, when I am laid out,
   They then may feed in quiet.   [*They strangle her.*

Bos. Where 's the waiting-woman?
   Fetch her: some other strangle the children.

     [*Cariola and Children are brought in by the Executioners;*
           who presently strangle the Children.

   Look you, there sleeps your mistress.

Cari. O, you are damned
   Perpetually for this! My turn is next;
   Is 't not so ordered?

Bos. Yes, and I am glad
   You are so well prepared for 't.

Cari. You are deceived, sir,
   I am not prepared for 't, I will not die;
   I will first come to my answer, and know
   How I have offended.

Bos. Come, dispatch her. –
   You kept her counsel; now you shall keep ours.

Cari. I will not die, I must not; I am contracted
   To a young gentleman.

First Execut. Here 's your wedding-ring.

Cari. Let me but speak with the duke; I 'll discover
   Treason to his person.

Bos. Delays: – throttle her.

First Execut. She bites and scratches.

Cari. If you kill me now,

I am damned; I have not been at confession
This two years.
Bos. [*to Executioners*]. When?
Cari. I am quick with child.
Bos. Why, then,
Your credit 's saved. [*The Executioners strangle Cariola.*
Bear her into the next room;
Let these lie still.
    [*Exeunt the Executioners with the body of Cariola.*

Enter FERDINAND

Ferd. Is she dead?
Bos. She is what
You 'd have her. But here begin your pity:
            [*Shows the Children strangled.*
Alas, how have these offended?
Ferd. The death
Of young wolves is never to be pitied.
Bos. Fix your eye here.
Ferd. Constantly.
Bos. Do you not weep?
Other sins only speak; murder shrieks out:
The element of water moistens the earth,
But blood flies upwards and bedews the heavens.
Ferd. Cover her face; mine eyes dazzle: she died young.
Bos. I think not so; her infelicity
Seemed to have years too many.
Ferd. She and I were twins;
And should I die this instant, I had lived
Her time to a minute.
Bos. It seems she was born first:
You have bloodily approved the ancient truth,
That kindred commonly do worse agree
Than remote strangers.
Ferd. Let me see her face

Again. Why didst not thou pity her? What
An excellent honest man might'st thou have been,
If thou hadst borne her to some sanctuary!
Or, bold in a good cause, opposed thyself,
With thy advanced sword above thy head,
Between her innocence and my revenge!
I bade thee, when I was distracted of my wits,
Go kill my dearest friend, and thou hast done 't.
For let me but examine well the cause:
What was the meanness of her match to me?
Only I must confess I had a hope,
Had she continued widow, to have gained
An infinite mass of treasure by her death:
And what was the main cause? her marriage,
That drew a stream of gall quite through my heart.
For thee, as we observe in tragedies
That a good actor many times is cursed
For playing a villain's part, I hate thee for 't,
And, for my sake, say, thou hast done much ill well.

Bos. Let me quicken your memory, for I perceive
   You are falling into ingratitude: I challenge
   The reward due to my service.

Ferd. I 'll tell thee
   What I 'll give thee.

Bos. Do.

Ferd. I 'll give thee a pardon
   For this murder.

Bos. Ha!

Ferd. Yes, and 'tis
   The largest bounty I can study to do thee.
   By what authority didst thou execute
   This bloody sentence?

Bos. By yours.

Ferd. Mine! was I her judge?
   Did any ceremonial form of law
   Doom her to not-being? Did a complete jury

Deliver her conviction up i' the court?
Where shalt thou find this judgement registered,
Unless in hell? See, like a bloody fool,
Thou 'st forfeited thy life, and thou shalt die for 't.

Bos. The office of justice is perverted quite
When one thief hangs another. Who shall dare
To reveal this?

Ferd. O, I 'll tell thee;
The wolf shall find her grave, and scrape it up,
Not to devour the corpse, but to discover
The horrid murder.

Bos. You, not I, shall quake for 't.

Ferd. Leave me.

Bos. I will first receive my pension.

Ferd. You are a villain.

Bos. When your ingratitude
Is judge, I am so.

Ferd. O, horror,
That not the fear of him which binds the devils
Can prescribe man obedience! —
Never look upon me more.

Bos. Why, fare thee well.
Your brother and yourself are worthy men:
You have a pair of hearts are hollow graves,
Rotten, and rotting others; and your vengeance,
Like two chained bullets, still goes arm in arm:
You may be brothers; for treason, like the plague,
Doth take much in a blood. I stand like one
That long hath ta'en a sweet and golden dream:
I am angry with myself, now that I wake.

Ferd. Get thee into some unknown part o' the world,
That I may never see thee.

Bos. Let me know
Wherefore I should be thus neglected. Sir,
I served your tyranny, and rather strove
To satisfy yourself than all the world:

And though I loathed the evil, yet I loved
You that did counsel it; and rather sought
To appear a true servant than an honest man.

Ferd. I 'll go hunt the badger by owl-light:
'Tis a deed of darkness.   [*Exit.*

Bos. He 's much distracted. Off, my painted honour!
While with vain hopes our faculties we tire,
We seem to sweat in ice and freeze in fire.
What would I do, were this to do again?
I would not change my peace of conscience
For all the wealth of Europe. She stirs; here 's life:
Return, fair soul, from darkness, and lead mine
Out of this sensible hell: she 's warm, she breathes:
Upon thy pale lips I will melt my heart,
To store them with fresh colour. — Who's there!
Some cordial drink! — Alas! I dare not call:
So pity would destroy pity. — Her eye opes,
And heaven in it seems to ope, that late was shut,
To take me up to mercy.

Duch. Antonio!

Bos. Yes, madam, he is living;
The dead bodies you saw were but feigned statues:
He 's reconciled to your brothers; the Pope hath
    wrought
The atonement.

Duch. Mercy!   [*Dies.*

Bos. O, she 's gone again! there the cords of life broke.
O sacred innocence, that sweetly sleeps
On turtles' feathers, whilst a guilty conscience
Is a black register wherein is writ
All our good deeds and bad, a perspective
That shows us hell! That we cannot be suffered
To do good when we have a mind to it!
This is manly sorrow;
These tears, I am very certain, never grew
In my mother's milk: my estate is sunk

Below the degree of fear: where were
These penitent fountains while she was living?
O, they were frozen up! Here is a sight
As direful to my soul as is the sword
Unto a wretch hath slain his father. Come,
I 'll bear thee hence,
And execute thy last will; that 's deliver
Thy body to the reverend dispose
Of some good women: that the cruel tyrant
Shall not deny me. Then I 'll post to Milan,
Where somewhat I will speedily enact
Worth my dejection.   [*Exit.*

ACT V, SCENE 1

Enter ANTONIO *and* DELIO

Ant. What think you of my hope of reconcilement
  To the Arragonian brethren?
Delio. I misdoubt it;
  For though they have sent their letters of safe-conduct
  For your repair to Milan, they appear
  But nets to entrap you. The Marquis of Pescara,
  Under whom you hold certain land in cheat,
  Much 'gainst his noble nature hath been moved
  To seize those lands; and some of his dependants
  Are at this instant making it their suit
  To be invested in your revenues.
  I cannot think they mean well to your life
  That do deprive you of your means of life,
  Your living.
Ant. You are still an heretic
  To any safety I can shape myself.
Delio. Here comes the marquis: I will make myself
  Petitioner for some part of your land,
  To know whither it is flying.
Ant. I pray, do.

Enter PESCARA

Delio. Sir, I have a suit for you.
Pes. To me?
Delio. An easy one:
  There is the Citadel of Saint Bennet,
  With some demesnes, of late in the possession
  Of Antonio Bologna – please you bestow them on me.
Pes. You are my friend; but this is such a suit,
  Nor fit for me to give, nor you to take.
Delio. No, sir?

Pes. I will give you ample reason for 't
   Soon in private: – here 's the cardinal's mistress.

Enter JULIA

Julia. My lord, I am grown your poor petitioner,
   And should be an ill beggar, had I not
   A great man's letter here, the cardinal's,
   To court you in my favour.   *[Gives a letter.*
Pes. He entreats for you
   The Citadel of Saint Bennet, that belonged
   To the banished Bologna.
Julia. Yes.
Pes. I could not have thought of a friend I could rather
   Pleasure with it: 'tis yours.
Julia. Sir, I thank you;
   And he shall know how doubly I am engaged
   Both in your gift, and speediness of giving
   Which makes your grant the greater.   *[Exit.*
Ant. How they fortify
   Themselves with my ruin!
Delio. Sir, I am
   Little bound to you.
Pes. Why?
Delio. Because you denied this suit to me, and gave 't
   To such a creature.
Pes. Do you know what it was?
   It was Antonio's land; not forfeited
   By course of law, but ravished from his throat
   By the cardinal's entreaty: it were not fit
   I should bestow so main a piece of wrong
   Upon my friend; 'tis a gratification
   Only due to a strumpet, for it is injustice.
   Shall I sprinkle the pure blood of innocents
   To make those followers I call my friends
   Look ruddier upon me? I am glad
   This land, ta'en from the owner by such wrong,

Returns again unto so foul an use
As salary for his lust. Learn, good Delio,
To ask noble things of me, and you shall find
I 'll be a noble giver.

Delio. You instruct me well.

Ant. Why, here 's a man now would fright impudence
From sauciest beggars.

Pes. Prince Ferdinand 's come to Milan,
Sick, as they give out, of an apoplexy;
But some say 'tis a frenzy; I am going
To visit him.   [*Exit.*

Ant. 'Tis a noble old fellow.

Delio. What course do you mean to take, Antonio?

Ant. This night I mean to venture all my fortune,
Which is no more than a poor lingering life,
To the cardinal's worst of malice: I have got
Private access to his chamber; and intend
To visit him about the mid of night,
As once his brother did our noble duchess.
It may be that the sudden apprehension
Of danger – for I 'll go in mine own shape –
When he shall see it fraught with love and duty,
May draw the poison out of him, and work
A friendly reconcilement: if it fail,
Yet it shall rid me of this infamous calling:
For better fall once than be ever falling,

Delio. I 'll second you in all danger; and, howe'er,
My life keeps rank with yours.

Ant. You are still my loved and best friend.   [*Exeunt.*

Enter PESCARA *and* DOCTOR

Pes. Now, doctor, may I visit your patient?
Doc. If 't please your lordship: but he 's instantly
  To take the air here in the gallery
  By my direction.
Pes. Pray thee, what 's his disease?
Doc. A very pestilent disease, my lord,
  They call lycanthropia.
Pes. What 's that?
  I need a dictionary to 't.
Doc. I 'll tell you.
  In those that are possessed with 't there o'erflows
  Such melancholy humour they imagine
  Themselves to be transformed into wolves;
  Steal forth to churchyards in the dead of night,
  And dig dead bodies up: as two nights since
  One met the duke 'bout midnight in a lane
  Behind Saint Mark's Church, with the leg of a man
  Upon his shoulder; and he howled fearfully;
  Said he was a wolf, only the difference
  Was, a wolf's skin was hairy on the outside,
  His on the inside; bade them take their swords,
  Rip up his flesh, and try: straight I was sent for,
  And, having ministered to him, found his grace
  Very well recovered.
Pes. I am glad on 't.
Doc. Yet not without some fear
  Of a relapse. If he grow to his fit again,
  I 'll go a nearer way to work with him
  Than ever Paracelsus dreamed of; if
  They 'll give me leave, I 'll buffet his madness out of
    him.
  Stand aside; he comes.

Enter FERDINAND, CARDINAL, MALATESTE,
and BOSOLA

Ferd. Leave me.

Mal. Why doth your lordship love this solitariness?

Ferd. Eagles commonly fly alone: they are crows, daws, and starlings that flock together. Look, what 's that follows me?

Mal. Nothing, my lord.

Ferd. Yes.

Mal. 'Tis your shadow.

Ferd. Stay it; let it not haunt me.

Mal. Impossible, if you move, and the sun shine.

Ferd. I will throttle it.   [*Throws himself down on his shadow.*

Mal. O, my lord, you are angry with nothing.

Ferd. You are a fool: how is 't possible I should catch my shadow, unless I fall upon 't? When I go to hell, I mean to carry a bribe; for, look you, good gifts evermore make way for the worst persons.

Pes. Rise, good my lord.

Ferd. I am studying the art of patience.

Pes. 'Tis a noble virtue.

Ferd. To drive six snails before me from this town to Moscow; neither use goad nor whip to them, but let them take their own time; – the patient'st man i' the world match me for an experiment; – and I 'll crawl after like a sheep-biter.

Card. Force him up.   [*They raise him.*

Ferd. Use me well, you were best. What I have done, I have done: I 'll confess nothing.

Doc. Now let me come to him. – Are you mad, my lord? are you out of your princely wits?

Ferd. What 's he?

Pes. Your doctor.

Ferd. Let me have his beard sawed off, and his eyebrows filed more civil.

Doc. I must do mad tricks with him, for that 's the only
way on 't. – I have brought your grace a salamander's skin to keep you from sun-burning.

Ferd. I have cruel sore eyes.

Doc. The white of a cockatrix's egg is present remedy.

Ferd. Let it be a new-laid one, you were best. –
Hide me from him: physicians are like kings, –
They brook no contradiction.

Doc. Now he begins to fear me: now let me alone with
him.

Card. How now! put off your gown!

Doc. Let me have some forty urinals filled with rose water:
he and I 'll go pelt one another with them. – Now he
begins to fear me. – Can you fetch a frisk, sir? – Let
him go, let him go, upon my peril: I find by his eye
he stands in awe of me; I 'll make him as tame as a
dormouse.

Ferd. Can you fetch your frisks, sir! – I will stamp him
into a cullis, flay off his skin, to cover one of the
anatomies this rogue hath set i' the cold yonder in
Barber-Chirurgeons' Hall. – Hence, hence! you are
all of you like beasts for sacrifice: there 's nothing
left of you but tongue and belly, flattery and lechery.
[*Exit.*

Pes. Doctor, he did not fear you throughly.

Doc. True; I was somewhat too forward.

Bos. Mercy upon me, what a fatal judgement
Hath fallen upon this Ferdinand!

Pes. Knows your grace
What accident hath brought unto the prince
This strange distraction?

Card. [*aside*]. I must feign somewhat. – Thus they say it
grew.
You have heard it rumoured, for these many years
None of our family dies but there is seen
The shape of an old woman, which is given

By tradition to us to have been murdered
By her nephews for her riches. Such a figure
One night, as the prince sat up late at 's book,
Appeared to him; when crying out for help,
The gentlemen of 's chamber found his grace
All on a cold sweat, altered much in face
And language: since which apparition,
He hath grown worse and worse, and I much fear
He cannot live.

Bos. Sir, I would speak with you.

Pes. We 'll leave your grace,
  Wishing to the sick prince, our noble lord,
  All health of mind and body.

Card. You are most welcome.

                [Exeunt Pescara, Malateste, and Doctor.
  Are you come? so. – [*Aside.*] This fellow must not know
  By any means I had intelligence
  In our duchess' death; for, though I counselled it,
  The full of all the engagement seemed to grow
  From Ferdinand. – Now, sir, how fares our sister?
  I do not think but sorrow makes her look
  Like to an oft-dyed garment: she shall now
  Taste comfort from me. Why do you look so wildly?
  O, the fortune of your master here the prince
  Dejects you; but be you of happy comfort:
  If you 'll do one thing for me I 'll entreat,
  Though he had a cold tombstone o'er his bones, ·
  I 'd make you what you would be.

Bos. Anything;
  Give it me in a breath, and let me fly to 't:
  They that think long small expedition win,
  For musing much o' the end cannot begin.

Enter JULIA

Julia. Sir, will you come in to supper?

Card. I am busy; leave me.

Julia. [*aside*]. What an excellent shape hath that fellow!
[*Exit.*

Card. 'Tis thus, Antonio lurks here in Milan:
Inquire him out, and kill him. While he lives,
Our sister cannot marry; and I have thought
Of an excellent match for her. Do this, and style
me
Thy advancement.

Bos. But by what means shall I find him out?

Card. There is a gentleman called Delio
Here in the camp, that hath been long approved
His loyal friend. Set eye upon that fellow;
Follow him to mass; may be Antonio,
Although he do account religion
But a school-name, for fashion of the world—
May accompany him; or else go inquire out
Delio's confessor, and see if you can bribe
Him to reveal it. There are a thousand ways
A man might find to trace him; as to know
What fellows haunt the Jews for taking up
Great sums of money, for sure he's in want;
Or else to go to the picture-makers, and learn
Who bought her picture lately: some of these
Happily may take.

Bos. Well, I'll not freeze i' the business:
I would see that wretched thing, Antonio,
Above all sights i' the world.

Card. Do, and be happy.   [*Exit.*

Bos. This fellow doth breed basilisks in 's eyes,
He's nothing else but murder; yet he seems
Not to have notice of the duchess' death.
'Tis his cunning: I must follow his example;
There cannot be a surer way to trace
Than that of an old fox.

Re-enter JULIA

Julia. So, sir, you are well met.

Bos. How now!

Julia. Nay, the doors are fast enough:
   Now, sir, I will make you confess your treachery.

Bos. Treachery!

Julia. Yes, confess to me
   Which of my women 'twas you hired to put
   Love-powder into my drink?

Bos. Love-powder!

Julia. Yes, when I was at Malfy.
   Why should I fall in love with such a face else?
   I have already suffered for thee so much pain,
   The only remedy to do me good
   Is to kill my longing.

Bos. Sure, your pistol holds
   Nothing but perfumes or kissing-comfits.
   Excellent lady!
   You have a pretty way on 't to discover
   Your longing. Come, come, I 'll disarm you,
   And arm you thus: yet this is wondrous strange.

Julia. Compare thy form and my eyes together,
   You 'll find my love no such great miracle.
   Now you 'll say
   I am wanton: this nice modesty in ladies
   Is but a troublesome familiar
   That haunts them.

Bos. Know you me, I am a blunt soldier.

Julia. The better:
   Sure, there wants fire where there are no lively
      sparks
   Of roughness.

Bos. And I want compliment.

Julia. Why, ignorance
   In courtship cannot make you do amiss,
   If you have a heart to do well.

Bos. You are very fair.

Julia. Nay, if you lay beauty to my charge,
  I must plead unguilty.
Bos. Your bright eyes
  Carry a quiver of darts in them sharper
  Than sunbeams.
Julia. You will mar me with commendation.
  Put yourself to the charge of courting me,
  Whereas now I woo you.
Bos. [*aside*]. I have it, I will work upon this creature. –
  Let us grow most amorously familiar:
  If the great cardinal now should see me thus,
  Would he not count me a villain?
Julia. No; he might count me a wanton,
  Not lay a scruple of offence on you;
  For if I see and steal a diamond,
  The fault is not i' the stone, but in me the thief
  That purloins it. I am sudden with you:
  We that are great women of pleasure use to cut off
  These uncertain wishes and unquiet longings,
  And in an instant join the sweet delight
  And the pretty excuse together. Had you been i' the
      street,
  Under my chamber-window, even there
  I should have courted you.
Bos. O, you are an excellent lady!
Julia. Bid me do somewhat for you presently
  To express I love you.
Bos. I will; and if you love me,
  Fail not to effect it.
  The cardinal is grown wondrous melancholy;
  Demand the cause, let him not put you off
  With feigned excuse; discover the main ground on 't.
Julia. Why would you know this?
Bos. I have depended on him,
  And I hear that he is fall'n in some disgrace
  With the emperor: if he be, like the mice

That forsake falling houses, I would shift
To other dependence.
Julia. You shall not need
Follow the wars: I 'll be your maintenance.
Bos. And I your loyal servant: but I cannot
Leave my calling.
Julia. Not leave an ungrateful
General for the love of a sweet lady!
You are like some cannot sleep in feather-beds,
But must have blocks for their pillows.
Bos. Will you do this?
Julia. Cunningly.
Bos. To-morrow I 'll expect the intelligence.
Julia. To-morrow! get you into my cabinet;
You shall have it with you. Do not delay me,
No more than I do you: I am like one
That is condemned; I have my pardon promised,
But I would see it sealed. Go, get you in:
You shall see me wind my tongue about his heart
Like a skein of silk.   [*Exit Bosola.*

Re-enter CARDINAL

Card. Where are you?

Enter SERVANTS

Serv. Here.
Card. Let none, upon your lives, have conference
With the Prince Ferdinand, unless I know it. —
[*Aside.*] In this distraction he may reveal
The murder.   [*Exeunt Servants.*
Yond 's my lingering consumption:
I am weary of her, and by any means
Would be quit of.
Julia. How now, my lord! what ails you?
Card. Nothing.
Julia. O, you are much altered:

Come, I must be your secretary, and remove
This lead from off your bosom: what 's the matter?
Card. I may not tell you.
Julia. Are you so far in love with sorrow
You cannot part with part of it? or think you
I cannot love your grace when you are sad
As well as merry? or do you suspect
I, that have been a secret to your heart
These many winters, cannot be the same
Unto your tongue?
Card. Satisfy thy longing, —
The only way to make thee keep my counsel
Is, not to tell thee.
Julia. Tell your echo this,
Or flatterers, that like echoes still report
What they hear though most imperfect, and not me;
For if that you be true unto yourself,
I 'll know.
Card. Will you rack me?
Julia. No, judgement shall
Draw it from you: it is an equal fault,
To tell one's secrets unto all or none.
Card. The first argues folly.
Julia. But the last tyranny.
Card. Very well: why, imagine I have committed
Some secret deed which I desire the world
May never hear of.
Julia. Therefore may not I know it?
You have concealed for me as great a sin
As adultery. Sir, never was occasion
For perfect trial of my constancy
Till now: sir, I beseech you —
Card. You 'll repent it.
Julia. Never.
Card. It hurries thee to ruin: I'll not tell thee.
Be well advised, and think what danger 'tis

To receive a prince's secrets: they that do,
Had need have their breasts hooped with adamant
To contain them. I pray thee, yet be satisfied;
Examine thine own frailty; 'tis more easy
To tie knots than unloose them: 'tis a secret
That, like a lingering poison, may chance lie
Spread in thy veins, and kill thee seven year hence.

Julia. Now you dally with me.

Card. No more; thou shalt know it.
By my appointment the great Duchess of Malfy
And two of her young children, four nights since,
Were strangled.

Julia. O heaven! sir, what have you done!

Card. How now? How settles this? Think you your bosom
Will be a grave dark and obscure enough
For such a secret?

Julia. You have undone yourself, sir.

Card. Why?

Julia. It lies not in me to conceal it.

Card. No?
Come, I will swear you to 't upon this book.

Julia. Most religiously.

Card. Kiss it.   [*She kisses the book.*
Now you shall never utter it; thy curiosity
Hath undone thee: thou 'rt poisoned with that book;
Because I knew thou couldst not keep my counsel,
I have bound thee to 't by death.

Re-enter BOSOLA

Bos. For pity sake, hold!

Card. Ha, Bosola!

Julia. I forgive you
This equal piece of justice you have done:
For I betrayed your counsel to that fellow:
He overheard it; that was the cause I said
It lay not in me to conceal it.

Bos. O, foolish woman,
    Couldst not thou have poisoned him?
Julia. 'Tis weakness,
    Too much to think what should have been done. I go,
    I know not whither.   [*Dies.*
Card. Wherefore com'st thou hither?
Bos. That I might find a great man like yourself,
    Not out of his wits as the Lord Ferdinand,
    To remember my service.
Card. I 'll have thee hewed in pieces.
Bos. Make not yourself such a promise of that life
    Which is not yours to dispose of.
Card. Who placed thee here?
Bos. Her lust, as she intended.
Card. Very well:
    Now you know me for your fellow-murderer.
Bos. And wherefore should you lay fair marble colours
    Upon your rotten purposes to me?
    Unless you imitate some that do plot great treasons,
    And when they have done, go hide themselves i' the
        graves
    Of those were actors in 't?
Card. No more; there is
    A fortune attends thee.
Bos. Shall I go sue to Fortune any longer?
    'Tis the fool's pilgrimage.
Card. I have honours in store for thee.
Bos. There are many ways that conduct to seeming
        honour,
    And some of them very dirty ones.
Card. Throw to the devil
    Thy melancholy. The fire burns well;
    What need we keep a stirring of 't, and make
    A greater smother? Thou wilt kill Antonio?
Bos. Yes.
Card. Take up that body.

Bos. I think I shall
Shortly grow the common bier for churchyards.

Card. I will allow thee some dozen of attendants
To aid thee in the murder.

Bos. O, by no means. Physicians that apply horse-
leeches to any rank swelling use to cut off their tails,
that the blood may run through them the faster: let
me have no train when I go to shed blood, lest it
make me have a greater when I ride to the gallows.

Card. Come to me after midnight, to help to remove
That body to her own lodging: I 'll give out
She died o' the plague; 'twill breed the less inquiry
After her death.

Bos. Where 's Castruccio her husband?

Card. He 's rode to Naples, to take possession
Of Antonio's citadel.

Bos. Believe me, you have done a very happy turn.

Card. Fail not to come: there is the master-key
Of our lodgings; and by that you may conceive
What trust I plant in you.

Bos. You shall find me ready.   [*Exit Cardinal.*
O poor Antonio, though nothing be so needful
To thy estate as pity, yet I find
Nothing so dangerous! I must look to my footing:
In such slippery ice-pavements men had need
To be frost-nailed well, they may break their necks
else;
The precedent 's here afore me. How this man
Bears up in blood! seems fearless! Why, 'tis well:
Security some men call the suburbs of hell,
Only a dead wall between. Well, good Antonio,
I 'll seek thee out; and all my care shall be
To put thee into safety from the reach
Of these most cruel biters that have got
Some of thy blood already. It may be,
I 'll join with thee in a most just revenge:

The weakest arm is strong enough that strikes
With the sword of justice. Still methinks the duchess
Haunts me: there, there! – 'Tis nothing but my melan-
    choly.
O Penitence, let me truly taste thy cup,
That throws men down only to raise them up! [*Exit.*

———

ACT V, SCENE 3

Enter ANTONIO *and* DELIO

Delio. Yond 's the cardinal's window. This fortification
    Grew from the ruins of an ancient abbey;
    And to yond side o' the river lies a wall,
    Piece of a cloister, which in my opinion
    Gives the best echo that you ever heard,
    So hollow and so dismal, and withal
    So plain in the distinction of our words,
    That many have supposed it is a spirit
    That answers.
Ant. I do love these ancient ruins.
    We never tread upon them but we set
    Our foot upon some reverend history:
    And, questionless, here in this open court,
    Which now lies naked to the injuries
    Of stormy weather, some men lie interred
    Loved the church so well, and gave so largely to 't,
    They thought it should have canopied their bones
    Till doomsday; but all things have their end:
    Churches and cities, which have diseases like to men,
    Must have like death that we have.
Echo. Like death that we have.
Delio. Now the echo hath caught you.
Ant. It groaned, methought, and gave
    A very deadly accent.

Echo. Deadly accent.

Delio. I told you 'twas a pretty one: you may make it
  A huntsman, or a falconer, a musician,
  Or a thing of sorrow.

Echo. *A thing of sorrow.*

Ant. Ay, sure, that suits it best.

Echo. *That suits it best.*

Ant. 'Tis very like my wife's voice.

Echo. *Ay, wife's voice.*

Delio. Come, let us walk farther from 't.
  I would not have you go to the cardinal's to-night:
  Do not.

Echo. *Do not.*

Delio. Wisdom doth not more moderate wasting sorrow
  Than time: take time for 't; be mindful of thy safety.

Echo. *Be mindful of thy safety.*

Ant. Necessity compels me:
  Make scrutiny throughout the passages
  Of your own life, you 'll find it impossible
  To fly your fate.

Echo. *O, fly your fate!*

Delio. Hark! the dead stones seem to have pity on you,
  And give you good counsel.

Ant. Echo, I will not talk with thee,
  For thou art a dead thing.

Echo. *Thou art a dead thing.*

Ant. My duchess is asleep now,
  And her little ones, I hope, sweetly: O heaven,
  Shall I never see her more?

Echo. *Never see her more.*

Ant. I marked not one repetition of the echo
  But that; and on the sudden a clear light
  Presented me a face folded in sorrow.

Delio. Your fancy merely.

Ant. Come, I 'll be out of this ague,
  For to live thus is not indeed to live;

It is a mockery and abuse of life:
I will not henceforth save myself by halves;
Lose all, or nothing.
Delio. Your own virtue save you!
I 'll fetch your eldest son, and second you:
It may be that the sight of his own blood
Spread in so sweet a figure may beget
The more compassion. However, fare you well.
Though in our miseries Fortune have a part,
Yet in our noble sufferings she hath none:
Contempt of pain, that we may call our own. [*Exeunt.*

———

ACT V, SCENE 4

Enter CARDINAL, PESCARA, MALATESTE, RODERIGO, *and* GRISOLAN

Card. You shall not watch to-night by the sick prince;
His grace is very well recovered.
Mal. Good my lord, suffer us.
Card. O, by no means;
The noise, and change of object in his eye,
Doth more distract him: I pray, all to bed;
And though you hear him in his violent fit,
Do not rise, I entreat you.
Pes. So, sir; we shall not.
Card. Nay, I must have you promise
Upon your honours, for I was enjoined to 't
By himself; and he seemed to urge it sensibly.
Pes. Let our honours bind this trifle.
Card. Nor any of your followers.
Mal. Neither.
Card. It may be, to make trial of your promise,
When he 's asleep, myself will rise and feign

  Some of his mad tricks, and cry out for help,
  And feign myself in danger.
Mal. If your throat were cutting,
  I 'd not come at you, now I have protested against it.
Card. Why, I thank you.
Gris. 'Twas a foul storm to-night.
Rod. The Lord Ferdinand's chamber shook like an osier.
Mal. 'Twas nothing but pure kindness in the devil,
  To rock his own child. [*Exeunt all except the Cardinal.*
Card. The reason why I would not suffer these
  About my brother, is, because at midnight
  I may with better privacy convey
  Julia's body to her own lodging. O, my conscience!
  I would pray now; but the devil takes away my heart
  For having any confidence in prayer.
  About this hour I appointed Bosola
  To fetch the body: when he hath served my turn,
  He dies.   [*Exit.*

Enter BOSOLA

Bos. Ha! 'twas the cardinal's voice; I heard him name
  Bosola and my death. Listen: I hear one's footing.

Enter FERDINAND

Ferd. Strangling is a very quiet death.
Bos. [*aside*]. Nay, then, I see I must stand upon my guard.
Ferd. What say you to that? Whisper softly; do you agree
  to 't? So; it must be done i' the dark: the cardinal
  would not for a thousand pounds the doctor should
  see it.   [*Exit.*
Bos. My death is plotted; here 's the consequence of
  murder.
  We value not desert nor Christian breath,
  When we know black deeds must be cured with death.

Enter ANTONIO *and* SERVANT

Serv. Here stay, sir, and be confident, I pray:
   I 'll fetch you a dark lantern.   *[Exit.*
Ant. Could I take him at his prayers,
   There were hope of pardon.
Bos. Fall right, my sword! –   *[Stabs him.*
   I 'll not give thee so much leisure as to pray.
Ant. O, I am gone! Thou hast ended a long suit
   In a minute.
Bos. What art thou?
Ant. A most wretched thing,
   That only have thy benefit in death,
   To appear myself.

Re-enter SERVANT *with a lantern*

Serv. Where are you, sir?
Ant. Very near my home. – Bosola!
Serv. O, misfortune!
Bos. Smother thy pity, thou art dead else. – Antonio!
   The man I would have saved 'bove mine own life!
   We are merely the stars' tennis-balls, struck and bandied
   Which way please them. – O, good Antonio,
   I 'll whisper one thing in thy dying ear
   Shall make thy heart break quickly! thy fair duchess
   And two sweet children —
Ant. Their very names
   Kindle a little life in me.
Bos. Are murdered.
Ant. Some men have wished to die
   At the hearing of sad tidings; I am glad
   That I shall do 't in sadness: I would not now
   Wish my wounds balmed nor healed, for I have no use
   To put my life to. In all our quest of greatness,
   Like wanton boys, whose pastime is their care,
   We follow after bubbles blown in the air.
   Pleasure of life, what is 't? only the good hours
   Of an ague; merely a preparative to rest,

To endure vexation. I do not ask
The process of my death; only commend me
To Delio.

Bos. Break, heart!

Ant. And let my son fly the courts of princes.   [*Dies.*

Bos. Thou seem'st to have loved Antonio?

Serv. I brought him hither,
To have reconciled him to the cardinal.

Bos. I do not ask thee that.
Take him up, if thou tender thine own life,
And bear him where the lady Julia
Was wont to lodge. – O, my fate moves swift!
I have this cardinal in the forge already;
Now I 'll bring him to the hammer. O direful mis-
        prision!
I will not imitate things glorious,
No more than base; I 'll be mine own example. –
On, on! and look thou represent, for silence,
The thing thou bear'st.   [*Exeunt.*

———

ACT V, SCENE 5

Enter CARDINAL, *with a book*

Card. I am puzzled in a question about hell:
He says, in hell there 's one material fire,
And yet it shall not burn all men alike.
Lay him by. How tedious is a guilty conscience!
When I look into the fish-ponds in my garden,
Methinks I see a thing armed with a rake,
That seems to strike at me.

Enter BOSOLA *and* SERVANT *bearing Antonio's body*

                    Now, art thou come?
Thou look'st ghastly:

There sits in thy face some great determination
Mixed with some fear.

Bos. Thus it lightens into action;
I am come to kill thee.

Card. Ha! – Help! our guard!

Bos. Thou art deceived;
They are out of thy howling.

Card. Hold; and I will faithfully divide
Revenues with thee.

Bos. Thy prayers and proffers
Are both unseasonable.

Card. Raise the watch! We are betrayed!

Bos. I have confined your flight:
I 'll suffer your retreat to Julia's chamber,
But no farther.

Card. Help! we are betrayed!

Enter, above, PESCARA, MALATESTE, RODERIGO,
and GRISOLAN

Mal. Listen.

Card. My dukedom for rescue!

Rod. Fie upon his counterfeiting!

Mal. Why, 'tis not the cardinal.

Rod. Yes, yes, 'tis he:
But I 'll see him hanged ere I 'll go down to him.

Card. Here 's a plot upon me; I am assaulted! I am lost,
Unless some rescue!

Gris. He doth this pretty well;
But it will not serve to laugh me out of mine honour.

Card. The sword 's at my throat!

Rod. You would not bawl so loud then.

Mal. Come, come, let 's go
To bed: he told us thus much aforehand.

Pes. He wished you should not come at him; but, believe 't,
The accent of the voice sounds not in jest:

I 'll down to him, howsoever, and with engines
Force ope the doors.   [*Exit above.*
Rod. Let 's follow him aloof,—
And note how the cardinal will laugh at him.
        [*Exeunt, above, Malateste, Roderigo, and Grisolan.*
Bos. There 's for you first,
    'Cause you shall not unbarricade the door
    To let in rescue.   [*Kills the Servant.*
Card. What cause hast thou to pursue my life?
Bos. Look there.
Card. Antonio!
Bos. Slain by my hand unwittingly.
    Pray, and be sudden: when thou killedst thy sister,
    Thou took'st from Justice her most equal balance,
    And left her naught but her sword.
Card. O, mercy!
Bos. Now it seems thy greatness was only outward;
    For thou fall'st faster of thyself than calamity
    Can drive thee. I 'll not waste longer time; there!
                                [*Stabs him.*
Card. Thou hast hurt me.
Bos. Again!   [*Stabs him again.*
Card. Shall I die like a leveret,
    Without any resistance? – Help! help! help!
    I am slain!

Enter FERDINAND

Ferd. The alarum! give me a fresh horse;
    Rally the vaunt-guard, or the day is lost.
    Yield, yield! I give you the honour of arms,
    Shake my sword over you; will you yield?
Card. Help me; I am your brother!
Ferd. The devil!
    My brother fight upon the adverse party!
        [*He wounds the Cardinal, and, in the scuffle, gives Bosola
                                his death-wound.*

There flies your ransom.

Card. O justice!
I suffer now for what hath former bin:
Sorrow is held the eldest child of sin.

Ferd. Now you 're brave fellows. Caesar's fortune was
harder than Pompey's; Caesar died in the arms of
prosperity, Pompey at the feet of disgrace. You both
died in the field. The pain 's nothing: pain many
times is taken away with the apprehension of greater,
as the toothache with the sight of a barber that
comes to pull it out; there 's philosophy for you.

Bos. Now my revenge is perfect. – Sink, thou main cause
[*Kills Ferdinand.*
Of my undoing! The last part of my life
Hath done me best service.

Ferd. Give me some wet hay; I am broken-winded.
I do account this world but a dog-kennel:
I will vault credit and affect high pleasures
Beyond death.

Bos. He seems to come to himself,
Now he 's so near the bottom.

Ferd. My sister, O my sister! there 's the cause on 't.
Whether we fall by ambition, blood, or lust,
Like diamonds, we are cut with our own dust. [*Dies.*

Card. Thou hast thy payment too.

Bos. Yes, I hold my weary soul in my teeth;
'Tis ready to part from me. I do glory
That thou, which stoodest like a huge pyramid
Begun upon a large and ample base,
Shalt end in a little point, a kind of nothing.

Enter, below, PESCARA, MALATESTE, RODERIGO,
and GRISOLAN

Pes. How now, my lord!
Mal. O, sad disaster!
Rod. How comes this?

Bos. Revenge for the Duchess of Malfy murdered
   By the Arragonian brethren; for Antonio
   Slain by this hand; for lustful Julia
   Poisoned by this man; and lastly for myself,
   That was an actor in the main of all
   Much 'gainst mine own good nature, yet i' the end
   Neglected.

Pes. How now, my lord!

Card. Look to my brother:
   He gave us these large wounds, as we were struggling
   Here i' the rushes. And now, I pray, let me
   Be laid by and never thought of.   [*Dies.*

Pes. How fatally, it seems, he did withstand
   His own rescue!

Mal. Thou wretched thing of blood,
   How came Antonio by his death?

Bos. In a mist; I know not how:
   Such a mistake as I have often seen
   In a play. O, I am gone!
   We are only like dead walls or vaulted graves,
   That, ruined, yield no echo. Fare you well.
   It may be pain, but no harm, to me to die
   In so good a quarrel. O, this gloomy world!
   In what a shadow, or deep pit of darkness,
   Doth womanish and fearful mankind live!
   Let worthy minds ne'er stagger in distrust
   To suffer death or shame for what is just:
   Mine is another voyage.   [*Dies.*

Pes. The noble Delio, as I came to the palace,
   Told me of Antonio's being here, and showed me
   A pretty gentleman, his son and heir.

Enter DELIO *and* ANTONIO'S SON

Mal. O, sir, you come too late!

Delio. I heard so, and
   Was armed for 't, ere I came. Let us make noble use

Of this great ruin; and join all our force
To establish this young hopeful gentleman
In 's mother's right. These wretched eminent things
Leave no more fame behind 'em, than should one
Fall in a frost, and leave his print in snow;
As soon as the sun shines, it ever melts,
Both form and matter. I have ever thought
Nature doth nothing so great for great men
As when she 's pleased to make them lords of truth:
Integrity of life is fame's best friend,
Which nobly, beyond death, shall crown the end.

[*Exeunt.*

JOHN DRYDEN

—

ALL FOR LOVE
or, The World well Lost

PERSONS REPRESENTED

MARK ANTONY
VENTIDIUS, *his general*
DOLABELLA, *his friend*
ALEXAS, *the Queen's eunuch*
SERAPION, *Priest of Isis*
MYRIS, *another priest*
SERVANTS *to* ANTONY

CLEOPATRA, *Queen of Egypt*
OCTAVIA, *Antony's wife*
CHARMION, ⎫
IRAS, ⎬ *Cleopatra's maids*
ANTONY'S TWO LITTLE DAUGHTERS

Scene — Alexandria

ALL FOR LOVE

OR, THE WORLD WELL LOST

PROLOGUE

What flocks of critics hover here today,
As vultures wait on armies for their prey,
All gaping for the carcass of a play!
With croaking notes they bode some dire event,
And follow dying poets by the scent.
Ours gives himself for gone; y' have watched your time!
He fights this day unarmed – without his rhyme; –
And brings a tale which often has been told,
As sad as Dido's; and almost as old.
His hero, whom you wits his bully call,
Bates of his mettle, and scarce rants at all:
He's somewhat lewd; but a well-meaning mind;
Weeps much; fights little; but is wondrous kind.
In short, a pattern, and companion fit,
For all the keeping Tonies of the pit.
I could name more: a wife, and mistress too;
Both (to be plain) too good for most of you:
The wife well-natured, and the mistress true.
Now, poets, if your fame has been his care,
Allow him all the candour you can spare.
A brave man scorns to quarrel once a day;
Like Hectors in at every petty fray.
Let those find fault whose wit's so very small
They've need to show that they can think at all:
Errors like straws upon the surface flow;
He who would search for pearls must dive below.
Fops may have leave to level all they can,
As pigmies would be glad to lop a man.
Half-wits are fleas; so little and so light,

We scarce could know they live, but that they bite.
But, as the rich, when tired with daily feasts,
For change, become their next poor tenant's guests;
Drink hearty draughts of ale from plain brown bowls,
And snatch the homely rasher from the coals:
So you, retiring from much better cheer,
For once, may venture to do penance here.
And since that plenteous autumn now is past,
Whose grapes and peaches have indulged your taste,
Take in good part, from our poor poet's board,
Such rivelled fruits as winter can afford.

—

ACT I, SCENE 1

The Temple of Isis

Enter SERAPION, MYRIS, Priests of Isis

Serap. Portents and prodigies are grown so frequent,
That they have lost their name. Our fruitful Nile
Flowed ere the wonted season, with a torrent
So unexpected, and so wondrous fierce,
That the wild deluge overtook the haste
Ev'n of the hinds that watched it: men and beasts
Were borne above the tops of trees, that grew
On th' utmost margin of the water-mark.
Then, with so swift an ebb the flood drove backward,
It slipt from underneath the scaly herd:
Here monstrous phocae panted on the shore;
Forsaken dolphins there, with their broad tails,
Lay lashing the departing waves: hard by 'em,
Sea-horses flound'ring in the slimy mud,
Tossed up their heads, and dashed the ooze about 'em.

Enter ALEXAS behind them

Myr. Avert these omens, heav'n!

Serap. Last night, between the hours of twelve and one,
  In a lone aisle o' th' temple while I walked,
  A whirlwind rose, that, with a violent blast,
  Shook all the dome: the doors around me clapt;
  The iron wicket, that defends the vault,
  Where the long race of Ptolemies is laid,
  Burst open, and disclosed the mighty dead.
  From out each monument, in order placed,
  An armed ghost start up: the boy-king last
  Reared his inglorious head. A peal of groans
  Then followed, and a lamentable voice
  Cried, 'Egypt is no more!' My blood ran back,
  My shaking knees against each other knocked;
  On the cold pavement down I fell entranced,
  And so unfinished left the horrid scene.

Alex. And dreamed you this? or did invent the story,
                              [*Showing himself.*
  To frighten our Egyptian boys withal,
  And train 'em up betimes in fear of priesthood?

Serap. My lord, I saw you not,
  Nor meant my words should reach your ears; but
    what
  I uttered was most true.

Alex.   A foolish dream,
  Bred from the fumes of indigested feasts
  And holy luxury.

Serap.   I know my duty:
  This goes no farther.

Alex.   'Tis not fit it should;
  Nor would the times now bear it, were it true.
  All southern, from yon hills, the Roman camp
  Hangs o'er us black and threat'ning, like a storm
  Just breaking on our heads.

Serap. Our faint Egyptians pray for Antony;
  But in their servile hearts they own Octavius.

F.T.—10

Myr. Why then does Antony dream out his hours,
   And tempts not fortune for a noble day
   Which might redeem what Actium lost?
Alex. He thinks 'tis past recovery.
Serap.   Yet the foe
   Seems not to press the siege.
Alex.   O, there's the wonder.
   Maecenas and Agrippa, who can most
   With Caesar, are his foes. His wife Octavia,
   Driv'n from his house, solicits her revenge;
   And Dolabella, who was once his friend,
   Upon some private grudge now seeks his ruin:
   Yet still war seems on either side to sleep.
Serap. 'Tis strange that Antony, for some days past,
   Has not beheld the face of Cleopatra;
   But here, in Isis' temple, lives retired,
   And makes his heart a prey to black despair.
Alex. 'Tis true; and we much fear he hopes by absence
   To cure his mind of love.
Serap.   If he be vanquished,
   Or make his peace, Egypt is doomed to be
   A Roman province; and our plenteous harvests
   Must then redeem the scarceness of their soil.
   While Antony stood firm, our Alexandria
   Rivalled proud Rome (dominion's other seat),
   And Fortune striding, like a vast Colossus,
   Could fix an equal foot of empire here.
Alex. Had I my wish, these tyrants of all nature
   Who lord it o'er mankind, should perish – perish,
   Each by the other's sword; but, since our will
   Is lamely followed by our pow'r, we must
   Depend on one, with him to rise or fall.
Serap. How stands the queen affected?
Alex.   O, she dotes,
   She dotes, Serapion, on this vanquished man,
   And winds herself about his mighty ruins;

Whom would she yet forsake, yet yield him up,
This hunted prey, to his pursuers' hands,
She might preserve us all; but 'tis in vain –
This changes my designs, this blasts my counsels,
And makes me use all means to keep him here,
Whom I could wish divided from her arms
Far as the earth's deep centre. Well, you know
The state of things; no more of your ill omens
And black prognostics; labour to confirm
The people's hearts.

Enter VENTIDIUS, *talking aside with a Gentleman of*
ANTONY'S

Serap.   These Romans will o'erhear us.
  But who's that stranger? By his warlike port,
  His fierce demeanour, and erected look,
  He's of no vulgar note.
Alex.   O, 'tis Ventidius,
  Our emp'ror's great lieutenant in the East,
  Who first showed Rome that Parthia could be con-
  quered.
  When Antony returned from Syria last,
  He left this man to guard the Roman frontiers.
Serap. You seem to know him well.
Alex. Too well. I saw him in Cilicia first,
  When Cleopatra there met Antony:
  A mortal foe he was to us, and Egypt.
  But, let me witness to the worth I hate,
  A braver Roman never drew a sword;
  Firm to his prince, but as a friend, not slave.
  He ne'er was of his pleasures; but presides
  O'er all his cooler hours, and morning counsels:
  In short, the plainness, fierceness, rugged virtue
  Of an old true-stamped Roman lives in him.
  His coming bodes I know not what of ill
  To our affairs. Withdraw, to mark him better;

And I'll acquaint you why I sought you here,
And what's our present work.

> [*They withdraw to a corner of the stage; and Ventidius,*
> *with the other, comes forwards to the front.*

Vent.   Not see him, say you?
I say, I must, and will.

Gent.   He has commanded,
On pain of death, none should approach his presence.

Vent. I bring him news will raise his drooping spirits,
Give him new life.

Gent.   He sees not Cleopatra.

Vent. Would he had never seen her!

Gent. He eats not, drinks not, sleeps not, has no use
Of anything, but thought; or, if he talks,
'Tis to himself, and then 'tis perfect raving:
Then he defies the world, and bids it pass;
Sometimes he gnaws his lip, and curses loud
The boy Octavius; then he draws his mouth
Into a scornful smile, and cries, 'Take all,
The world's not worth my care.'

Vent.   Just, just his nature.
Virtue's his path; but sometimes 'tis too narrow
For his vast soul; and then he starts out wide,
And bounds into a vice that bears him far
From his first course, and plunges him in ills:
But, when his danger makes him find his fault,
Quick to observe, and full of sharp remorse,
He censures eagerly his own misdeeds,
Judging himself with malice to himself,
And not forgiving what as man he did,
Because his other parts are more than man.
He must not thus be lost.

ALEXAS *and the Priests come forward*

Alex. You have your full instructions, now advance;
Proclaim your orders loudly.

Serap. Romans, Egyptians, hear the queen's command.
  Thus Cleopatra bids: 'Let labour cease,
  To pomp and triumphs give this happy day,
  That gave the world a lord: 'tis Antony's.'
  Live, Antony; and Cleopatra live!
  Be this the general voice sent up to heav'n,
  And every public place repeat this echo.
Vent. Fine pageantry!   [*Aside.*
Serap.   Set out before your doors
  The images of all your sleeping fathers,
  With laurels crowned; with laurels wreathe your posts,
  And strow with flow'rs the pavement; let the priests
  Do present sacrifice; pour out the wine,
  And call the gods to join with you in gladness.
Vent. Curse on the tongue that bids this general joy!
  Can they be friends of Antony, who revel
  When Antony's in danger? Hide, for shame,
  You Romans, your great grandsires' images,
  For fear their souls should animate their marbles,
  To blush at their degenerate progeny.
Alex. A love which knows no bounds to Antony,
  Would mark the day with honours, when all heaven
  Laboured for him, when each propitious star
  Stood wakeful in his orb, to watch that hour,
  And shed his better influence. Her own birthday
  Our queen neglected, like a vulgar fate
  That passed obscurely by.
Vent.   Would it had slept,
  Divided far from his; till some remote
  And future age had called it out, to ruin
  Some other prince, not him.
Alex.   Your emperor,
  Though grown unkind, would be more gentle than
  T' upbraid my queen for loving him too well.
Vent. Does the mute sacrifice upbraid the priest?
  He knows him not his executioner.

O, she has decked his ruin with her love,
Led him in golden bands to gaudy slaughter,
And made perdition pleasing; she has left him
The blank of what he was;
I tell thee, eunuch, she has quite unmanned him.
Can any Roman see, and know him now,
Thus altered from the lord of half mankind,
Unbent, unsinewed, made a woman's toy,
Shrunk from the vast extent of all his honours,
And cramped within a corner of the world?
O Antony!
Thou bravest soldier, and thou best of friends!
Bounteous as nature; next to nature's God!
Couldst thou but make new worlds, so wouldst thou
    give 'em,
As bounty were thy being: rough in battle,
As the first Romans when they went to war;
Yet, after victory, more pitiful
Than all their praying virgins left at home!

Alex. Would you could add, to those more shining virtues,
His truth to her who loves him.

Vent.   Would I could not!
But wherefore waste I precious hours with thee?
Thou art her darling mischief, her chief engine,
Antony's other fate. Go, tell thy queen,
Ventidius is arrived, to end her charms.
Let your Egyptian timbrels play alone;
Nor mix effeminate sounds with Roman trumpets.
You dare not fight for Antony; go pray,
And keep your cowards' holiday in temples.
                          [*Exeunt Alexas, Serapion.*

Enter a Gentleman of M. ANTONY

2nd Gent. The emperor approaches, and commands,
On pain of death, that none presume to stay.
1st Gent. I dare not disobey him.   [*Going out with the other.*

Vent.   Well, I dare.
　But I'll observe him first unseen, and find
　Which way his humour drives: the rest I'll venture.
                                    [*Withdraws*.

Enter ANTONY, *walking with a disturbed motion before
　　　　　　　he speaks*

Ant. They tell me 'tis my birthday, and I'll keep it
　With double pomp of sadness.
　'Tis what the day deserves, which gave me breath.
　Why was I raised the meteor of the world,
　Hung in the skies, and blazing as I travelled,
　Till all my fires were spent; and then cast downward
　To be trod out by Caesar?
Vent. [*aside*].   On my soul,
　'Tis mournful, wondrous mournful!
Ant.   Count thy gains.
　Now, Antony, wouldst thou be born for this?
　Glutton of fortune, thy devouring youth
　Has starved thy wanting age.
Vent. [*aside*].   How sorrow shakes him!
　So, now the tempest tears him up by th' roots,
　And on the ground extends the noble ruin.
Ant. [*having thrown himself down*]. Lie there, thou shadow
　　of an emperor;
　The place thou pressest on thy mother earth
　Is all thy empire now: now it contains thee;
　Some few days hence, and then 'twill be too large,
　When thou'rt contracted in thy narrow urn,
　Shrunk to a few cold ashes; then Octavia
　(For Cleopatra will not live to see it),
　Octavia then will have thee all her own,
　And bear thee in her widowed hand to Caesar;
　Caesar will weep, the crocodile will weep,
　To see his rival of the universe
　Lie still and peaceful there. I'll think no more on't.

Give me some music; look that it be sad:
I'll soothe my melancholy, till I swell,
And burst myself with sighing. –   [*Soft music.*
'Tis somewhat to my humour. Stay, I fancy
I'm now turned wild, a commoner of nature,
Of all forsaken, and forsaking all;
Live in a shady forest's sylvan scene;
Stretched at my length beneath some blasted oak,
I lean my head upon the mossy bark,
And look just of a piece as I grew from it:
My uncombed locks, matted like mistletoe,
Hang o'er my hoary face; a murm'ring brook
Runs at my foot.

Vent.   Methinks I fancy
Myself there too.

Ant.   The herd come jumping by me,
And, fearless, quench their thirst, while I look on,
And take me for their fellow-citizen.
More of this image, more; it lulls my thoughts.

[*Soft music again.*

Vent. I must disturb him; I can hold no longer.

[*Stands before him.*

Ant. [*starting up*]. Art thou Ventidius?

Vent.   Are you Antony?
I'm liker what I was, than you to him
I left you last.

Ant.   I'm angry.

Vent.   So am I.

Ant. I would be private: leave me.

Vent.   Sir, I love you,
And therefore will not leave you.

Ant.   Will not leave me!
Where have you learnt that answer? Who am I?

Vent. My emperor; the man I love next heaven;
If I said more, I think 'twere scarce a sin;
Y'are all that's good, and good-like.

Ant.   All that's wretched.
  You will not leave me then?

Vent.   'Twas too presuming
  To say I would not; but I dare not leave you:
  And, 'tis unkind in you to chide me hence
  So soon, when I so far have come to see you.

Ant. Now thou hast seen me, art thou satisfied?
  For, if a friend, thou hast beheld enough;
  And, if a foe, too much.

Vent. Look, emperor, this is no common dew. [*Weeping.*
  I have not wept this forty year; but now
  My mother comes afresh into my eyes;
  I cannot help her softness.

Ant. By heav'n, he weeps, poor good old man, he weeps!
  The big round drops course one another down
  The furrows of his cheeks. Stop 'em, Ventidius,
  Or I shall blush to death: they set my shame,
  That caused 'em, full before me.

Vent.   I'll do my best.

Ant. Sure there's contagion in the tears of friends:
  See, I have caught it too. Believe me, 'tis not
  For my own griefs, but thine. – Nay, father.

Vent.   Emperor.

Ant. Emperor! Why, that's the style of victory;
  The conqu'ring soldier, red with unfelt wounds,
  Salutes his general so: but never more
  Shall that sound reach my ears.

Vent.   I warrant you.

Ant. Actium, Actium! O! —

Vent.   It sits too near you.

Ant. Here, here it lies; a lump of lead by day,
  And, in my short, distracted, nightly slumbers,
  The hag that rides my dreams. —

Vent. Out with it; give it vent.

Ant.   Urge not my shame.
  I lost a battle.

Vent.   So has Julius done.

Ant. Thou favour'st me, and speak'st not half thou
     think'st;

  For Julius fought it out, and lost it fairly:

  But Antony —

Vent. ○   Nay, stop not.

Ant.   Antony,

  (Well, thou wilt have it) like a coward, fled,

  Fled while his soldiers fought; fled first, Ventidius.

  Thou long'st to curse me, and I give thee leave.

  I know thou cam'st prepared to rail.

Vent.   I did.

Ant. I'll help thee. – I have been a man, Ventidius –

Vent. Yes, and a brave one; but —

Ant.   I know thy meaning.

  But I have lost my reason, have disgraced

  The name of soldier, with inglorious ease.

  In the full vintage of my flowing honours,

  Sat still, and saw it pressed by other hands.

  Fortune came smiling to my youth, and wooed it,

  And purple greatness met my ripened years.

  When first I came to empire, I was borne

  On tides of people, crowding to my triumphs,

  The wish of nations; and the willing world

  Received me as its pledge of future peace;

  I was so great, so happy, so beloved,

  Fate could not ruin me; till I took pains,

  And worked against my fortune, chid her from me,

  And turned her loose; yet still she came again.

  My careless days, and my luxurious nights,

  At length have wearied her, and now she's gone,

  Gone, gone, divorced for ever. Help me, soldier,

  To curse this madman, this industrious fool,

  Who laboured to be wretched: pr'ythee, curse me.

Vent. No.

Ant.   Why?

Vent.   You are too sensible already
  Of what y'have done, too conscious of your failings;
  And, like a scorpion, whipped by others first
  To fury, sting yourself in mad revenge.
  I would bring balm, and pour it in your wounds,
  Cure your distempered mind, and heal your fortunes.
Ant. I know thou would'st.
Vent.   I will.
Ant.   Ha, ha, ha, ha!
Vent. You laugh.
Ant.   I do, to see officious love
  Give cordials to the dead.
Vent.   You would be lost, then?
Ant. I am.
Vent.   I say you are not. Try your fortune.
Ant. I have, to th' utmost. Dost thou think me desperate,
  Without just cause? No, when I found all lost
  Beyond repair, I hid me from the world,
  And learned to scorn it here; which now I do
  So heartily, I think it is not worth
  The cost of keeping.
Vent.   Caesar thinks not so;
  He'll thank you for the gift he could not take.
  You would be killed like Tully, would you? Do,
  Hold out your throat to Caesar, and die tamely.
Ant. No, I can kill myself; and so resolve.
Vent. I can die with you too, when time shall serve;
  But fortune calls upon us now to live,
  To fight, to conquer.
Ant.   Sure thou dream'st, Ventidius.
Vent. No; 'tis you dream; you sleep away your hours
  In desperate sloth, miscalled philosophy.
  Up, up, for honour's sake; twelve legions wait you,
  And long to call you chief; by painful journeys
  I led 'em, patient both of heat and hunger,
  Down from the Parthian marches to the Nile.

'Twill do you good to see their sunburnt faces,
Their scarred cheeks, and chopped hands; there's
   virtue in 'em.
They'll sell those mangled limbs at dearer rates
Than yon trim bands can buy.

Ant.   Where left you them?

Vent. I said in Lower Syria.

Ant.   Bring 'em hither;
There may be life in these.   ,

Vent.   They will not come.

Ant. Why didst thou mock my hopes with promised
   aids,
  To double my despair? They're mutinous.

Vent. Most firm and loyal.

Ant.   Yet they will not march
To succour me. O trifler!

Vent.   They petition '
You would make haste to head 'em.

Ant.   I'm besieged.

Vent. There's but one way shut up: how came I hither?

Ant. I will not stir.

Vent.   They would perhaps desire
A better reason.

Ant.   I have never used
My soldiers to demand a reason of
My actions. Why did they refuse to march?

Vent. They said they would not fight for Cleopatra.

Ant. What was't they said?

Vent. They said they would not fight for Cleopatra.
Why should they fight indeed, to make her conquer,
And make you more a slave? to gain you kingdoms,
Which, for a kiss, at your next midnight feast,
You'll sell to her? Then she new-names her jewels,
And calls this diamond such or such a tax;
Each pendant in her ear shall be a province.

Ant. Ventidius, I allow your tongue free license

On all my other faults; but, on your life,
No word of Cleopatra: she deserves
More worlds than I can lose.

Vent.   Behold, you pow'rs,
To whom you have intrusted humankind;
See Europe, Afric, Asia, put in balance,
And all weighed down by one light, worthless woman!
I think the gods are Antonies, and give,
Like prodigals, this nether world away
To none but wasteful hands.

Ant.   You grow presumptuous.

Vent. I take the privilege of plain love to speak.

Ant. Plain love! plain arrogance, plain insolence!
Thy men are cowards; thou, an envious traitor,
Who, under seeming honesty, hast vented
The burden of thy rank, o'erflowing gall.
O, that thou wert my equal, great in arms
As the first Caesar was, that I might kill thee
Without a stain to honour!

Vent.   You may kill me;
You have done more already – called me traitor.

Ant. Art thou not one?

Vent.   For showing you yourself,
Which none else durst have done? But had I been
That name, which I disdain to speak again,
I needed not have sought your abject fortunes,
Come to partake your fate, to die with you.
What hindered me t' have led my conqu'ring eagles
To fill Octavius' bands? I could have been
A traitor then, a glorious, happy traitor,
And not have been so called.

Ant.   Forgive me, soldier:
I've been too passionate.

Vent.   You thought me false;
Thought my old age betrayed you. Kill me, sir;
Pray, kill me; yet you need not, your unkindness

Has left your sword no work.

Ant.   I did not think so;
I said it in my rage: pr'ythee, forgive me.
Why didst thou tempt my anger, by discovery
Of what I would not hear?

Vent.   No prince but you
Could merit that sincerity I used,
Nor durst another man have ventured it;
But you, ere love misled your wand'ring eyes,
Were sure the chief and best of human race,
Framed in the very pride and boast of nature;
So perfect, that the gods, who formed you, wondered
At their own skill, and cried, 'A lucky hit
Has mended our design.' Their envy hindered,
Else you had been immortal, and a pattern,
When heav'n would work for ostentation sake,
To copy out again.

Ant.   But Cleopatra –
Go on; for I can bear it now.

Vent.   No more.

Ant. Thou dar'st not trust my passion, but thou may'st;
Thou only lov'st, the rest have flattered me.

Vent. Heav'n's blessing on your heart for that kind word!
May I believe you love me? Speak again.

Ant. Indeed I do. Speak this, and this, and this.

                                        [*Hugging him.*
Thy praises were unjust; but I'll deserve 'em.
And yet mend all. Do with me what thou wilt;
Lead me to victory, thou know'st the way.

Vent. And, will you leave this —

Ant.   Pr'ythee, do not curse her,
And I will leave her; though, heav'n knows, I love
Beyond life, conquest, empire, all but honour;
But I will leave her.

Vent.   That's my royal master;
And, shall we fight?

Ant.   I warrant thee, old soldier,
Thou shalt behold me once again in iron;
And at the head of our old troops, that beat
The Parthians, cry aloud, 'Come, follow me!'
Vent. O, now I hear my emperór! In that word
Octavius fell. Gods, let me see that day,
And, if I have ten years behind, take all;
I'll thank you for the exchange.
Ant.   O Cleopatra!
Vent. Again?
Ant.   I've done: in that last sigh, she went.
Caesar shall know what 'tis to force a lover
From all he holds most dear.
Vent.   Methinks you breathe
Another soul: your looks are more divine;
You speak a hero, and you move a god.
Ant. O, thou hast fired me; my soul's up in arms,
And mans each part about me. Once again,
That noble eagerness of fight has seized me;
That eagerness with which I darted upward
To Cassius' camp; in vain the steepy hill
Opposed my way; in vain a war of spears
Sung round my head, and planted on my shield;
I won the trenches, while my foremost men
Lagged on the plain below.
Vent.   Ye gods, ye gods,
For such another hour!
Ant.   Come on, my soldier!
Our hearts and arms are still the same: I long
Once more to meet our foes, that thou and I,
Like Time and Death, marching before our troops,
May taste fate to them; mow them out a passage,
And, entering where the foremost squadrons yield,
Begin the noble harvest of the field.   [*Exeunt.*

Enter CLEOPATRA, IRAS, *and* ALEXAS

Cleo. What shall I do, or whither shall I turn?
  Ventidius has o'ercome, and he will go.
Alex. He goes to fight for you.
Cleo. Then he would see me, ere he went to fight.
  Flatter me not: if once he goes, he's lost,
  And all my hopes destroyed.
Alex.   Does this weak passion
  Become a mighty queen?
Cleo.   I am no queen:
  Is this to be a queen, to be besieged
  By yon insulting Roman, and to wait
  Each hour the victor's chain? These ills are small:
  For Antony is lost, and I can mourn
  For nothing else but him. Now come, Octavius,
  I have no more to lose; prepare thy bands;
  I'm fit to be a captive: Antony
  Has taught my mind the fortune of a slave.
Iras. Call reason to assist you.
Cleo.   I have none,
  And none would have: my love's a noble madness,
  Which shows the cause deserved it. Moderate sorrow
  Fits vulgar love, and for a vulgar man:
  But I have loved with such transcendent passion,
  I soared, at first, quite out of reason's view,
  And now am lost above it. No, I'm proud
  'Tis thus; would Antony could see me now!
  Think you he would not sigh? Though he must leave
    me,
  Sure he would sigh; for he is noble-natured,
  And bears a tender heart; I know him well.
  Ah, no, I know him not; I knew him once,
  But now 'tis past.

Iras.   Let it be past with you:
  Forget him, madam.
Cleo.   Never, never, Iras.
  He once was mine; and once, though now 'tis gone,
  Leaves a faint image of possession still.
Alex. Think him unconstant, cruel, and ungrateful.
Cleo. I cannot: if I could, those thoughts were vain.
  Faithless, ungrateful, cruel, though he be,
  I still must love him.

Enter CHARMION

         Now, what news, my Charmion?
  Will he be kind? and will he not forsake me?
  Am I to live, or die? – nay, do I live?
  Or am I dead? for when he gave his answer,
  Fate took the word, and then I lived or died.
Char. I found him, madam —
Cleo.   A long speech preparing?
  If thou bring'st comfort, haste, and give it me,
  For never was more need.
Iras.   I know he loves you.
Cleo. Had he been kind, her eyes had told me so,
  Before her tongue could speak it: now she studies,
  To soften what he said; but give me death,
  Just as he sent it, Charmion, undisguised,
  And in the words he spoke.
Char.   I found him, then,
  Encompassed round, I think, with iron statues;
  So mute, so motionless his soldiers stood,
  While awfully he cast his eyes about,
  And every leader's hopes or fears surveyed:
  Methought he looked resolved, and yet not pleased.
  When he beheld me struggling in the crowd,
  He blushed, and bade make way.
Alex.   There's comfort yet.
Char. Ventidius fixed his eyes upon my passage

Severely, as he meant to frown me back,
And sullenly gave place: I told my message,
Just as you gave it, broken and disordered;
I numbered in it all your sighs and tears,
And while I moved your pitiful request,
That you but only begged a last farewell,
He fetched an inward groan, and every time
I named you, sighed, as if his heart were breaking,
But shunned my eyes, and guiltily looked down:
He seemed not now that awful Antony
Who shook an armed assembly with his nod;
But, making show as he would rub his eyes,
Disguised and blotted out a falling tear.

Cleo. Did he then weep? And was I worth a tear?
If what thou hast to say be not as pleasing,
Tell me no more, but let me die contented.

Char. He bid me say, he knew himself so well,
He could deny you nothing, if he saw you;
And therefore —

Cleo. Thou wouldst say, he would not see me?

Char. And therefore begged you not to use a power,
Which he could ill resist; yet he should ever
Respect you as he ought.

Cleo. Is that a word
For Antony to use to Cleopatra?
O that faint word, *respect!* how I disdain it!
Disdain myself, for loving after it!
He should have kept that word for cold Octavia.
Respect is for a wife: am I that thing,
That dull, insipid lump, without desires,
And without power to give them?

Alex. You misjudge;
You see through love, and that deludes your sight,
As, what is straight, seems crooked through the water;
But I, who bear my reason undisturbed,
Can see this Antony, this dreaded man,

A fearful slave, who fain would run away,
And shuns his master's eyes: if you pursue him,
My life on't, he still drags a chain along,
That needs must clog his flight.

Cleo.   Could I believe thee! –

Alex. By every circumstance I know he loves.
True, he's hard pressed, by interest and by honour;
Yet he but doubts, and parleys, and casts out
Many a long look for succour.

Cleo.   He sends word,
He fears to see my face.

Alex.   And would you more?
He shows his weakness who declines the combat,
And you must urge your fortune. Could he speak
More plainly? To my ears, the message sounds –
'Come to my rescue, Cleopatra, come;
Come, free me from Ventidius; from my tyrant:
See me, and give me a pretence to leave him!' –
I hear his trumpets. This way he must pass.
Please you, retire a while; I'll work him first,
That he may bend more easy.

Cleo.   You shall rule me;
But all, I fear, in vain.   [*Exit with Charmion and Iras.*

Alex.   I fear so too;
Though I concealed my thoughts, to make her bold;
But 'tis our utmost means, and fate befriend it!
                                        [*Withdraws.*

Enter Lictors with Fasces, one bearing the Eagle: then enter
ANTONY *with* VENTIDIUS, *followed by other Commanders*

Ant. Octavius is the minion of blind chance,
But holds from virtue nothing.

Vent.   Has he courage?

Ant. But just enough to season him from coward.
O, 'tis the coldest youth upon a charge,
The most deliberate fighter! If he ventures

  (As in Illyria once they say he did,
  To storm a town), 'tis when he cannot choose;
  When all the world have fixed their eyes upon him;
  And then he lives on that for seven years after;
  But, at a close revenge he never fails.
Vent. I heard you challenged him.
Ant.   I did, Ventidius.
  What think'st thou was his answer? 'Twas so tame!
  He said, he had more ways than one to die;
  I had not.
Vent. Poor!
Ant.   He has more ways than one;
  But he would choose them all before that one.
Vent. He first would choose an ague, or a fever.
Ant. No; it must be an ague, not a fever;
  He has not warmth enough to die by that.
Vent. Or old age and a bed.
Ant.   Aye, there's his choice,
  He would live, like a lamp, to the last wink,
  And crawl upon the utmost verge of life.
  O Hercules! Why should a man like this,
  Who dares not trust his fate for one great action,
  Be all the care of heaven? Why should he lord it
  O'er fourscore thousand men, of whom each one
  Is braver than himself?
Vent.   You conquered for him:
  Philippi knows it; there you shared with him
  That empire, which your sword made all your own.
Ant. Fool that I was, upon my eagle's wings
  I bore this wren, till I was tired with soaring,
  And now he mounts above me.
  Good heavens, is this — is this the man who braves me?
  Who bids my age make way, drives me before him,
  To the world's ridge, and sweeps me off like rubbish?
Vent. Sir, we lose time; the troops are mounted all.
Ant. Then give the word to march:

I long to leave this prison of a town,
To join thy legions; and, in open field,
Once more to show my face. Lead, my deliverer.

Enter ALEXAS

Alex. Great emperor,
 In mighty arms renowned above mankind,
 But, in soft pity to the oppressed, a god,
 This message sends the mournful Cleopatra
 To her departing lord.
Vent.   Smooth sycophant!
Alex. A thousand wishes, and ten thousand prayers,
 Millions of blessings wait you to the wars;
 Millions of sighs and tears she sends you too,
 And would have sent
 As many dear embraces to your arms,
 As many parting kisses to your lips;
 But those, she fears, have wearied you already.
Vent. [*aside*]. False crocodile!
Alex. And yet she begs not now, you would not leave her;
 That were a wish too mighty for her hopes,
 Too presuming
 For her low fortune, and your ebbing love;
 That were a wish for her more prosperous days,
 Her blooming beauty, and your growing kindness.
Ant. [*aside*]. Well, I must man it out! — What would the
 queen?
Alex. First, to these noble warriors, who attend
 Your daring courage in the chase of fame —
 Too daring, and too dangerous for her quiet —
 She humbly recommends all she holds dear,
 All her own cares and fears, — the care of you.
Vent. Yes, witness Actium.
Ant.   Let him speak, Ventidius.
Alex. You, when his matchless valour bears him forward,
 With ardour too heroic, on his foes,

Fall down, as she would do, before his feet;
Lie in his way, and stop the paths of death.
Tell him, this god is not invulnerable;
That absent Cleopatra bleeds in him;
And, that you may remember her petition,
She begs you wear these trifles, as a pawn,
Which, at your wished return, she will redeem

        [Gives jewels to the Commanders.
With all the wealth of Egypt:
This to the great Ventidius she presents,
Whom she can never count her enemy,
Because he loves her lord.

Vent.   Tell her, I'll none on't;
I'm not ashamed of honest poverty:
Not all the diamonds of the east can bribe
Ventidius from his faith. I hope to see
These, and the rest of all her sparkling store,
Where they shall more deservingly be placed.

Ant. And who must wear them then?

Vent.   The wronged Octavia.

Ant. You might have spared that word.

Vent.   And he that bribe.

Ant. But have I no remembrance?

Alex.   Yes, a dear one:
Your slave the queen —

Ant.   My mistress.

Alex.   Then your mistress;
Your mistresss would, she says, have sent her soul,
But that you had long since; she humbly begs
This ruby bracelet, set with bleeding hearts,
The emblems of her own, may bind your arm.

        [Presenting a bracelet.

Vent. Now, my best lord, in honour's name, I ask you,
For manhood's sake, and for your own dear safety,
Touch not these poisoned gifts,
Infected by the sender; touch them not;

Myriads of bluest plagues lie underneath them,
And more than aconite has dipped the silk.
Ant. Nay, now you grow too cynical, Ventidius:
A lady's favours may be worn with honour.
What, to refuse her bracelet! On my soul,
When I lie pensive in my tent alone,
'Twill pass the wakeful hours of winter nights,
To tell these pretty beads upon my arm,
To count for every one a soft embrace,
A melting kiss at such and such a time,
And now and then the fury of her love,
When — And what harm's in this?
Alex.   None, none, my lord,
But what's to her, that now 'tis past for ever.
Ant. [*going to tie it*]. We soldiers are so awkward – help me
tie it.
Alex. In faith, my lord, we courtiers too are awkward
In these affairs: so are all men indeed;
Even I, who am not one. But shall I speak?
Ant. Yes, freely.
Alex.   Then, my lord, fair hands alone
Are fit to tie it; she, who sent it, can.
Vent. Hell, death! this eunuch pander ruins you.
You will not see her?
                    [*Alexas whispers an Attendant, who goes out.*
Ant.   But to take my leave.
Vent. Then I have washed an Aethiop. Y'are undone;
Y'are in the toils; y'are taken; y'are destroyed:
Her eyes do Caesar's work.
Ant.   You fear too soon.
I'm constant to myself; I know my strength;
And yet she shall not think me barbarous neither,
Born in the depths of Afric: I am a Roman,
Bred to the rules of soft humanity.
A guest, and kindly used, should bid farewell.
Vent. You do not know

How weak you are to her, how much an infant:
You are not proof against a smile, or glance;
A sigh will quite disarm you.

Ant.   See, she comes!
Now you shall find your error. Gods, I thank you:
I formed the danger greater than it was,
And now 'tis near, 'tis lessened.

Vent.   Mark the end yet.

Enter CLEOPATRA, CHARMION, *and* IRAS

Ant. Well, madam, we are met.

Cleo.   Is this a meeting?
Then, we must part?

Ant.   We must.

Cleo.   Who says we must?

Ant. Our own hard fates.

Cleo.   We make those fates ourselves.

Ant. Yes, we have made them; we have loved each other
Into our mutual ruin.

Cleo. The gods have seen my joys with envious eyes;
I have no friends in heaven; and all the world,
As 'twere the business of mankind to part us
Is armed against my love: even you yourself
Join with the rest; you, you are armed against me.

Ant. I will be justified in all I do.
To late posterity, and therefore hear me.
If I mix a lie
With any truth, reproach me freely with it;
Else, favour me with silence.

Cleo.   You command me,
And I am dumb.

Vent. I like this well: he shows authority.

Ant. That I derive my ruin
From you alone —

Cleo.   O heavens! I ruin you!

Ant. You promised me your silence, and you break it
 Ere I have scarce begun.
Cleo.   Well, I obey you.
Ant. When I beheld you first, it was in Egypt,
 Ere Caesar saw your eyes; you gave me love,
 And were too young to know it; that I settled
 Your father in his throne, was for your sake;
 I left the acknowledgement for time to ripen.
 Caesar stepped in, and with a greedy hand
 Plucked the green fruit, ere the first blush of red,
 Yet cleaving to the bough. He was my lord,
 And was, beside, too great for me to rival;
 But, I deserved you first, though he enjoyed you.
 When, after, I beheld you in Cilicia,
 An enemy to Rome, I pardoned you.
Cleo. I cleared myself —
Ant.   Again you break your promise.
 I loved you still, and took your weak excuses,
 Took you into my bosom, stained by Caesar,
 And not half mine: I went to Egypt with you,
 And hid me from the business of the world,
 Shut out enquiring nations from my sight,
 To give whole years to you.
Vent. [*aside*]. Yes, to your shame be't spoken.
Ant.   How I loved,
 Witness, ye days and nights, and all your hours,
 That danced away with down upon your feet,
 As all your business were to count my passion!
 One day passed by, and nothing saw but love;
 Another came, and still 'twas only love:
 The suns were wearied out with looking on,
 And I untired with loving.
 I saw you every day, and all the day;
 And every day was still but as the first,
 So eager was I still to see you more.
Vent. 'Tis all too true.

Ant.   Fulvia, my wife, grew jealous,
  As she indeed had reason; raised a war
  In Italy, to call me back.
Vent.   But yet
  You went not.
Ant.   While within your arms I lay,
  The world fell mouldering from my hands each hour,
  And left me scarce a grasp – I thank your love for't.
Vent. Well pushed: that last was home.
Cleo.   Yet may I speak?
Ant. If I have urged a falsehood, yes; else, not.
  Your silence says I have not. Fulvia died,
  (Pardon, you gods, with my unkindness died);
  To set the world at peace, I took Octavia,
  This Caesar's sister; in her pride of youth
  And flower of beauty did I wed that lady,
  Whom blushing I must praise, because I left her.
  You called; my love obeyed the fatal summons:
  This raised the Roman arms; the cause was yours.
  I would have fought by land, where I was stronger;
  You hindered it: yet, when I fought at sea,
  Forsook me fighting; and (O stain to honour!
  O lasting shame!) I knew not that I fled;
  But fled to follow you.
Vent. What haste she made to hoist her purple sails!
  And, to appear magnificent in flight,
  Drew half our strength away.
Ant.   All this you caused.
  And would you multiply more ruins on me?
  This honest man, my best, my only friend,
  Has gathered up the shipwreck of my fortunes;
  Twelve legions I have left, my last recruits,
  And you have watched the news, and bring your
    eyes
  To seize them too. If you have aught to answer,
  Now speak, you have free leave.

Alex. [*aside*].   She stands confounded:
   Despair is in her eyes.
Vent. Now lay a sigh in the way to stop his passage:
   Prepare a tear, and bid it for his legions;
   'Tis like they shall be sold.
Cleo. How shall I plead my cause, when you, my judge,
   Already have condemned me? Shall I bring
   The love you bore me for my advocate?
   That now is turned against me, that destroys me;
   For love, once past, is, at the best, forgotten;
   But oftener sours to hate: 'twill please my lord
   To ruin me, and therefore I'll be guilty.
   But, could I once have thought it would have pleased
     you,
   That you would pry, with narrow searching eyes,
   Into my faults, severe to my destruction,
   And watching all advantages with care,
   That serve to make me wretched? Speak, my lord,
   For I end here. Though I deserve this usage,
   Was it like you to give it?
Ant.   Oh, you wrong me,
   To think I sought this parting, or desired
   To accuse you more than what will clear myself,
   And justify this breach.
Cleo.   Thus low I thank you.
   And, since my innocence will not offend,
   I shall not blush to own it.
Vent.   After this,
   I think she'll blush at nothing.
Cleo.   You seemed grieved
   (And therein you are kind) that Caesar first
   Enjoyed my love, though you deserved it better;
   I grieve for that, my lord, much more than you;
   For, had I first been yours, it would have saved
   My second choice: I never had been his,
   And ne'er had been but yours. But Caesar first,

You say, possessed my love. Not so, my lord:
He first possessed my person; you, my love:
Caesar loved me; but I loved Antony.
If I endured him after, 'twas because
I judged it due to the first name of men;
And, half constrained, I gave, as to a tyrant,
What he would take by force.

Vent.   O siren! siren!
Yet grant that all the love she boasts were true,
Has she not ruined you? I still urge that,
The fatal consequence.

Cleo.   The consequence indeed,
For I dare challenge him, my greatest foe,
To say it was designed: 'tis true, I loved you,
And kept you far from an uneasy wife —
Such Fulvia was.
Yes, but he'll say, you left Octavia for me; —
And, can you blame me to receive that love,
Which quitted such desert, for worthless me?
How often have I wished some other Caesar,
Great as the first, and as the second young,
Would court my love, to be refused for you!

Vent. Words, words; but Actium, sir, remember Actium.

Cleo. Even there, I dare his malice. True, I counselled
To fight at sea; but I betrayed you not.
I fled, but not to the enemy. 'Twas fear;
Would I had been a man, not to have feared!
For none would then have envied me your friendship,
Who envy me your love.

Ant.   We're both unhappy:
If nothing else, yet our ill fortune parts us.
Speak; would you have me perish by my stay?

Cleo. If as a friend you ask my judgement, go;
If as a lover, stay. If you must perish —
'Tis a hard word — but stay.

Vent. See now the effects of her so boasted love!

She strives to drag you down to ruin with her:
But, could she 'scape without you, oh, how soon
Would she let go her hold, and haste to shore,
And never look behind!

Cleo. Then judge my love by this.

> [*Giving Antony a writing.*
>
> Could I have borne

A life or death, a happiness or woe,
From yours divided, this had given me means.

Ant. By Hercules, the writing of Octavius!
I know it well: 'tis that proscribing hand,
Young as it was, that led the way to mine,
And left me but the second place in murder. —
See, see, Ventidius! here he offers Egypt,
And joins all Syria to it, as a present,
So, in requital, she forsake my fortunes,
And join her arms with his.

Cleo.   And yet you leave me!
You leave me, Antony; and yet I love you,
Indeed I do: I have refused a kingdom;
That's a trifle:
For I could part with life, with anything,
But only you. O, let me die but with you!
Is that a hard request?

Ant.   Next living with you,
'Tis all that heav'n can give.

Alex. [*aside*].   He melts; we conquer.

Cleo. No; you shall go; your interest calls you hence;
Yes; your dear interest pulls too strong, for these
Weak arms to hold you here. —   [*Takes his hand.*

> Go; leave me, soldier

(For you're no more a lover); leave me dying:
Push me, all pale and panting, from your bosom,
And, when your march begins, let one run after,
Breathless almost for joy, and cry, 'She's dead.'
The soldiers shout; you then, perhaps, may sigh,

    And muster all your Roman gravity:
    Ventidius chides; and straight your brow clears up,
    As I had never been.

Ant.   Gods, 'tis too much;
    Too much for man to bear!

Cleo.   What is't for me then,
    A weak, forsaken woman, and a lover? –
    Here let me breathe my last: envy me not
    This minute in your arms: I'll die apace,
    As fast as e'er I can, and end your trouble.

Ant. Die! rather let me perish: loosened nature
    Leap from its hinges! Sink the props of heaven,
    And fall the skies to crush the nether world!
    My eyes, my soul, my all! –   *[Embraces her.*

Vent.   And what's this toy,
    In balance with your fortune, honour, fame?

Ant. What is't, Ventidius? – it outweighs them all;
    Why, we have more than conquered Caesar now:
    My queen's not only innocent, but loves me.
    This, this is she who drags me down to ruin!
    'But, could she 'scape without me, with what haste
    Would she let slip her hold, and make to shore,
    And never look behind!'
    Down on thy knees, blasphemer as thou art,
    And ask forgiveness of wronged innocence.

Vent. I'll rather die, than take it. Will you go?

Ant. Go! whither? Go from all that's excellent?
    Faith, honour, virtue, all good things forbid,
    That I should go from her, who sets my love
    Above the price of kingdoms! Give, you gods,
    Give to your boy, your Caesar,
    This rattle of a globe to play withal,
    This gewgaw world, and put him cheaply off:
    I'll not be pleased with less than Cleopatra.

Cleo. She's wholly yours. My heart's so full of joy,
    That I shall do some wild extravagance

Of love, in public; and the foolish world,
Which knows not tenderness, will think me mad.
Vent. O women! women! women! all the gods
Have not such power of doing good to man,
As you of doing harm.   [*Exit.*
Ant.   Our men are armed.
Unbar the gate that looks to Caesar's camp;
I would revenge the treachery he meant me;
And long security makes conquest easy.
I'm eager to return before I go;
For all the pleasures I have known beat thick
On my remembrance. How I long for night!
That both the sweets of mutual love may try,
And triumph once o'er Caesar ere we die.
                    [*Exeunt.*

At one door, enter CLEOPATRA, CHARMION, IRAS, *and*
ALEXAS, *a Train of Egyptians: at the other,* ANTONY
*and Romans. The entrance on both sides is prepared by music;
the trumpets first sounding on* ANTONY'S *part, then answered
by timbrels, etc., on* CLEOPATRA'S. CHARMION *and*
IRAS *hold a laurel wreath betwixt them. A dance of Egyptians.
After the ceremony,* CLEOPATRA *crowns* ANTONY.

Ant. I thought how those white arms would fold me in,
   And strain me close, and melt me into love;
   So pleased with that sweet image, I sprung forwards,
   And added all my strength to every blow.
Cleo. Come to me, come, my soldier, to my arms!
   You've been too long away from my embraces;
   But, when I have you fast, and all my own,
   With broken murmurs, and with amorous sighs,
   I'll say, you were unkind, and punish you,
   And mark you red with many an eager kiss.
Ant. My brighter Venus!
Cleo.   O my greater Mars!
Ant. Thou join'st us well, my love!
   Suppose me come from the Phlegraean plains,
   Where gasping giants lay, cleft by my sword,
   And mountain-tops pared off each other blow,
   To bury those I slew. Receive me, goddess!
   Let Caesar spread his subtle nets, like Vulcan;
   In thy embraces I would be beheld
   By heaven and earth at once;
   And make their envy what they meant their sport.
   Let those who took us blush; I would love on
   With awful state, regardless of their frowns,
   As their superior god.
   There's no satiety of love in thee;

Enjoyed, thou still art new; perpetual spring
Is in thy arms; the ripened fruit but falls,
And blossoms rise to fill its empty place;
And I grow rich by giving.

Enter VENTIDIUS, *and stands apart*

Alex. O, now the danger's past, your general comes!
   He joins not in your joys, nor minds your triumphs;
   But, with contracted brows, looks frowning on,
   As envying your success.
Ant. Now, on my soul, he loves me; truly loves me;
   He never flattered me in any vice,
   But awes me with his virtue: even this minute,
   Methinks, he has a right of chiding me.
   Lead to the temple: I'll avoid his presence;
   It checks too strong upon me.
     [*Exeunt the rest. As Antony is going, Ventidius pulls him*
                          by the robe.
Vent.   Emperor!
Ant. [*looking back*].' Tis the old argument; I pr'ythee, spare
   me.
Vent. But this one hearing, emperor.
Ant.   Let go.
   My robe; or, by my father Hercules –
Vent. By Hercules his father, that's yet greater,
   I bring you somewhat you would wish to know.
Ant. Thou seest we are observed; attend me here,
   And I'll return.   [*Exit.*
Vent. I'm waning in his favour, yet I love him;
   I love this man, who runs to meet his ruin;
   And sure the gods, like me, are fond of him:
   His virtues lie so mingled with his crimes,
   As would confound their choice to punish one,
   And not reward the other.

Enter ANTONY

Ant.   We can conquer,
  You see, without your aid.
  We have dislodged their troops;
  They look on us at distance, and, like curs
  'Scaped from the lion's paws, they bay far off,
  And lick their wounds, and faintly threaten war.
  Five thousand Romans, with their faces upward,
  Lie breathless on the plain.
Vent.   'Tis well: and he,
  Who lost them, could have spared ten thousand more.
  Yet if, by this advantage, you could gain
  An easier peace, while Caesar doubts the chance
  Of arms —
Ant.   O, think not on't, Ventidius!
  The boy pursues my ruin, he'll no peace;
  His malice is considerate in advantage;
  Oh, he's the coolest murderer! so staunch,
  He kills, and keeps his temper.
Vent.   Have you no friend
  In all his army, who has power to move him?
  Maecenas, or Agrippa, might do much.
Ant. They're both too deep in Caesar's interests.
  We'll work it out by dint of sword, or perish.
Vent. Fain I would find some other.
Ant.   Thank thy love.
  Some four or five such victories as this
  Will save thy farther pains.
Vent. Expect no more; Caesar is on his guard:
  I know, sir, you have conquered against odds;
  But still you draw supplies from one poor town,
  And of Egyptians: he has all the world,
  And, at his back, nations come pouring in,
  To fill the gaps you make. Pray, think again.
Ant. Why dost thou drive me from myself, to search
  For foreign aids? – to hunt my memory,
  And range all o'er a waste and barren place,

To find a friend? The wretched have no friends. –
Yet I had one, the bravest youth of Rome,
Whom Caesar loves beyond the love of women;
He could resolve his mind, as fire does wax,
From that hard rugged image melt him down,
And mould him in what softer form he pleased.

Vent. Him would I see, that man of all the world;
Just such a one we want.

Ant.   He loved me too,
I was his soul; he lived not but in me;
We were so closed within each other's breasts,
The rivets were not found that joined us first.
That does not reach us yet: we were so mixed,
As meeting streams, both to ourselves were lost;
We were one mass; we could not give or take,
But from the same; for he was I, I he!

Vent. [*aside*]. He moves as I would wish him.

Ant.   After this,
I need not tell his name – 'twas Dolabella.

Vent. He's now in Caesar's camp.

Ant.   No matter where,
Since he's no longer mine. He took unkindly
That I forbade him Cleopatra's sight,
Because I feared he loved her: he confessed
He had a warmth, which, for my sake, he stifled;
For 'twere impossible that two, so one,
Should not have loved the same. When he departed,
He took no leave; and that confirmed my thoughts.

Vent. It argues that he loved you more than her,
Else he had stayed; but he perceived you jealous,
And would not grieve his friend: I know he loves
    you.

Ant. I should have seen him, then, ere now.

Vent.   Perhaps
He has thus long been labouring for your peace.

Ant. Would he were here!

Vent.   Would you believe he loved you?
  I read your answer in your eyes; you would.
  Not to conceal it longer, he has sent
  A messenger from Caesar's camp, with letters.
Ant. Let him appear.
Vent.   I'll bring him instantly.

  Exit VENTIDIUS, *and re-enters immediately with*
                    DOLABELLA

Ant. 'Tis he himself! himself! by holy friendship!
                              [*Runs to embrace him.*
  Art thou returned at last, my better half?
  Come, give me all myself!
  Let me not live,
  If the young bridegroom, longing for his night,
  Was ever half so fond.
Dola. I must be silent, for my soul is busy
  About a nobler work: she's new come home,
  Like a long-absent man, and wanders o'er
  Each room, a stranger to her own, to look
  If all be safe.
Ant.   Thou hast what's left of me;
  For I am now so sunk from what I was,
  Thou find'st me at my lowest water-mark.
  The rivers that ran in, and raised my fortunes,
  Are all dried up, or take another course.
  What I have left is from my native spring;
  I've still a heart that swells, in scorn of fate,
  And lifts me to my banks.
Dola. Still you are lord of all the world to me.
Ant. Why, then I yet am so; for thou art all.
  If I had any joy when thou wert absent,
  I grudged it to myself; methought I robbed
  Thee of thy part. But, O my Dolabella!
  Thou hast beheld me other than I am.
  Hast thou not seen my morning chambers filled

With sceptred slaves, who waited to salute me?
With eastern monarchs, who forgot the sun,
To worship my uprising? Menial kings
Ran coursing up and down my palace-yard,
Stood silent in my presence, watched my eyes,
And, at my least command, all started out,
Like racers to the goal.

Dola.   Slaves to your fortune.

Ant. Fortune is Caesar's now; and what am I?

Vent. What you have made yourself; I will not flatter.

Ant. Is this friendly done?

Dola. Yes, when his end is so, I must join with him;
Indeed I must, and yet you must not chide:
Why am I else your friend?

Ant.   Take heed, young man
How thou upbraid'st my love; the queen has eyes,
And thou too hast a soul. Canst thou remember,
When, swelled with hatred, thou beheld'st her first,
As accessory to thy brother's death?

Dola. Spare my remembrance; 'twas a guilty day,
And still the blush hangs here.

Ant.   To clear herself
For sending him no aid, she came from Egypt.
Her galley down the silver Cydnos rowed,
The tackling silk, the streamers waved with gold;
The gentle winds were lodged in purple sails;
Her nymphs, like Nereids, round her couch were
   placed,
Where she, another sea-born Venus, lay.

Dola. No more: I would not hear it.

Ant.   Oh, you must!
She lay, and leant her cheek upon her hand,
And cast a look so languishingly sweet,
As if, secure of all beholders' hearts,
Neglecting, she could take 'em: boys, like Cupids,
Stood fanning with their painted wings the winds

That played about her face: but if she smiled,
A darting glory seemed to blaze abroad,
That men's desiring eyes were never wearied,
But hung upon the object. To soft flutes
The silver oars kept time; and while they played,
The hearing gave new pleasure to the sight,
And both to thought. 'Twas heaven, or somewhat more;
For she so charmed all hearts, that gazing crowds
Stood panting on the shore, and wanted breath
To give their welcome voice.
Then, Dolabella, where was then thy soul?
Was not thy fury quite disarmed with wonder?
Didst thou not shrink behind me from those eyes,
And whisper in my ear, 'Oh, tell her not
That I accused her with my brother's death'?
Dola. And should my weakness be a plea for yours?
Mine was an age when love might be excused,
When kindly warmth, and when my springing youth
Made it a debt to nature. Yours —
Vent.   Speak boldly.
Yours, he would say, in your declining age,
When no more heat was left but what you forced,
When all the sap was needful for the trunk,
When it went down, then you constrained the course,
And robbed from nature, to supply desire;
In you (I would not use so harsh a word)
But 'tis plain dotage.
Ant.   Ha!
Dola.   'Twas urged too home.
But yet the loss was private that I made;
'Twas but myself I lost: I lost no legions;
I had no world to lose, no people's love.
Ant. This from a friend?
Dola.   Yes, Antony, a true one;
A friend so tender, that each word I speak
Stabs my own heart, before it reach your ear.

O, judge me not less kind, because I chide!
To Caesar I excuse you.
Ant.   O ye gods!
Have I then lived to be excused to Caesar?
Dola. As to your equal.
Ant.   Well, he's but my equal;
While I wear this, he never shall be more.
Dola. I bring conditions from him.
Ant.   Are they noble?
Methinks thou shouldst not bring 'em else; yet he
Is full of deep dissembling; knows no honour
Divided from his int'rest. Fate mistook him;
For nature meant him for an usurer;
He's fit indeed to buy, not conquer, kingdoms.
Vent. Then, granting this,
What pow'r was theirs who wrought so hard a temper
To honourable terms?
Ant. It was my Dolabella, or some god.
Dola. Nor I, nor yet Maecenas, nor Agrippa:
They were your enemies; and I, a friend,
Too weak alone; yet 'twas a Roman's deed.
Ant. 'Twas like a Roman done: show me that man,
Who has preserved my life, my love, my honour;
Let me but see his face.
Vent.   That task is mine,
And, heaven, thou know'st how pleasing.
                              [*Exit Ventidius.*
Dola.   You'll remember
To whom you stand obliged?
Ant.   When I forget it,
Be thou unkind, and that's my greatest curse.
My queen shall thank him too.
Dola.   I fear she will not.
Ant. But she shall do it – the queen, my Dolabella!
Hast thou not still some grudgings of thy fever?
Dola. I would not see her lost.

Ant.   When I forsake her,
　Leave me, my better stars! for she has truth
　Beyond her beauty. Caesar tempted her,
　At no less price than kingdoms, to betray me;
　But she resisted all: and yet thou chidest me
　For loving her too well. Could I do so?
Dola. Yes; there's my reason.

> *Re-enter* VENTIDIUS, *with* OCTAVIA, *leading*
> ANTONY'S *two little daughters*

Ant. [*starting back*].   Where? – Octavia there!
Vent. What, is she poison to you? – a disease?
　Look on her, view her well, and those she brings:
　Are they all strangers to your eyes? Has nature
　No secret call, no whisper they are yours?
Dola. For shame, my lord, if not for love, receive them
　With kinder eyes. If you confess a man,
　Meet them, embrace them, bid them welcome to you.
　Your arms should open, even without your knowledge,
　To clasp them in; your feet should turn to wings,
　To bear you to them; and your eyes dart out
　And aim a kiss, ere you could reach the lips.
Ant. I stood amazed to think how they came hither.
Vent. I sent for them; I brought them in, unknown
　To Cleopatra's guards.
Dola.   Yet are you cold?
Octav. Thus long I have attended for my welcome,
　Which, as a stranger, sure I might expect.
　Who am I?
Ant.   Caesar's sister.
Octav.   That's unkind.
　Had I been nothing more than Caesar's sister,
　Know, I had still remained in Caesar's camp;
　But your Octavia, your much injured wife,
　Though banished from your bed, driven from your
　　house

In spite of Caesar's sister, still is yours.
'Tis true, I have a heart disdains your coldness,
And prompts me not to seek what you should offer;
But a wife's virtue still surmounts that pride:
I come to claim you as my own; to show
My duty first; to ask, nay beg, your kindness:
Your hand, my lord; 'tis mine, and I will have it.

                              [*Taking his hand.*

Vent. Do, take it; thou deserv'st it.

Dola.   On my soul,
  And so she does: she's neither too submissive,
  Nor yet too haughty; but so just a mean
  Shows, as it ought, a wife and Roman too.

Ant. I fear, Octavia, you have begged my life.

Octav. Begged it, my lord?

Ant.   Yes, begged it, my ambassadress,
  Poorly and basely begged it of your brother.

Octav. Poorly and basely I could never beg;
  Nor could my brother grant.

Ant. Shall I, who, to my kneeling slave, could say,
  'Rise up, and be a king,' shall I fall down
  And cry, 'Forgive me, Caesar'? Shall I set
  A man, my equal, in the place of Jove,
  As he could give me being? No; that word,
  'Forgive', would choke me up,
  And die upon my tongue.

Dola.   You shall not need it.

Ant. I will not need it. Come, you've all betrayed me –
  My friend too! – to receive some vile conditions.
  My wife has bought me, with her prayers and tears;
  And now I must become her branded slave.
  In every peevish mood, she will upbraid
  The life she gave: if I but look awry,
  She cries, 'I'll tell my brother.'

Octav.   My hard fortune
  Subjects me still to your unkind mistakes.

But the conditions I have brought are such
You need not blush to take: I love your honour,
Because 'tis mine; it never shall be said,
Octavia's husband was her brother's slave.
Sir, you are free – free, ev'n from her you loathe;
For, though my brother bargains for your love,
Makes me the price and cement of your peace,
I have a soul like yours; I cannot take
Your love as alms, nor beg what I deserve.
I'll tell my brother we are reconciled;
He shall draw back his troops, and you shall march
To rule the East: I may be dropped at Athens;
No matter where, I never will complain,
But only keep the barren name of wife,
And rid you of the trouble.

Vent. Was ever such a strife of sullen honour!
    Both scorn to be obliged.

Dola. Oh, she has touched him in the tenderest part;
    See how he reddens with despite and shame,
    To be outdone in generosity!   *[Apart.*

Vent. See how he winks! how he dries up a tear,
    That fain would fall!   *[Apart.*

Ant. Octavia, I have heard you, and must praise
    The greatness of your soul;
    But cannot yield to what you have proposed;
    For I can ne'er be conquered but by love;
    And you do all for duty. You would free me,
    And would be dropped at Athens; was't not so?

Octav. It was, my lord.

Ant.   Then I must be obliged
    To one who loves me not, who, to herself,
    May call me thankless and ungrateful man: –
    I'll not endure it; no.

Vent. [*aside*]. I'm glad it pinches there.

Octav. Would you triumph o'er poor Octavia's virtue?
    That pride was all I had to bear me up;

That you might think you owed me for your life,
And owed it to my duty, not my love.
I have been injured, and my haughty soul
Could brook but ill the man who slights my bed.
Ant. Therefore you love me not.
Octav.   Therefore, my lord,
I should not love you.
Ant.   Therefore you would leave me?
Octav. And therefore I should leave you — if I could.
Dola. Her soul's too great, after such injuries,
To say she loves; and yet she lets you see it.
Her modesty and silence plead her cause.
Ant. O Dolabella, which way shall I turn?
I find a secret yielding in my soul;
But Cleopatra, who would die with me,
Must she be left? Pity pleads for Octavia;
But does it not plead more for Cleopatra?
Vent. Justice and pity both plead for Octavia;
For Cleopatra, neither.
One would be ruined with you, but she first
Had ruined you: the other, you have ruined,
And yet she would preserve you.
In everything their merits are unequal.
Ant. O my distracted soul!
Octav.   Sweet heaven compose it!
Come, come, my lord, if I can pardon you,
Methinks you should accept it. Look on these;
Are they not yours? Or stand they thus neglected,
As they are mine? Go to him, children, go;
Kneel to him, take him by the hand, speak to him;
For you may speak, and he may own you too,
Without a blush, and so he cannot all
His children: go, I say, and pull him to me,
And pull him to yourselves, from that bad woman.
You, Agrippina, hang upon his arms;
And you, Antonia, clasp about his waist:

If he will shake you off, if he will dash you
Against the pavement, you must bear it, children;
For you are mine, and I was born to suffer.

      [Here the Children go to him, etc.

Vent. Was ever sight so moving? – Emperor!
Dola. Friend!
Octav.   Husband!
Both Child.   Father!
Ant.   I am vanquished; take me,
 Octavia; take me, children; share me all.

         [Embracing them.

 I've been a thriftless debtor to your loves,
 And run out much, in riot, from your stock;
 But all shall be amended.
Octav.   O blest hour!
Dola. O happy change!
Vent.   My joy stops at my tongue;
 But it has found two channels here for one,
 And bubbles out above.
Ant. [*to Octavia*]. This is thy triumph; lead me where
  thou wilt;
 Ev'n to thy brother's camp.
Octav.   All there are yours.

Enter ALEXAS *hastily*

Alex. The queen, my mistress, sir, and yours —
Ant.   'Tis past. –
 Octavia, you shall stay this night; tomorrow,
 Caesar and we are one.

  [Exit leading Octavia; Dolabella and the Children follow.

Vent. There's news for you; run, my officious eunuch,
 Be sure to be the first; haste forward;
 Haste, my dear eunuch, haste!
Alex. This downright fighting fool, this thick-skulled
  hero,
 This blunt, unthinking instrument of death,

With plain dull virtue has outgone my wit.
Pleasure forsook my earliest infancy;
The luxury of others robbed my cradle,
And ravished thence the promise of a man.
Cast out from nature, disinherited
Of what her meanest children claim by kind,
Yet greatness kept me from contempt: that's gone.
Had Cleopatra followed my advice,
Then he had been betrayed who now forsakes.
She dies for love; but she has known its joys:
Gods, is this just, that I, who know no joys,
Must die, because she loves?

Enter CLEOPATRA, CHARMION, IRAS, *and train*

O madam, I have seen what blasts my eyes!
Octavia's here!
Cleo.   Peace with that raven's note.
  I know it too; and now am in
  The pangs of death.
Alex.   You are no more a queen;
  Egypt is lost.
Cleo.   What tell'st thou me of Egypt?
  My life, my soul is lost! Octavia has him! –
  O fatal name to Cleopatra's love!
  My kisses, my embraces now are hers;
  While I — but thou hast seen my rival; speak,
  Does she deserve this blessing? Is she fair?
  Bright as a goddess? And is all perfection
  Confined to her? It is. Poor I was made
  Of that coarse matter, which, when she was finished,
  The gods threw by, for rubbish.
Alex. She's indeed a very miracle.
Cleo. Death to my hopes, a miracle!
Alex. [*bowing*].   A miracle;
  I mean of goodness; for in beauty, madam,
  You make all wonders cease.

Cleo.   I was too rash:
 Take this in part of recompense. But oh!

         [Giving a ring.

 I fear thou flatterest me.

Char. She comes! she's here!

Iras.   Fly, madam, Cæsar's sister!

Cleo. Were she the sister of the thunderer Jove,
 And bore her brother's lightning in her eyes,
 Thus would I face my rival.

   *[Meets Octavia with Ventidius. Octavia bears up to her.
        Their trains come up on either side*

Octav. I need not ask if you are Cleopatra;
 Your haughty carriage —

Cleo.   Shows I am a queen:
 Nor need I ask you who you are.

Octav.   A Roman:
 A name that makes and can unmake a queen.

Cleo. Your lord, the man who serves me, is a Roman.

Octav. He was a Roman, till he lost that name,
 To be a slave in Egypt; but I come
 To free him thence.

Cleo.   Peace, peace, my lover's Juno.
 When he grew weary of that household clog,
 He chose my easier bonds.

Octav.   I wonder not
 Your bonds are easy; you have long been practised
 In that lascivious art: he's not the first
 For whom you spread your snares: let Caesar witness.

Cleo. I loved not Caesar; 'twas but gratitude
 I paid his love. The worst your malice can,
 Is but to say the greatest of mankind
 Has been my slave. The next, but far above him
 In my esteem, is he whom law calls yours,
 But whom his love made mine.

Octav. [*coming up close to her*]. I would view nearer
 That face which has so long usurped my right,

    To find the inevitable charms that catch
    Mankind so sure, that ruined my dear lord.
Cleo. Oh, you do well to search; for had you known
    But half these charms, you had not lost his heart.
Octav. Far be their knowledge from a Roman lady,
    Far from a modest wife! Shame of our sex,
    Dost thou not blush to own those black endearments
    That make sin pleasing?
Cleo.   You may blush, who want them.
    If bounteous nature, if indulgent heaven
    Have given me charms to please the bravest man,
    Should I not thank them? Should I be ashamed,
    And not be proud? I am, that he has loved me;
    And, when I love not him, heaven change this face
    For one like that.
Octav.   Thou lov'st him not so well.
Cleo. I love him better, and deserve him more.
Octav. You do not — cannot: you have been his ruin.
    Who made him cheap at Rome, but Cleopatra?
    Who made him scorned abroad, but Cleopatra?
    At Actium, who betrayed him? Cleopatra.
    Who made his children orphans, and poor me
    A wretched widow? only Cleopatra.
Cleo. Yet she who loves him best is Cleopatra.
    If you have suffered, I have suffered more.
    You bear the specious title of a wife,
    To gild your cause, and draw the pitying world
    To favour it: the world contemns poor me,
    For I have lost my honour, lost my fame,
    And stained the glory of my royal house,
    And all to bear the branded name of mistress.
    There wants but life, and that too I would lose
    For him I love.
Octav.   Be't so, then; take thy wish.
                            [*Exit with her train.*
Cleo. And 'tis my wish,

Now he is lost for whom alone I lived.
My sight grows dim, and every object dances,
And swims before me, in the maze of death.
My spirits, while they were opposed, kept up;
They could not sink beneath a rival's scorn:
But now she's gone, they faint.

Alex.   Mine have had leisure
To recollect their strength, and furnish counsel,
To ruin her, who else must ruin you.

Cleo.   Vain promiser!
Lead me, my Charmion; nay, your hand too, Iras:
My grief has weight enough to sink you both.
Conduct me to some solitary chamber,
And draw the curtains round;
Then leave me to myself, to take alone
My fill of grief.
    There I till death will his unkindness weep;
    As harmless infants moan themselves asleep.

                                   [*Exeunt.*

Enter ANTONY, DOLABELLA

Dola. Why would you shift it from yourself on me?
  Can you not tell her you must part?
Ant.   I cannot.
  I could pull out an eye, and bid it go,
  And t'other should not weep. O Dolabella,
  How many deaths are in this word 'depart!'
  I dare not trust my tongue to tell her so:
  One look of hers would thaw me into tears,
  And I should melt till I were lost again.
Dola. Then let Ventidius;
  He's rough by nature.
Ant.   O, he'll speak too harshly;
  He'll kill her with the news: thou, only thou.
Dola. Nature has cast me in so soft a mould,
  That but to hear a story feigned for pleasure
  Of some sad lover's death, moistens my eyes,
  And robs me of my manhood. I should speak
  So faintly, with such fear to grieve her heart,
  She'd not believe it earnest.
Ant.   Therefore – therefore
  Thou only, thou art fit; think thyself me,
  And when thou speak'st (but let it first be long),
  Take off the edge from every sharper sound,
  And let our parting be as gently made
  As other loves begin: wilt thou do this?
Dola. What you have said so sinks into my soul,
  That, if I must speak, I shall speak just so.
Ant. I leave you then to your sad task. Farewell!
  I sent her word to meet you.
                              [*Goes to the door, and comes back.*
                                I forgot;
  Let her be told, I'll make her peace with mine:

Her crown and dignity shall be preserved,
If I have power with Caesar. — O, be sure
To think on that.
Dola.   Fear not, I will remember.
              [*Antony goes again to the door, and comes back.*
Ant. And tell her, too, how much I was constrained;
I did not this, but with extremest force:
Desire her not to hate my memory,
For I still cherish hers; — insist on that.
Dola. Trust me, I'll not forget it.
Ant.   Then that's all.
              [*Goes out, and returns again.*
Wilt thou forgive my fondness this once more?
Tell her, though we shall never meet again,
If I should hear she took another love,
The news would break my heart. — Now I must go;
For every time I have returned, I feel
My soul more tender; and my next command
Would be to bid her stay, and ruin both.   [*Exit.*
Dola. Men are but children of a larger growth;
Our appetites as apt to change as theirs,
And full as craving too, and full as vain;
And yet the soul, shut up in her dark room,
Viewing so clear abroad, at home sees nothing;
But, like a mole in earth, busy and blind,
Works all her folly up, and casts it outward
To the world's open view: thus I discovered,
And blamed the love of ruined Antony;
Yet wish that I were he, to be so ruined.

Enter VENTIDIUS *above*

Vent. Alone? and talking to himself? concerned too?
Perhaps my guess is right; he loved her once,
And may pursue it still.
Dola.   O friendship! friendship!
Ill canst thou answer this; and reason, worse:

Unfaithful in the attempt; hopeless to win;
And if I win, undone: mere madness all.
And yet the occasion's fair. What injury
To him, to wear the robe which he throws by?
Vent. None, none at all. This happens as I wish,
To ruin her yet more with Antony.

Enter CLEOPATRA, *talking with* ALEXAS; CHARMION,
IRAS, *on the other side*

Dola. She comes! What charms have sorrow on that face!
Sorrow seems pleased to dwell with so much sweetness;
Yet, now and then, a melancholy smile
Breaks loose, like lightning in a winter's night,
And shows a moment's day.
Vent. If she should love him too! her eunuch there!
That porc'pisce bodes ill weather. Draw, draw nearer,
Sweet devil, that I may hear.
Alex.   Believe me; try
    [*Dolabella goes over to Charmion and Iras; seems to talk
                                                        with them.*
To make him jealous; jealousy is like
A polished glass held to the lips when life's in doubt:
If there be breath, 'twill catch the damp, and show it.
Cleo. I grant you, jealousy's a proof of love,
But 'tis a weak and unavailing med'cine;
It puts out the disease, and makes it show,
But has no power to cure.
Alex. 'Tis your last remedy, and strongest too:
And then this Dolabella – who so fit
To practise on? He's handsome, valiant, young,
And looks as he were laid for nature's bait
To catch weak women's eyes.
He stands already more than half suspected
Of loving you: the least kind word or glance
You give this youth will kindle him with love:
Then, like a burning vessel set adrift,

You'll send him down amain before the wind,
To fire the heart of jealous Antony.

Cleo. Can I do this? Ah, no; my love's so true
That I can neither hide it where it is,
Nor show it where it is not. Nature meant me
A wife, a silly, harmless, household dove,
Fond without art, and kind without deceit;
But Fortune, that has made a mistress of me,
Has thrust me out to the wide world, unfurnished
Of falsehood to be happy.

Alex.   Force yourself.
Th' event will be, your lover will return
Doubly desirous to possess the good
Which once he feared to lose.

Cleo.   ,   I must attempt it;
But, oh with what regret!

                    [*Exit Alexas. She comes up to Dolabella.*

Vent. So, now the scene draws near; they're in my reach.

Cleo. [*to Dolabella*]. Discoursing with my women! might
   not I
Share in your entertainment?

Char.   You have been
The subject of it, madam.

Cleo.   How! and how?

Iras. Such praises of your beauty!

Cleo.   Mere poetry.
Your Roman wits, your Gallus and Tibullus,
Have taught you this from Cytheris and Delia.

Dola. Those Roman wits have never been in Egypt;
Cytheris and Delia else had been unsung:
I, who have seen — had I been born a poet,
Should choose a nobler name.

Cleo.   You flatter me.
But, 'tis your nation's vice: all of your country
Are flatterers, and all false. Your friend's like you.
I'm sure he sent you not to speak these words.

Dola. No, madam; yet he sent me —

Cleo.   Well, he sent you —

Dola. Of a less pleasing errand.

Cleo.   How less pleasing?
Less to yourself, or me?

Dola   Madam, to both;
For you must mourn, and I must grieve to cause it.

Cleo. You, Charmion, and your fellow, stand at distance. –
[*Aside.*] Hold up, my spirits. — Well, now your
mournful matter;
For I'm prepared, perhaps can guess it too.

Dola. I wish you would; for 'tis a thankless office
To tell ill news: and I, of all your sex,
Most fear displeasing you.

Cleo.   Of all your sex,
I soonest could forgive you, if you should.

Vent. Most delicate advances! Woman! Woman!
Dear, damned, inconstant sex!

Cleo.   In the first place,
I am to be forsaken; is't not so?

Dola. I wish I could not answer to that question.

Cleo. Then pass it o'er, because it troubles you:
I should have been more grieved another time.
Next, I'm to lose my kingdom. — Farewell, Egypt!
Yet is there any more?

Dola.   Madam, I fear
Your too deep sense of grief has turned your reason.

Cleo. No, no, I'm not run mad; I can bear fortune:
And love may be expelled by other love,
As poisons are by poisons.

Dola. You o'erjoy me, madam,
To find your griefs so moderately borne.
You've heard the worst; all are not false like him.

Cleo. No; heaven forbid they should.

Dola.   Some men are constant.

Cleo. And constancy deserves reward, that's certain.

Dola. Deserves it not; but give it leave to hope.

Vent. I'll swear thou hast my leave. I have enough.
    But how to manage this! Well, I'll consider.   [*Exit.*

Dola. I came prepared
    To tell you heavy news; news, which I thought
    Would fright the blood from your pale cheeks to
       hear:
    But you have met it with a cheerfulness
    That makes my task more easy; and my tongue,
    Which on another's message was employed,
    Would gladly speak its own.

Cleo.   Hold, Dolabella.
    First tell me, were you chosen by my lord?
    Or sought you this employment?

Dola. He picked me out; and, as his bosom friend,
    He charged me with his words.

Cleo.   The message then
    I know was tender, and each accent smooth,
    To mollify that rugged word 'depart'.

Dola. Oh, you mistake: he chose the harshest words;
    With fiery eyes, and with contracted brows,
    He coined his face in the severest stamp:
    And fury shook his fabric, like an earthquake;
    He heaved for vent, and burst like bellowing Etna,
    In sounds scarce human – 'Hence, away for ever:
    Let her begone, the blot of my renown,
    And bane of all my hopes!

       [*All the time of this speech, Cleopatra seems more and*
                 more concerned, till she sinks quite down.

    Let her be driven as far as men can think
    From man's commerce! She'll poison to the centre.'

Cleo. O, I can bear no more!

Dola. Help, help! – O wretch! O cursed, cursed wretch!
    What have I done!

Char.   Help, chafe her temples, Iras.

Iras. Bend, bend her forward quickly.

Char.   Heaven be praised,
   She comes again.
Cleo.   O, let him not approach me.
   Why have you brought me back to this loathed being,
   The abode of falsehood, violated vows,
   And injured love? For pity, let me go;
   For, if there be a place of long repose,
   I'm sure I want it. My disdainful lord
   Can never break that quiet; nor awake
   The sleeping soul with hollowing in my tomb
   Such words as fright her hence. – Unkind, unkind!
Dola. [*kneeling*]. Believe me, 'tis against myself I speak;
   That sure deserves belief; I injured him:
   My friend ne'er spoke those words. O, had you
      seen
   How often he came back, and every time
   With something more obliging and more kind,
   To add to what he said; what dear farewells;
   How almost vanquished by his love he parted,
   And leaned to what unwillingly he left!
   I, traitor as I was, for love of you
   (But what can you not do, who made me false!)
   I forged that lie; for whose forgiveness kneels
   This self-accused, self-punished criminal.
Cleo. With how much ease believe we what we wish!
   Rise, Dolabella; if you have been guilty,
   I have contributed, and too much love
   Has made me guilty too.
   The advance of kindness which I made was feigned,
   To call back fleeting love by jealousy;
   But 'twould not last. O, rather let me lose,
   Than so ignobly trifle with his heart.
Dola. I find your breast fenced round from human reach,
   Transparent as a rock of solid crystal,
   Seen through, but never pierced. My friend, my friend!
   What endless treasure hast thou thrown away,

And scattered, like an infant, in the ocean,
Vain sums of wealth, which none can gather thence!
Cleo. Could you not beg
An hour's admittance to his private ear?
Like one who wanders through long barren wilds,
And yet foreknows no hospitable inn
Is near to succour hunger, eats his fill,
Before his painful march:
So would I feed a while my famished eyes
Before we part; for I have far to go,
If death be far, and never must return.

VENTIDIUS *with* OCTAVIA, *behind*

Vent. From hence you may discover – oh, sweet, sweet!
Would you indeed? the pretty hand in earnest?
Dola. I will, for this reward. –   [*Takes her hand.*
Draw it not back,
'Tis all I e'er will beg.
Vent. They turn upon us.
Octav.   What quick eyes has guilt!
Vent. Seem not to have observed them, and go on.

They enter

Dola. Saw you the emperor, Ventidius?
Vent.   No.
I sought him; but I heard that he was private,
None with him but Hipparchus, his freedman.
Dola. Know you his business?
Vent.   Giving him instructions,
And letters to his brother Caesar.
Dola.   Well,
He must be found.
                    [*Exeunt Dolabella and Cleopatra.*
Octav.   Most glorious impudence!
Vent. She looked, methought,
As she would say, 'Take your old man, Octavia;

Thank you, I'm better here.' Well, but what use
Make we of this discovery?
Octav.   Let it die.
Vent. I pity Dolabella; but she's dangerous:
Her eyes have power beyond Thessalian charms
To draw the moon from heaven; for eloquence,
The sea-green Sirens taught her voice their flattery;
And, while she speaks, night steals upon the day,
Unmarked of those that hear. Then she's so charming,
Age buds at sight of her, and swells to youth:
The holy priests gaze on her when she smiles;
And with heaved hands, forgetting gravity,
They bless her wanton eyes: even I, who hate her,
With a malignant joy behold such beauty;
And, while I curse, desire it. Antony
Must needs have some remains of passion still,
Which may ferment into a worse relapse,
If now not fully cured. I know, this minute,
With Caesar he's endeavouring her peace.
Octav. You have prevailed: — but for a farther purpose
                                         [*Walks off.*
I'll prove how he will relish this discovery.
What, make a strumpet's peace! It swells my heart:
It must not, shall not be.
Vent.   His guards appear.
Let me begin, and you shall second me.

Enter ANTONY

Ant. Octavia, I was looking you, my love:
What, are your letters ready? I have given
My last instructions.
Octav.   Mine, my lord, are written.
Ant. Ventidius!   [*Drawing him aside.*
Vent.   My lord?
Ant.   A word in private.
When saw you Dolabella?

Vent.   Now, my lord,
  He parted hence; and Cleopatra with him.
Ant. Speak softly. – 'Twas by my command he went,
  To bear my last farewell.
Vent. [*aloud*].   It looked indeed
  Like your farewell.
Ant.   More softly. – My farewell?
  What secret meaning have you in those words
  Of 'my farewell'? He did it by my order.
Vent. [*aloud*]. Then he obeyed your order. I suppose
  You bid him do it with all gentleness,
  All kindness, and all — love.
Ant.   How she mourned,
  The poor forsaken creature!
Vent. She took it as she ought; she bore your parting
  As she did Caesar's, as she would another's,
  Were a new love to come.
Ant. [*aloud*].   Thou dost belie her;
  Most basely, and maliciously belie her.
Vent. I thought not to displease you; I have done.
Octav. [*coming up*]. You seemed disturbed, my lord.
Ant.   A very trifle.
  Retire, my love.
Vent.   It was indeed a trifle.
  He sent —
Ant. [*angrily*]. No more. Look how thou disobey'st me;
  Thy life shall answer it.
Octav.   Then 'tis no trifle.
Vent. [*to Octavia*]. 'Tis less, a very nothing; you too saw it,
  As well as I, and therefore 'tis no secret.
Ant. She saw it!
Vent.   Yes: she saw young Dolabella —
Ant. Young Dolabella!
Vent.   Young, I think him young,
  And handsome too; and so do others think him.
  But what of that? He went by your command,

Indeed 'tis probable, with some kind message;
For she received it graciously; she smiled;
And then he grew familiar with her hand,
Squeezed it, and worried it with ravenous kisses;
She blushed, and sighed, and smiled, and blushed
 again;
At last she took occasion to talk softly,
And brought her cheek up close, and leaned on his;
At which, he whispered kisses back on hers;
And then she cried aloud that constancy
Should be rewarded.
Octav.   This I saw and heard.
Ant. What woman was it, whom you heard and saw
So playful with my friend? Not Cleopatra?
Vent. Even she, my lord.
Ant.   My Cleopatra?
Vent. Your Cleopatra;
 Dolabella's Cleopatra;
 Every man's Cleopatra.
Ant. Thou liest.
Vent.   I do not lie, my lord.
 Is this so strange? Should mistresses be left,
 And not provide against a time of change?
 You know she's not much used to lonely nights.
Ant. I'll think no more on't.
 I know 'tis false, and see the plot betwixt you.
 You needed not have gone this way, Octavia.
 What harms it you that Cleopatra's just?
 She's mine no more. I see, and I forgive:
 Urge it no farther, love.
Octav.   Are you concerned,
 That she's found false?
Ant.   I should be, were it so;
 For, though 'tis past, I would not that the world
 Should tax my former choice, that I loved one
 Of so light note; but I forgive you both.

Vent. What has my age deserved, that you should think
    I would abuse your ears with perjury?
    If heaven be true, she's false.
Ant.   Though heaven and earth
    Should witness it, I'll not believe her tainted.
Vent. I'll bring you, then, a witness
    From hell, to prove her so [*Seeing Alexas just entering, and
        starting back.*] – Nay, go not back;
    For stay you must and shall.
Alex.   What means my lord?
Vent. To make you do what most you hate, – speak truth.
    You are of Cleopatra's private counsel,
    Of her bed-counsel, her lascivious hours;
    Are conscious of each nightly change she makes,
    And watch her, as Chaldeans do the moon,
    Can tell what signs she passes through, what day.
Alex. My noble lord!
Vent.   My most illustrious pander,
    No fine set speech, no cadence, no turned periods,
    But a plain homespun truth, is what I ask:
    I did, myself, o'erhear your queen make love
    To Dolabella. Speak; for I will know,
    By your confession, what more passed betwixt 'em;
    How near the business draws to your employment;
    And when the happy hour.
Ant. Speak truth, Alexas; whether it offend
    Or please Ventidius, care not: justify
    Thy injured queen from malice: dare his worst.
Octav. [*aside*]. See how he gives him courage ! how he
        fears
    To find her false! and shuts his eyes to truth,
    Willing to be misled!
Alex. As far as love may plead for woman's frailty,
    Urged by desert and greatness of the lover,
    So far, divine Octavia, may my queen
    Stand even excused to you for loving him

Who is your lord: so far, from brave Ventidius,
  May her past actions hope a fair report.
Ant. 'Tis well, and truly spoken: mark, Ventidius.
Alex. To you, most noble emperor, her strong passion
  Stands not excused, but wholly justified.
  Her beauty's charms alone, without her crown,
  From Ind and Meroe drew the distant vows
  Of sighing kings; and at her feet were laid
  The sceptres of the earth, exposed on heaps,
  To choose where she would reign:
  She thought a Roman only could deserve her,
  And, of all Romans, only Antony.
  And, to be less than wife to you, disdained
  Their lawful passion.
Ant.   'Tis but truth.
Alex. And yet, though love, and your unmatched desert,
  Have drawn her from the due regard of honour,
  At last heaven opened her unwilling eyes
  To see the wrongs she offered fair Octavia,
  Whose holy bed she lawlessly usurped.
  The sad effects of this improsperous war
  Confirmed those pious thoughts.
Vent. [*aside*].   Oh, wheel you there?
  Observe him now; the man begins to mend,
  And talk substantial reason. – Fear not, eunuch;
  The emperor has given thee leave to speak.
Alex. Else had I never dared to offend his ears
  With what the last necessity has urged
  On my forsaken mistress; yet I must not
  Presume to say her heart is wholly altered.
Ant. No, dare not for thy life, I charge thee dare not
  Pronounce that fatal word!
Octav. [*aside*]. Must I bear this? Good heaven, afford me
  patience.
Vent. On, sweet eunuch; my dear half-man, proceed.
Alex. Yet Dolabella

Has loved her long; he, next my god-like lord,
Deserves her best; and should she meet his passion,
Rejected, as she is, by him she loved —

Ant. Hence, from my sight! for I can bear no more:
Let Furies drag thee quick to hell; let all
The longer damned have rest; each torturing hand
Do thou employ, till Cleopatra comes;
Then join thou too, and help to torture her!

                         [*Exit Alexas, thrust out by Antony.*

Octav. 'Tis not well,
Indeed, my lord, 'tis much unkind to me,
To show this passion, this extreme concernment,
For an abandoned, faithless prostitute.

Ant. Octavia, leave me: I am much disordered.
Leave me, I say.

Octav.   My lord!

Ant.   I bid you leave me.

Vent. Obey him, madam: best withdraw a while,
And see how this will work.

Octav. Wherein have I offended you, my lord,
That I am bid to leave you? Am I false,
Or infamous? Am I a Cleopatra?
Were I she,
Base as she is, you would not bid me leave you;
But hang upon my neck, take slight excuses,
And fawn upon my falsehood.

Ant.   'Tis too much,
Too much, Octavia; I am pressed with sorrows
Too heavy to be borne; and you add more:
I would retire, and recollect what's left
Of man within, to aid me.

Octav.   You would mourn,
In private, for your love, who has betrayed you;
You did but half return to me: your kindness
Lingered behind with her. I hear, my lord,
You make conditions for her,

And would include her treaty. Wondrous proofs
  Of love to me!
Ant.   Are you my friend, Ventidius?
  Or are you turned a Dolabella too,
  And let this Fury loose?
Vent.   Oh, be advised,
  Sweet madam, and retire.
Octav. Yes, I will go; but never to return.
  You shall no more be haunted with this Fury.
  My lord, my lord, love will not always last,
  When urged with long unkindness and disdain;
  Take her again whom you prefer to me;
  She stays but to be called. Poor cozened man!
  Let a feigned parting give her back your heart,
  Which a feigned love first got; for injured me,
  Though my just sense of wrongs forbid my stay,
  My duty shall be yours.
  To the dear pledges of our former love
  My tenderness and care shall be transferred,
  And they shall cheer, by turns, my widowed nights:
  So, take my last farewell; for I despair
  To have you whole, and scorn to take you half.
                        [*Exit.*

Vent. I combat heaven, which blasts my best designs:
  My last attempt must be to win her back;
  But oh! I fear, in vain.   [*Exit.*
Ant. Why was I framed with this plain, honest heart,
  Which knows not to disguise its griefs and weak-
    ness,
  But bears its workings outward to the world?
  I should have kept the mighty anguish in,
  And forced a smile at Cleopatra's falsehood:
  Octavia had believed it, and had stayed.
  But I am made a shallow-forded stream,
  Seen to the bottom, – all my clearness scorned,
  And all my faults exposed! – See where he comes,

Enter DOLABELLA

Who has profaned the sacred name of friend,
And worn it into vileness!
With how secure a brow, and specious form,
He gilds the secret villain! Sure that face
Was meant for honesty; but heaven mismatched it,
And furnished treason out with nature's pomp,
To make its work more easy.

Dola.   O my friend!
Ant. Well, Dolabella, you performed my message?
Dola. I did, unwillingly.
Ant.   Unwillingly?
Was it so hard for you to bear our parting?
You should have wished it.
Dola.   Why?
Ant.   Because you love me.
And she received my message with as true,
With as unfeigned a sorrow as you brought it?
Dola. She loves you, even to madness.
Ant.   Oh, I know it.
You, Dolabella, do not better know
How much she loves me. And should I
Forsake this beauty, this all-perfect creature?
Dola. I could not, were she mine.
Ant.   And yet you first
Persuaded me: how come you altered since?
Dola. I said at first I was not fit to go;
I could not hear her sighs, and see her tears,
But pity must prevail: and so, perhaps,
It may again with you; for I have promised,
That she should take her last farewell: and, see,
She comes to claim my word.

Enter CLEOPATRA

Ant.   False Dolabella!
Dola. What's false, my lord?

Ant.   Why, Dolabella's false,
    And Cleopatra's false: both false and faithless.
    Draw near, you well-joined wickedness, you serpents,
    Whom I have in my kindly bosom warmed
    Till I am stung to death.
Dola.   My lord, have I
    Deserved to be thus used?
Cleo.   Can heaven prepare
    A newer torment? Can it find a curse
    Beyond our separation?
Ant.   Yes, if fate
    Be just, much greater: heaven should be ingenious
    In punishing such crimes. The rolling stone,
    And gnawing vulture, were slight pains, invented
    When Jove was young, and no examples known
    Of mighty ills; but you have ripened sin
    To such a monstrous growth, 'twill pose the gods
    To find an equal torture. Two, two such! –
    O, there's no farther name, two such! – to me,
    To me, who locked my soul within your breasts,
    Had no desires, no joys, no life, but you;
    When half the globe was mine, I gave it you
    In dowry with my heart; I had no use,
    No fruit of all, but you: a friend and mistress
    Was what the world could give. O Cleopatra!
    O Dolabella! how could you betray
    This tender heart, which with an infant fondness
    Lay lulled betwixt your bosoms, and there slept,
    Secure of injured faith?
Dola.   If she has wronged you,
    Heaven, hell, and you revenge it.
Ant.   If she wronged me!
    Thou wouldst evade thy part of guilt; but swear
    Thou lov'st not her.
Dola.   Not so as I love you.
Ant. Not so! Swear, swear, I say; thou dost not love her.

F.T.—12

Dola. No more than friendship will allow.

Ant.   No more?
    Friendship allows thee nothing; thou art perjured —
    And yet thou didst not swear thou lov'st her not;
    But not so much, no more. O trifling hypocrite,
    Who dar'st not own to her, thou dost not love,
    Nor own to me, thou dost! Ventidius heard it;
    Octavia saw it.

Cleo.   They are enemies.

Ant. Alexas is not so: he, he confessed it:
    He, who, next hell, best knew it, he avowed it.
    [*To Dolabella.*] Why do I seek a proof beyond your-
        self?
    You, whom I sent to bear my last farewell,
    Returned to plead her stay.

Dola.   What shall I answer?
    If to have loved be guilt, then I have sinned;
    But if to have repented of that love
    Can wash away my crime, I have repented.
    Yet, if I have offended past forgiveness,
    Let not her suffer: she is innocent.

Cleo. Ah, what will not a woman do, who loves!
    What means will she refuse, to keep that heart
    Where all her joys are placed? 'Twas I encouraged,
    'Twas I blew up the fire that scorched his soul,
    To make you jealous, and by that regain you.
    But all in vain; I could not counterfeit.
    In spite of all the dams my love broke o'er,
    And drowned my heart again. Fate took the occasion;
    And thus one minute's feigning has destroyed
    My whole life's truth.

Ant.   Thin cobweb arts of falsehood,
    Seen, and broke through at first.

Dola.   Forgive your mistress.

Cleo. Forgive your friend.

Ant.   You have convinced yourselves,

You plead each other's cause. What witness have you,
That you but meant to raise my jealousy?
Cleo. Ourselves, and heaven.
Ant. Guilt witnesses for guilt. Hence, love and friendship!
You have no longer place in human breasts,
These two have driv'n you out. Avoid my sight!
I would not kill the man whom I have loved,
And cannot hurt the woman; but avoid me;
I do not know how long I can be tame.
For, if I stay one minute more to think
How I am wronged, my justice and revenge
Will cry so loud within me, that my pity
Will not be heard for either.
Dola.   Heaven has but
Our sorrow for our sins; and then delights
To pardon erring man: sweet mercy seems
Its darling attribute, which limits justice;
As if there were degrees in infinite,
And infinite would rather want perfection
Than punish to extent.
Ant.   I can forgive
A foe, but not a mistress and a friend.
Treason is there in its most horrid shape,
Where trust is greatest: and the soul resigned
Is stabbed by its own guards. I'll hear no more;
Hence from my sight for ever!
Cleo.   How? for ever!
I cannot go one moment from your sight,
And must I go for ever?
My joys, my only joys, are centred here.
What place have I to go to? My own kingdom?
That I have lost for you. Or to the Romans?
They hate me for your sake. Or must I wander
The wide world o'er, a helpless, banished woman,
Banished for love of you, banished from you?
Aye, there's the banishment! Q, hear me! hear me,

With strictest justice, for I beg no favour;
And if I have offended you, then kill me,
But do not banish me.

Ant.   I must not hear you.
I have a fool within me takes your part;
But honour stops my ears.

Cleo.   For pity hear me!
Would you cast off a slave who followed you?
Who crouched beneath your spurn? – He has no pity!
See, if he gives one tear to my departure,
One look, one kind farewell: O iron heart!
Let all the gods look down, and judge betwixt us
If he did ever love!

Ant.   No more. Alexas!

Dola. A perjured villain!

Ant. [*to Cleopatra*].   Your Alexas, yours!

Cleo. Oh, 'twas his plot, his ruinous design,
To engage you in my love by jealousy.
Hear him; confront him with me; let him speak.

Ant. I have; I have.

Cleo.   And if he clear me not —

Ant. Your creature! one who hangs upon your smiles!
Watches your eye, to say or to unsay
Whate'er you please! I am not to be moved.

Cleo. Then must we part? Farewell, my cruel lord!
The appearance is against me; and I go,
Unjustified, for ever from your sight.
How I have loved, you know; how yet I love,
My only comfort is, I know myself:
I love you more, even now you are unkind,
Than when you loved me most: so well, so truly,
I'll never strive against it; but die pleased,
To think you once were mine.

Ant. Good heaven, they weep at parting!
Must I weep too? That calls them innocent.
I must not weep; and yet I must, to think

That I must not forgive. —
Live, but live wretched; 'tis but just you should,
Who made me so. Live from each other's sight:
Let me not hear you meet: set all the earth,
And all the seas, betwixt your sundered loves:
View nothing common but the sun and skies.
Now, all take several ways;
    And each your own sad fate, with mine, deplore;
    That you were false, and I could trust no more.

                                        [*Exeunt severally*.

Enter CLEOPATRA, CHARMION, IRAS

Char. Be juster, heaven: such virtue punished thus,
 Will make us think that chance rules all above,
 And shuffles, with a random hand, the lots
 Which man is forced to draw.
Cleo. I could tear out these eyes, that gained his heart,
 And had not power to keep it. O, the curse
 Of doting on, even when I find it dotage!
 Bear witness, gods, you heard him bid me go;
 You, whom he mocked with imprecating vows
 Of promised faith! — I'll die; I will not bear it.
          [*She pulls out her dagger, and they hold her.*
 You may hold me —
 But I can keep my breath; I can die inward,
 And choke this love.

Enter ALEXAS

Iras.   Help, O Alexas, help!
 The queen grows desperate; her soul struggles in
   her
 With all the agonies of love and rage,
 And strives to force its passage.
Cleo.   Let me go.
 Art thou there, traitor! – O!
 O, for a little breath, to vent my rage!
 Give, give me way, and let me loose upon him.
Alex. Yes, I deserve it, for my ill-timed truth.
 Was it for me to prop
 The ruins of a falling majesty?
 To place myself beneath the mighty flaw,
 Thus to be crushed, and pounded into atoms,
 By its o'erwhelming weight? 'Tis too presuming

For subjects to preserve that wilful power
Which courts its own destruction.
Cleo.   I would reason
   More calmly with you. Did not you o'errule,
   And force my plain, direct, and open love
   Into these crooked paths of jealousy?
   Now, what's the event? Octavia is removed;
   But Cleopatra's banished. Thou, thou, villain,
   Hast pushed my boat to open sea; to prove,
   At my sad cost, if thou canst steer it back.
   It cannot be; I'm lost too far; I'm ruined!
   Hence, thou impostor, traitor, monster, devil! –
   I can no more: thou, and my griefs, have sunk
   Me down so low, that I want voice to curse thee.
Alex. Suppose some shipwrecked seaman near the
      shore,
   Dropping and faint with climbing up the cliff,
   If, from above, some charitable hand
   Pull him to safety, hazarding himself
   To draw the other's weight; would he look back,
   And curse him for his pains? The case is yours;
   But one step more, and you have gained the height.
Cleo. Sunk, never more to rise.
Alex. Octavia's gone, and Dolabella banished.
   Believe me, madam, Antony is yours.
   His heart was never lost, but started off
   To jealousy, love's last retreat and covert;
   Where it lies hid in shades, watchful in silence,
   And listening for the sound that calls it back.
   Some other, any man ('tis so advanced),
   May perfect this unfinished work, which I
   (Unhappy only to myself) have left
   So easy to his hand.
Cleo.   Look well thou do't; else —
Alex. Else, what your silence threatens. – Antony
   Is mounted up the Pharos, from whose turret

He stands surveying our Egyptian galleys,
Engaged with Caesar's fleet. Now death or conquest!
If the first happen, fate acquits my promise;
If we o'ercome, the conqueror is yours.

[*A distant shout within.*

Char. Have comfort, madam: did you mark that shout?

[*Second shout nearer.*

Iras. Hark! they redouble it.
Alex.   'Tis from the port.
    The loudness shows it near: good news, kind heavens!
Cleo. Osiris make it so!

Enter SERAPION

Serap.   Where, where's the queen?
Alex. How frightfully the holy coward stares!
    As if not yet recovered of the assault,
    When all his gods, and, what's more dear to him,
    His offerings, were at stake.
Serap.   O horror, horror!
    Egypt has been; our latest hour is come:
    The queen of nations, from her ancient seat,
    Is sunk for ever in the dark abyss:
    Time has unrolled her glories to the last,
    And now closed up the volume.
Cleo.   Be more plain:
    Say, whence thou com'st; though fate is in thy face,
    Which from thy haggard eyes looks wildly out,
    And threatens ere thou speakest.
Serap.   I came from Pharos;
    From viewing (spare me, and imagine it)
    Our land's last hope, your navy —
Cleo.   Vanquished?
Serap.   No.
    They fought not.
Cleo.   Then they fled?
Serap.   Nor that. I saw,

With Antony, your well-appointed fleet
Row out; and thrice he waved his hand on high,
And thrice with cheerful cries they shouted back:
'Twas then false Fortune, like a fawning strumpet,
About to leave the bankrupt prodigal,
With a dissembled smile would kiss at parting,
And flatter to the last; the well-timed oars
Now dipped from every bank, now smoothly run
To meet the foe; and soon indeed they met,
But not as foes. In few, we saw their caps
On either side thrown up; the Egyptian galleys
Received like friends, passed through, and fell behind
The Roman rear; and now, they all come forward,
And ride within the port.

Cleo.   Enough, Serapion:
I've heard my doom. – This needed not, you gods:
When I lost Antony, your work was done;
'Tis but superfluous malice. – Where's my lord?
How bears he this last blow?

Serap. His fury cannot be expressed by words:
Thrice he attempted headlong to have fallen
Full on his foes, and aimed at Caesar's galley:
Withheld, he raves on you; cries, he's betrayed.
Should he now find you –

Alex.   Shun him; seek your safety,
Till you can clear your innocence.

Cleo.   I'll stay.

Alex. You must not; haste you to your monument,
While I make speed to Caesar.

Cleo.   Caesar! No,
I have no business with him.

Alex.   I can work him.
To spare your life, and let this madman perish.

Cleo. Base fawning wretch! wouldst thou betray him too?
Hence from my sight! I will not hear a traitor;

'Twas thy design brought all this ruin on us.
Serapion, thou art honest; counsel me:
But haste, each moment's precious.

Serap. Retire; you must not yet see Antony,
He who began this mischief,
'Tis just he tempt the danger: let him clear you;
And, since he offered you his servile tongue,
To gain a poor precarious life from Caesar,
Let him expose that fawning eloquence,
And speak to Antony.

Alex.   O heavens! I dare not;
I meet my certain death.

Cleo.   Slave, thou deservest it. –
Not that I fear my lord, will I avoid him;
I know him noble: when he banished me,
And thought me false, he scorned to take my life;
But I'll be justified, and then die with him.

Alex. O pity me, and let me follow you!

Cleo. To death, if thou stir hence. Speak, if thou canst,
Now for thy life, which basely thou wouldst save;
While mine I prize at – this! Come, good Serapion.

                [*Exeunt Cleopatra, Serapion, Charmion, Iras.*

Alex. O that I less could fear to lose this being,
Which, like a snowball in my coward hand,
The more 'tis grasped, the faster melts away.
Poor reason! what a wretched aid art thou!
For still, in spite of thee,
These two long lovers, soul and body, dread
Their final separation. Let me think:
What can I say, to save myself from death?
No matter what becomes of Cleopatra.

Ant. [*within*]. Which way? where?

Vent. [*within*].   This leads to the monument.

Alex. Ah me! I hear him; yet I'm unprepared:
My gift of lying's gone;
And this court-devil, which I so oft have raised,

Forsakes me at my need. I dare not stay;
Yet cannot far go hence.   [*Exit.*

Enter ANTONY *and* VENTIDIUS

Ant. O happy Caesar! thou hast men to lead:
Think not 'tis thou hast conquered Antony;
But Rome has conquered Egypt. I'm betrayed.
Vent. Curse on this treacherous train!
Their soil and heaven infect 'em all with baseness:
And their young souls come tainted to the world
With the first breath they draw.
Ant. The original villain sure no god created;
He was a bastard of the sun, by Nile,
Aped into man; with all his mother's mud
Crusted about his soul.
Vent.   The nation is
One universal traitor; and their queen
The very spirit and extract of them all.
Ant. Is there yet left
A possibility of aid from valour?
Is there one god unsworn to my destruction?
The least unmortgaged hope? for, if there be,
Methinks I cannot fall beneath the fate
Of such a boy as Caesar.
The world's one half is yet in Antony;
And from each limb of it that's hewed away,
The soul comes back to me.
Vent.   There yet remain
Three legions in the town – the last assault
Lopped off the rest. If death be your design
(As I must wish it now) these are sufficient
To make a heap about us of dead foes,
An honest pile for burial.
Ant.   They're enough.
We'll not divide our stars; but side by side
Fight emulous, and with malicious eyes

  Survey each other's acts: so every death
  Thou giv'st, I'll take on me, as a just debt,
  And pay thee back a soul.
Vent. Now you shall see I love you. Not a word
  Of chiding more. By my few hours of life,
  I am so pleased with this brave Roman fate,
  That I would not be Caesar, to outlive you.
  When we put off this flesh, and mount together,
  I shall be shown to all the ethereal crowd, —
  'Lo, this is he who died with Antony!'
Ant. Who knows but we may pierce through all their
   troops,
  And reach my veterans yet? 'Tis worth the tempting,
  To o'erleap this gulf of fate,
  And leave our wandering destinies behind.

    Enter ALEXAS, *trembling*

Vent. See, see, that villain!
  See Cleopatra stamped upon that face,
  With all her cunning, all her arts of falsehood!
  How she looks out through those dissembling eyes!
  How he has set his countenance for deceit,
  And promises a lie, before he speaks!
  Let me despatch him first.   [*Drawing.*
Alex.   O spare me, spare me!
Ant. Hold; he's not worth your killing. — On thy life
  Which thou may'st keep, because I scorn to take it,
  No syllable to justify thy queen;
  Save thy base tongue its office.
Alex.   Sir, she's gone,
  Where she shall never be molested more
  By love, or you.
Ant.   Fled to her Dolabella!
  Die, traitor! I revoke my promise! die!
        [*Going to kill him.*
Alex. O hold! she is not fled.

Ant.   She is: my eyes
   Are open to her falsehood; my whole life
   Has been a golden dream of love and friendship.
   But, now I wake, I'm like a merchant, roused
   From soft repose, to see his vessel sinking,
   And all his wealth cast o'er. Ingrateful woman!
   Who followed me, but as the swallow summer,
   Hatching her young ones in my kindly beams,
   Singing her flatteries to my morning wake;
   But, now my winter comes, she spreads her wings,
   And seeks the spring of Caesar.

Alex.   Think not so:
   Her fortunes have, in all things, mixed with yours.
   Had she betrayed her naval force to Rome,
   How easily might she have gone to Caesar,
   Secure by such a bribe!

Vent.   She sent it first,
   To be more welcome after.

Ant.   'Tis too plain;
   Else would she have appeared, to clear herself.

Alex. Too fatally she has; she could not bear
   To be accused by you; but shut herself
   Within her monument; looked down and sighed;
   While, from her unchanged face, the silent tears
   Dropped, as they had not leave, but stole their parting.
   Some undistinguished words she inly murmured;
   At last, she raised her eyes; and, with such looks
   As dying Lucrece cast —

Ant.   My heart forbodes —

Vent. All for the best; go on.

Alex.   She snatched her poniard,
   And ere we could prevent the fatal blow,
   Plunged it within her breast: then turned to me:
   'Go, bear my lord,' said she, 'my last farewell;
   And ask him if he yet suspect my faith.'
   More she was saying, but death rushed betwixt.

She half pronounced your name with her last breath,
And buried half within her.

Vent.   Heaven be praised!

Ant. Then art thou innocent, my poor dear love,
And art thou dead?
O those two words! their sound should be divided:
Hadst thou been false, and died; or hadst thou
lived,
And hadst been true. — But innocence and death!
This shows not well above. Then what am I,
The murderer of this truth, this innocence!
Thoughts cannot form themselves in words so horrid
As can express my guilt!

Vent. Is't come to this? The gods have been too gracious:
And thus you thank 'em for't!

Ant. [*to Alexas*].   Why stay'st thou here?
Is it for thee to spy upon my soul,
And see its inward mourning? Get thee hence!
Thou art not worthy to behold what now
Becomes a Roman emperor to perform.

Alex. [*aside*]. He loves her still:
His grief betrays it. Good! The joy to find
She's yet alive, completes the reconcilement.
I've saved myself, and her. But, oh! the Romans!
Fate comes too fast upon my wit,
Hunts me too hard, and meets me at each double.
                                        [*Exit.*

Vent. Would she had died a little sooner, though,
Before Octavia went; you might have treated:
Now 'twill look tame, and would not be received.
Come, rouse yourself, and let's die warm together.

Ant. I will not fight: there's no more work for war.
The business of my angry hour is done.

Vent. Caesar is at your gates.

Ant.   Why, let him enter;
He's welcome now.

Vent. What lethargy has crept into your soul?

Ant. 'Tis but a scorn of life, and just desire
　To free myself from bondage.

Vent.　　　　　　　　　Do it bravely.

Ant. I will; but not by fighting. O Ventidius!
　What should I fight for now? My queen is dead.
　I was but great for her; my power, my empire,
　Were but my merchandise to buy her love;
　And conquered kings, my factors. Now she's dead,
　Let Caesar take the world, –
　An empty circle, since the jewel's gone
　Which made it worth my strife: my being's nauseous;
　For all the bribes of life are gone away.

Vent. Would you be taken?

Ant.　　　　　　　Yes, I would be taken;
　But, as a Roman ought, – dead, my Ventidius:
　For I'll convey my soul from Caesar's reach,
　And lay down life myself. 'Tis time the world
　Should have a lord, and know whom to obey.
　We two have kept its homage in suspense,
　And bent the globe, on whose each side we trod,
　Till it was dinted inwards. Let him walk
　Alone upon't; I'm weary of my part.
　My torch is out; and the world stands before me
　Like a black desert at the approach of night:
　I'll lay me down, and stray no farther on.

Vent. I could be grieved,
　But that I'll not outlive you: choose your death;
　For I have seen him in such various shapes,
　I care not which I take: I'm only troubled,
　The life I bear is worn to such a rag,
　'Tis scarce worth giving. I could wish, indeed,
　We threw it from us with a better grace;
　That, like two lions taken in the toils,
　We might at least thrust out our paws, and wound
　The hunters that enclose us.

Ant. I have thought on't.
Ventidius, you must live.

Vent. I must not, sir.

Ant. Wilt thou not live, to speak some good of me?
To stand by my fair fame, and guard the approaches
From the ill tongues of men?

Vent. Who shall guard mine,
For living after you?

Ant. Say, I command it.

Vent. If we die well, our deaths will speak themselves
And need no living witness.

Ant. Thou hast loved me,
And fain I would reward thee. I must die;
Kill me, and take the merit of my death
To make thee friends with Caesar.

Vent. Thank your kindness.
You said I loved you; and, in recompense,
You bid me turn a traitor. Did I think
You would have used me thus? – that I should die
With a hard thought of you?

Ant. Forgive me, Roman.
Since I have heard of Cleopatra's death,
My reason bears no rule upon my tongue,
But lets my thoughts break all at random out.
I've thought better; do not deny me twice.

Vent. By heaven, I will not.
Let it not be to outlive you.

Ant. Kill me first,
And then die thou; for 'tis but just thou serve
Thy friend, before thyself.

Vent. Give me your hand.
We soon shall meet again. Now, farewell, emperor! –
[*Embrace.*
Methinks that word's too cold to be my last:
Since death sweeps all distinctions, farewell, friend!
That's all. —

I will not make a business of a trifle;
And yet I cannot look on you, and kill you;
Pray turn your face.

Ant.   I do: strike home, be sure.

Vent. Home as my sword will reach.   [*Kills himself.*

Ant.   Oh, thou mistak'st!
That wound was none of thine: give it me back:
Thou robb'st me of my death!

Vent.   I do indeed;
But think 'tis the first time I e'er deceived you,
If that may plead my pardon. – And you, gods,
Forgive me, if you will; for I die perjured,
Rather than kill my friend.   [*Dies.*

Ant. Farewell! Ever my leader, even in death!
My queen and thou have got the start of me,
And I'm the lag of honour. – Gone so soon?
Is Death no more? He used him carelessly,
With a familiar kindness; ere he knocked,
Ran to the door, and took him in his arms,
As who should say, 'Y'are welcome at all hours,
A friend need give no warning.' Books had spoiled
    him;
For all the learned are cowards by profession.
'Tis not worth
My farther thought; for death, for aught I know,
Is but to think no more. Here's to be satisfied.
                        [*Falls on his sword.*
I've missed my heart. O unperforming hand!
Thou never couldst have erred in a worse time.
My fortune jades me to the last; and Death,
Like a great man, takes state, and makes me wait
For my admittance. —   [*Trampling within.*
            Some, perhaps, from Caesar:
If he should find me living, and suspect
That I played booty with my life! I'll mend
My work, ere they can reach me. [*Rises upon his knees.*

Enter CLEOPATRA, CHARMION, IRAS

Cleo. Where is my lord! where is he?

Char.   There he lies,
  And dead Ventidius by him.

Cleo. My fears were prophets; I am come too late.
  O that accursed Alexas!   [*Runs to him.*

Ant.   Art thou living?
  Or am I dead before I knew, and thou
  The first kind ghost that meets me?

Cleo.   Help me seat him.
  Send quickly, send for help!   [*They place him in a chair.*

Ant.   I am answered.
  We live both. Sit thee down, my Cleopatra:
  I'll make the most I can of life, to stay
  A moment more with thee.

Cleo. How is it with you?

Ant.   'Tis as with a man
  Removing in a hurry; all packed up,
  But one dear jewel that his haste forgot;
  And he, for that, returns upon the spur:
  So I come back, for thee.

Cleo. Too long, you heavens, you have been cruel to
    me;
  Now show your mended faith, and give me back
  His fleeting life!

Ant.   It will not be, my love.
  I keep my soul by force.
  Say but thou art not false.

Cleo.   'Tis now too late
  To say I'm true: I'll prove it, and die with you.
  Unknown to me, Alexas feigned my death:
  Which, when I knew, I hasted to prevent
  This fatal consequence. My fleet betrayed
  Both you and me.

Ant.   And Dolabella —

Cleo.   Scarce
    Esteemed before he loved; but hated now.
Ant. Enough: my life's not long enough for more.
    Thou say'st, thou wilt come after: I believe thee;
    For I can now believe whate'er thou sayest
    That we may part more kindly.
Cleo.   I will come:
    Doubt not, my life, I'll come, and quickly too:
    Caesar shall triumph o'er no part of thee.
Ant. But grieve not, while thou stayest,
    My last disastrous times:
    Think we have had a clear and glorious day,
    And heaven did kindly to delay the storm,
    Just till our close of evening. Ten years' love,
    And not a moment lost, but all improved
    To the utmost joys, – what ages have we lived!
    And now to die each other's; and, so dying,
    While hand in hand we walk in groves below,
    Whole troops of lovers' ghosts shall flock about us,
    And all the train be ours.
Cleo. Your words are like the notes of dying swans,
    Too sweet to last. Were there so many hours
    For your unkindness, and not one for love?
Ant. No, not a minute. – This one kiss – more worth
    Than all I leave to Caesar.   [*Dies.*
Cleo. O, tell me so again,
    And take ten thousand kisses for that word.
    My lord, my lord! speak, if you yet have being;
    Sigh to me, if you cannot speak; or cast
    One look! Do anything that shows you live.
Iras. He's gone too far to hear you;
    And this you see, a lump of senseless clay,
    The leavings of a soul.
Char.   Remember, madam,
    He charged you not to grieve.
Cleo.   And I'll obey him.

I have not loved a Roman not to know
What should become his wife; his wife, my Charmion,
For 'tis to that high title I aspire,
And now I'll not die less! Let dull Octavia
Survive, to mourn him dead: my nobler fate
Shall knit our spousals with a tie too strong
For Roman laws to break.

Iras.   Will you then die?

Cleo. Why shouldst thou make that question?

Iras. Caesar is merciful.

Cleo.   Let him be so
To those that want his mercy: my poor lord
Made no such covenant with him, to spare me
When he was dead. Yield me to Caesar's pride?
What! to be led in triumph through the streets,
A spectacle to base plebeian eyes;
While some dejected friend of Antony's,
Close in a corner, shakes his head, and mutters
A secret curse on her who ruined him?
I'll none of that.

Char.   Whatever you resolve,
I'll follow, ev'n to death.

Iras.   I only feared
For you; but more should fear to live without you.

Cleo. Why, now 'tis as it should be. Quick, my friends,
Dispatch; ere this, the town's in Caesar's hands:
My lord looks down concerned, and fears my stay,
Lest I should be surprised;
Keep him not waiting for his love too long.
You, Charmion, bring my crown and richest jewels;
With them, the wreath of victory I made
(Vain augury!) for him who now lies dead.
You, Iras, bring the cure of all our ills.

Iras. The aspics, madam?

Cleo.   Must I bid you twice?

                              [*Exeunt Charmion and Iras.*

'Tis sweet to die, when they would force life on me,
To rush into the dark abode of Death,
And seize him first; if he be like my love,
He is not frightful, sure.
We're now alone, in secrecy and silence;
And is not this like lovers? I may kiss
These pale, cold lips; Octavia does not see me;
And, oh! 'tis better far to have him thus,
Than see him in her arms. – Oh, welcome, welcome!

Enter CHARMION *and* IRAS

Char. What must be done?
Cleo.   Short ceremony, friends;
But yet it must be decent. First, this laurel
Shall crown my hero's head: he fell not basely,
Nor left his shield behind him. – Only thou
Couldst triumph o'er thyself; and thou alone
Wert worthy so to triumph.
Char.   To what end
These ensigns of your pomp and royalty?
Cleo. Dull that thou art! why, 'tis to meet my love;
As when I saw him first, on Cydnos' bank,
All sparkling, like a goddess: so adorned,
I'll find him once again: my second spousals
Shall match my first in glory. Haste, haste, both,
And dress the bride of Antony.
Char.   'Tis done.
Cleo. Now seat me by my lord. I claim this place;
For I must conquer Caesar too, like him,
And win my share o' th' world. – Hail, you dear
 relics
Of my immortal love!
O, let no impious hand remove you hence;
But rest for ever here! Let Egypt give
His death that peace, which it denied his life. –
Reach me the casket.

Iras.   Underneath the fruit
     The aspic lies.
Cleo. [*putting aside the leaves*]. Welcome, thou kind deceiver!
     Thou best of thieves, who, with an easy key,
     Dost open life, and, unperceived by us,
     Ev'n steal us from ourselves; discharging so
     Death's dreadful office, better than himself;
     Touching our limbs so gently into slumber,
     That Death stands by, deceived by his own image,
     And thinks himself but Sleep.
Serap. [*within*].   The queen, where is she?
     The town is yielded, Caesar's at the gates.
Cleo. He comes too late to invade the rights of death.
     Haste, bare my arm, and rouse the serpent's fury.
                    [*Holds out her arm, and draws it back.*
     Coward flesh,
     Wouldst thou conspire with Caesar to betray me,
     As thou wert none of mine? I'll force thee to it,
     And not be sent by him,
     But bring, myself, my soul to Antony.
                    [*Turns aside, and then shows her arm bloody.*
     Take hence; the work is done.
Serap. [*within*].   Break ope the door,
     And guard the traitor well.
Char.   The next is ours.
Iras. Now, Charmion, to be worthy
     Of our great queen and mistress.
                    [*They apply the aspics.*
Cleo. Already, death, I feel thee in my veins;
     I go with such a will to find my lord,
     That we shall quickly meet.
     A heavy numbness creeps through every limb,
     And now 'tis at my head: my eyelids fall,
     And my dear love is vanished in a mist.
     Where shall I find him, where? O turn me to him,
     And lay me on his breast! – Caesar, thy worst;

Now part us, if thou canst.   [*Dies.*

[*Iras sinks down at her feet, and dies; Charmion stands
behind her chair, as dressing her head.*

Enter SERAPION, *two Priests*, ALEXAS *bound*,
Egyptians

Two Priests.   Behold, Serapion,
What havoc death has made!
Serap.   'Twas what I feared. –
Charmion, is this well done?
Char. Yes, 'tis well done, and like a queen, the last
Of her great race: I follow her.   [*Sinks down; dies.*
Alex.   Tis true,
She has done well: much better thus to die,
Than live to make a holiday in Rome.
Serap. See,
See how the lovers sit in state together,
As they were giving laws to half mankind!
The impression of a smile, left in her face,
Shows she died pleased with him for whom she lived,
And went to charm him in another world.
Caesar's just entering: grief has now no leisure.
Secure that villain, as our pledge of safety,
To grace the imperial triumph. – Sleep, blest pair,
Secure from human chance, long ages out,
While all the storms of fate fly o'er your tomb;
    And fame to late posterity shall tell,
    No lovers lived so great, or died so well.

EPILOGUE

Poets, like disputants, when reasons fail,
Have one sure refuge left – and that's to rail.
Fop, coxcomb, fool, are thundered through the pit;
And this is all their equipage of wit.
We wonder how the devil this diff'rence grows,
Betwixt our fools in verse, and yours in prose:
For, 'faith, the quarrel rightly understood,
'Tis civil war with their own flesh and blood.
The threadbare author hates the gaudy coat;
And swears at the gilt coach, but swears afoot:
For 'tis observed of every scribbling man,
He grows a fop as fast as e'er he can;
Prunes up, and asks his oracle, the glass,
If pink or purple best become his face.
For our poor wretch, he neither rails nor prays
Nor likes your wit just as you like his plays;
He has not yet so much of Mr Bayes.
He does his best; and if he cannot please,
Would quietly sue out his *writ of ease*.
Yet, if he might his own grand jury call,
By the fair sex he begs to stand or fall.
Let Caesar's pow'r the men's ambition move,
But grace you him who lost the world for love!
Yet if some antiquated lady say,
The last age is not copied in his play;
Heav'n help the man who for that face must drudge,
Which only has the wrinkles of a judge.
Let not the young and beauteous join with those;
For should you raise such numerous hosts of foes,
Young wits and sparks he to his aid must call;
'Tis more than one man's work to please you all.

*The following pages describe books in
various series published by Penguin Books including*

PELICANS, PENGUIN CLASSICS, KING PENGUINS

PENGUIN MINIATURE SCORES
and a new series
THE PELICAN HISTORY OF ART

*

SELECTED DRAMA

CHEHOV
Three Plays (L19)

New translations of *The Cherry Orchard, Three Sisters*, and *Ivanov* by Elisaveta Fen (2s 6d)

EURIPIDES
Three Plays (L31)

New translations of *Alcestis, Iphigenia in Tauris*, and *Hippolytus* by Philip Vellacott (2s)

SHAKESPEARE AND SHAW

Eleven volumes of the Penguin Shakespeare are now available – *Hamlet, King Lear, Macbeth, Henry IV (Part II), Sonnets and a Lover's Complaint, The Taming of the Shrew, Antony and Cleopatra, Romeo and Juliet, A Midsummer Night's Dream, Love's Labour's Lost,* and *Henry V;* as are Bernard Shaw's *Major Barbara, Androcles and the Lion, St Joan, The Doctor's Dilemma, Pygmalion, Man and Superman, Plays Pleasant, Plays Unpleasant, Three Plays for Puritans,* and *The Black Girl in Search of God* (1s 6d – 2s 6d each)

SOPHOCLES
Electra and Other Plays (L28)

New translations of *Electra, Ajax, The Women of Trachis,* and *Philoctetes* by E. F. Watling (2s)

JOHN M. SYNGE
Collected Plays (845)

All the plays of one of Ireland's greatest dramatists, a leader of the renaissance at the Abbey Theatre, Dublin, forty years ago (3s)

PELICANS

Pelicans, the non-fiction counterpart of Penguins, were launched in 1937, as a series of reprints of popular books with a serious, informative content. Since then their scope has widened considerably, and most of the books now appearing between the pale blue covers of a Pelican have never been published before. In all some 270 volumes have been issued, including introductions to almost every subject, a whole sub-series on the History of England, and others on Philosophy, Psychology, Religion, and Archaeology, all of which are still growing. Amongst them are:

JOHN STUART MILL – *Karl Britton*

A volume in the Pelican Philosophy series, introducing the teaching of a famous 19th-century political philosopher (A274) 2/-

AN OUTLINE OF EUROPEAN ARCHITECTURE – *Nikolaus Pevsner*

A well-illustrated account of the buildings of every period from the ninth to the twentieth century (A109) 3/6

THE GREEKS – *H. D. F. Kitto*

'The best introduction I have ever read to ancient Greece' – *Raymond Mortimer in the New Statesman* (A220) 2/-

HORSE-RACING – *Dennis Craig*

Not a punter's guide but a miniature encyclopaedia of the racing and breeding of thoroughbreds (A203) 2/-

VIRUSES AND MAN – *F. M. Burnet*

An account of many common varieties of the smallest living organism, which is responsible for most of to-day's infectious diseases (A265) 2/-

THE ANT WORLD – *Derek Wragge Morley*

The history of ants, their many varieties, the organization of their society and what makes them tick (A240) 2/-

KING PENGUINS

Described by Clive Bell as 'short, illustrated monographs, edited and written by scholars', the King Penguins, which are edited by Nikolaus Pevsner and R. B. Fishenden, were originally inspired by the Insel-Bücherei, a series published in Leipzig before the war. They have stiff board covers attractively designed, and special care has been taken to use the best possible methods of reproduction for the colour or black-and-white plates, which in each case are introduced by a brief descriptive essay. The various books include:

ACKERMANN'S CAMBRIDGE – *R. Ross Williamson*

A selection of colour plates from Ackermann's *History of the University of Cambridge* (1815), with an introduction (K 59)   4/–

EARLY BRITISH RAILWAYS – *Christian Barman*

An attractive account of the first railways in Britain. The plates are from old engravings and drawings (K 56)   3/–

MOUNTAIN BIRDS – *R. A. H. Coombes*

With sixteen plates by G. E. Lodge and an essay by R. A. H. Coombes of the Zoology Department of the British Museum (K 67)   4/6

MEDIEVAL CARVINGS IN EXETER CATHEDRAL – *C. J. P. Cave*

64 pages of photographs and an authoritative text describing the 13th- and 14th-century sculpture and decoration (K 62)   4/6

SEMI-PRECIOUS STONES – *Nora Wooster*

16 colour plates by Arthur Smith and an essay by Mrs Wooster of the Brooklyn Crystallographic Laboratory, Cambridge (K 65)   5/–

AN ATLAS OF TUDOR ENGLAND AND WALES – *E. G. R. Taylor*

Reproductions of forty-four colour plates from John Speed's Pocket Atlas of 1627, introduced by Professor Taylor (K 61)   4/–

A BOOK OF GREEK COINS – *Charles Seltman*

A condensed history of the beginnings of gold and silver coined money, with forty-eight black-and-white plates (K 63)   4/6

PENGUIN SCORES

Edited by Gordon Jacob

Each volume has a musical introduction and a biographical note
preceding the score.

BACH – *Brandenburg Concertos Nos. 1 and 2 in F* (SC7)   2s 6d

BACH – *Brandenburg Concerto No. 3 in G* (SC2)   2s 6d

BEETHOVEN – *Overtures: Coriolan and Egmont* (SC3)   2s 6d

BEETHOVEN – *Symphony No. 1 in C* (SC9)   2s 6d

BEETHOVEN – *Symphony No. 5 in C minor* (SC12)   3s 6d

BEETHOVEN – *Symphony No. 7 in A* (SC18)   5s

BRAHMS – *Variations on a Theme of Haydn* (SC17)   2s 6d

HAYDN – *Symphony No. 101 in D (The Clock)* (SC4)   2s 6d

MENDELSSOHN – *Overtures: A Midsummer Night's
Dream and Fingal's Cave* (SC5)   2s 6d

MENDELSSOHN – *Violin Concerto in E Minor* (SC14)   3s 6d

MOZART – *Overtures: The Magic Flute and Don
Giovanni* (SC15)   3s

MOZART – *Symphony No. 39 in E Flat* (SC16)   3s 6d

MOZART – *Symphony No. 40 in G minor* (SC1)   2s 6d

MOZART – *Symphony No. 41 in C (Jupiter)* (SC10)   2s 6d

SCHUBERT – *Symphony No. 8 in B minor (Unfinished)*
(SC6)   2s 6d

SCHUMANN – *Piano Concerto in A minor* (SC19)   5s

TSCHAIKOVSKY – *Fantasy-Overture, Romeo and Juliet*
(SC11)   2s 6d

WAGNER – *Siegfried Idyll* (SC13)   2s 6d

WEBER – *Overtures: Der Freischütz and Oberon* (SC8)   2s 6d